MARIA WOODWORTH-ETTER:

THE EVANGELIST

by Steven Phipps, Ph.D.

Tulsa, OK

10 9 8 7 6 5 4 3 2 1   17 18 19 20

Maria Woodworth-Etter: The Evangelist
© 2017 Steven Phipps
ISBN: 978-1-68031-116-7

Steven Phipps, Ph.D.
Kimmswick, MO 63053 U.S.

Cover photo ©Flower Pentecostal Heritage Center. Used by permission.

Published by Harrison House Publishers
Tulsa, OK 74145
www.harrisonhouse.com

ACKNOWLEDGMENTS AND
A NOTE ON SOURCES

Maria Woodworth-Etter was considered one of the most significant evangelists of the late 19th and early 20th centuries. She has been the subject of various articles, book chapters, and book sections. Her life formed the basis of a biography published in 2004 (Wayne Warner, *Maria Woodworth-Etter: For Such a Time as This*).[1] Then why another biography?

Earlier writings—book chapters and sections, as well as Warner's biography—have attempted to present a general overview of the life and ministry of Maria Woodworth-Etter. Instead, the present work focuses on the unique manifestations that set her apart from other ministers of her era, and on the persecution that they engendered. This new study also examines the results of that persecution on her life and ministry.

The basic thesis of the present biography is that the extreme dissonance between her ministry and that of most of her contemporaries led to extreme persecution. That persecution arose from three sources: (a) the press, (b) other ministers, especially within her own denomination, and (c) her husband. This persecution led to an eventual breakdown. When she finally reentered ministry, that ministry had largely "waned" in power. This theme forms the focus of this book.

As a result, this book emphasizes the period of her life from the time she entered ministry around 1880 until the time of her second marriage in 1901. In addition, coverage of her supposed "lost" years is included, which another scholar (Nancy

A. Hardesty, in a section of her book *Faith Cure*)[2] says Warner omitted. While Warner does very briefly touch on these years in a later edition, an expanded view is provided here, along with the reason for her apparent disappearance.

Most of my published historical research on other topics has consisted of revisionist history in the area of the media. Probably because I am primarily a media historian, my focus in the present volume has often turned to press coverage of this controversial individual. My primary aim has been to uncover aspects of her life that others have missed, and to use that as a basis for constructing a new image of Maria Woodworth-Etter.

In the process of following this approach, various major and significant facets of Maria Woodworth-Etter's life, and in the lives of those who surrounded her, are covered here which have not been discussed previously. In addition, far more detail is presented in some areas that have been previously glossed over.

Those areas include such matters as the strange demise of Maria's first husband, the death of a young man who was killed in her revival tent, her husband's lies and deceptions regarding his military career and previous marriage, and her eventual breakdown.

Also discussed, as already mentioned, is the "waning" nature of her ministry after her remarriage. This latter aspect of her life is a factor that appears to have been overlooked, perhaps in an effort to connect her with the fledgling Pentecostal movement following her second marriage.

As a result of comprehensive new research, I have identified Maria Woodworth's 1890 St. Louis meetings as the apex of her ministry career. That series of meetings, more than any other, came to define her ministry generally. While Warner has briefly mentioned those meetings, the present work provides an abundance of detail regarding them. In addition, attempts at that time to have her committed as insane are extensively discussed, which is an important matter which has previously escaped significant comment.

This new study also presents a tremendous amount of information regarding Maria's first husband, Philo Harris ("P. H.") Woodworth. (The previous biographer referred to him as Philo Harrison Woodworth.) P. H. Woodworth is correctly identified in this new study as a man who appears to have literally lied his way into her heart, and who became one of her leading antagonists in ministry.

The book also contains a number of more narrowly focused but still significant and insightful details which do not seem to be found elsewhere. These include such matters as Philo and Maria Woodworths' hotel management endeavors, the role played in Maria Woodworth's ministry by her favorite song "The Power," the sources of the tidal wave "prophecies," her husband's murder threats, a comparison of the manifestations present in her meetings with much earlier camp meetings, and details of some of her ministry associates and "followers." This study also connects Maria Woodworth's ministry with contextual events and movements.

Maria Woodworth, later known as Woodworth-Etter, was known in her early ministry as the "trance evangelist." While the previous biographer seemed to characterize reported "manifestations" in her ministry as generally either very similar to those in charismatic meetings of today or as exaggerated,[3] the present work adopts a different view.

The sheer number and extent of accounts appear to be far too numerous and detailed to pertain to something that was exaggerated or mundane. The Woodworths' ever-pragmatic friend A.B. Sibert was skeptical of the trances associated with her ministry, for instance, but was shocked when he found that an "entranced" woman did not respond to being pricked with a pin.[4]

The sheer number of highly detailed trance-related accounts, as well as the remarkable similarity in those accounts, suggests that the trance phenomenon present in Woodworth meetings was real. Much of this book focuses on the supernatural manifestations and their role and nature, while relating them to other similar or related movements and ministries.

Maria Woodworth was the subject of literally countless newspaper articles. Ironically, more appears to have survived in terms of press coverage about this woman than has been published in newspapers pertaining to at least most of the major evangelists who postdated her.

Some of those newspaper articles have been transcribed and published in two books. Kenneth Kline-Walczak's book *Testimonies of Signs and Wonders*[5] is a narrowly focused collection of news clippings pertaining to Moline, Illinois, Rock Island, Illinois, and Davenport, Iowa in 1902, 1903, and 1907. *Maria Woodworth Etter: The Complete Collection of Her Life Teachings*, compiled by Roberts Liardon,[6] is another published collection of news clippings.

Although Liardon's selection of articles is more expansive than that of Kline-Walczak, it is hardly a "complete collection." There could never be a literally complete collection of writings about Mrs. Woodworth. That is because she was the subject of extremely widespread press coverage, with her services having been oftentimes discussed in small town papers published far from the scene of her ministry. Many of those articles have been found, but some will never be found.

In most of my previous research leading to publication in other subject areas, I have relied most heavily on newspaper articles as source materials. That has been the case here as well.

Only a minority of the articles which were consulted appear in the bibliography; inclusion of a complete list would be impossible. Literally thousands of newspaper articles were consulted, many of which are not found in the substantial collection of the Flower Pentecostal Heritage Center.

In addition to newspaper articles, other substantial sources include coroners' reports of the deaths of Philo Harris Woodworth and Louis Burg, the young man who was killed in Woodworth's revival tent. Various other court records were consulted, as well as pension records and additional public records.

Valuable and even essential assistance was provided by a number of individuals and research institutions, for which I would like to express sincere gratitude. Darrin Rodgers, director of the Flower Pentecostal Heritage Center (FPHC) in Springfield, Missouri, has helped tremendously with editing suggestions.

Both Rodgers and Glenn Gohr, research archivist at the FPHC, offered very valuable help in the form of general encouragement regarding this project, and Wayne Warner, former FPHC director, provided editing suggestions. Some original Woodworth-Etter materials have been reproduced on an FPHC DVD-ROM, *Healing Evangelists 1881–1957*.

I would also like to thank the research staff of the Special Collections Department at the St. Louis County Library in Frontenac, Missouri for their extensive help with such materials as coroner's reports, military records, newspapers, census reports, city directories, and maps. Additional information came from the research libraries of Washington University in St. Louis, the University of Missouri at St. Louis, and St. Louis Community College at Meramec, as well as the St. Louis Public Library (not to be confused with the St. Louis County Library).

Extensive records pertaining to the death of Philo Harris Woodworth were generously provided by the Cuyahoga County

Archives in the Robert Russell Rhodes House in Cleveland, Ohio. Maria Woodworth's *Rules of the Church of God*, along with related materials, were graciously supplied by the Circuit Court of the Seventh Judicial Circuit Court, in Sangamon County, Illinois.

In addition, Theresa Dickman, Music Librarian, provided extensive assistance regarding the hymn book published by Maria Woodworth and housed in the Essex Hymnal Collection, a part of the Essex Music Collection in the Lovejoy Library at Southern Illinois University at Edwardsville. That assistance included photographing the entire hymn book, as well as helping to identify the melody of Mrs. Woodworth's favorite song, "The Power."

Substantial information was provided by the United Brethren Historical Center at Huntington University in Huntington, Indiana, even to the point of digitizing materials for my benefit. Additional materials were provided by Special Collections and Historical Archives at Winebrenner Theological Seminary in Findlay, Ohio.

Before his death in 2010, Jack Overmyer, former publisher of the *Rochester News-Sentinel* in Rochester, Indiana, helped with local news coverage of Maria Woodworth, as did the Fulton County Public Library in Rochester. That library also assisted with access to the very valuable writings of A.B. Sibert regarding his close personal friends, Philo and Maria Woodworth. Genealogist and descendant Daniel Slevin helped with family information.

Special thanks to Billye Brim for her assistance and encouragement with this research project.

TABLE OF CONTENTS

Foreword 1

Introduction 3

1 The Trance Evangelist 7

2 Lightning Across the Midwest 49

3 A Tidal Wave of Controversy 89

4 Hypnotism and Hysteria:
   The St. Louis Meetings of 1890 101

5 A New Wave of Persecution 139

6 Hope and Hardship 165

7 Breakdown and a New Start 189

FOREWORD

I first heard of this remarkable woman evangelist through the teachings of Dr. Kenneth E. Hagin. The accounts he gave of her miraculous ministry held me in wonder. He used examples of the unusual supernatural demonstrations that accompanied her in meetings to encourage believers, especially those studying for the ministry, to yearn for and expect God to show up in power.

Steven Phipps' research into how the power of God would come upon her in "holding" her in its grip for hours, for instance, took the work of an unusually dedicated and qualified researcher. I know Brother Hagin, as I called him when I edited his teachings into print, would have welcomed this book. I know I do.

I will recommend it when I write and teach about the coming move of God that will be punctuated with the supernatural as most Christians today have never seen. This well-researched book shows glorious things that did happen. And they will happen again.

John G. Lake called her Mother Etter and would say, "Pray for the sick like Mother Etter prays."

The office of the evangelist in the New Testament was marked by miracles. Maria Woodworth-Etter truly ministered in the New Testament pattern. May Steven Phipps scholarly, yet exciting and easy-to-read account awaken many to what God has done through a little woman, and what He will do through many of His own in these end of days.

Dr. Billye Brim, Founder,
Billye Brim Ministries

INTRODUCTION

The era of the late 19th and early 20th centuries was a time of numerous important revivals and revivalists. Perhaps none of this era's evangelists was, however, as unique as Maria Woodworth. In addition, perhaps no other individual's ministry so clearly straddled the dividing lines among several of the most significant religious movements of the late 19th and early 20th centuries: the 19th century holiness movement, the proto-Pentecostal movement which began to manifest itself in a variety of modes during the 1880s and 1890s, and the early Pentecostal movement which gained impetus by around 1906 and which eventually crystallized into denominations during the 1910s.

The career of this enigmatic woman, Maria Beulah (Underwood) Woodworth-Etter, can easily and quite justifiably be divided into two distinct periods: her 19th century ministry, when she was known most often as simply "Mrs. Woodworth," and her 20th century ministry, when she became Maria Woodworth-Etter, the "hyphenated evangelist." While her spiritual orientation and ministry methods during these two period naturally exhibited tremendous similarity, there were marked differences.

Maria Woodworth found herself propelled into ministry after a series of deaths in her family. Those death experiences left her desperately eager to see the heaven where so many of her family members resided. A series of visions of heaven, accompanied by additional related spiritual experiences, empowered her for a ministry that was shocking to those accustomed to traditional denominational religion. She became known as the "trance evangelist," a woman whose meetings resulted in countless claims of physical healing, but even more experiences of trances and visions.

Near the end of the 19th century, however, she appears to have suffered a physical collapse. After a painful divorce, intense criticism from an often hostile press, attempts by medical doctors to have her committed, and censure from her denomination, Mrs. Woodworth seemed exhausted. Her anointing, which had resulted in extensive press coverage of her meetings by papers across the country, seemed to have waned.

In 1894, Maria Woodworth was unable to attend a denominational convention because of "so long and continued labor" and her resultant "tired physical condition."[7] A few years later, a newspaper reported that she had been lying for weeks in a tiny hamlet in Indiana, "at the point of death."[8]

That was in 1899. On New Year's Day in 1902, however, she remarried. The "trance evangelist" then settled on a farm in a remote portion of Illinois and, evidently, continued the recuperation process. She continued to hold meetings, even as early in the new century as 1901, but only on a minuscule scale compared to her previous campaigns.

Gone were the notoriety and the intense press coverage. When she returned to Decatur, Illinois in 1903, a newspaper there remarked that she "was once a drawing card in this section."[9] Eventually, as she joined the ranks of the early 20th century Pentecostal movement, her ministry would largely recover, but it would never be the same. Clearly, the heyday of her ministry was during the 19th century.

Although she wrote and self-published several versions of her autobiography, published works by others about Mrs. Woodworth (aside from press coverage) have been very limited. These have consisted of a few brief articles or book chapters, a collection primarily consisting of some of the literally countless newspaper articles about her ministry, and a biography offering a general overview of her entire life and ministry career.

None of these secondary sources have particularly focused on the facets of her ministry that made her famous: the trances, the visions, and other evidences of what the public often termed "the power." Instead, the present volume will concentrate specifically on these controversial phenomena and on the criticism that they engendered, while focusing primarily on the first phase of her ministry. That phase extended from the time she first became an evangelist around 1880 until the time she became Maria Woodworth-Etter in 1902.

Chapter

1

THE TRANCE
EVANGELIST

One day in 1890, a most unusual court hearing took place in St. Louis. Two medical doctors were attempting to have an enigmatic woman committed as insane. The reason? In revival meetings in a tent in the north part of the city, this woman, who was an evangelist, seemed to be leading her flock into what the doctors considered to be a dangerous state of religious frenzy.

In her tent meetings, typically some would fall to the floor in a swoon. Others might make climbing motions, as though attempting to climb up to a heaven that they were able to see so close above them. Still others would become as rigid as a statue as they entered into a trance state. Those trances might last for a few hours, or perhaps even for several days. Some of those who attended her services claimed to receive physical healing in the presence of God's glory.

These sorts of experiences were not, according to the doctors, the only supposedly dangerous and pernicious activities going on in her tent. By her own admission, the woman claimed to speak, at times, directly to Jesus. She claimed to have seen both heaven and hell. The two medical doctors concluded that she must be committed before her strange influence affected others.

The woman was Maria Woodworth, more commonly known simply as "Mrs. Woodworth." She was one of the best known evangelists of the late 19th century, and certainly the most controversial.

MARIA WOODWORTH IN AN ERA OF REVIVALS

The 19th century was, in large measure, a time of evangelists and revivals. Fiery camp meetings marked the opening of the century, and later decades saw the development of prayer and evangelism movements wielding widespread impact.

Adherents of "holiness" groups believed that they had received a definite, separate experience which they tended to term "entire sanctification." By late in the century, some of these groups had begun to call themselves "Pentecostal." They began to search the scriptures for references to walking in the power of God, believing that such experiences of old must surely be for us today.

By the fourth quarter of the 19th century, all sorts of new holiness and Pentecostal groups were beginning to surface amidst controversy and criticism. The press lumped together sincere Christian believers and dangerous psychopaths, as long as they seemed to be "fanatics."

Since they tended to hold to views on religion that seemed unconventional compared to the traditional denominations, and since those views seemed extreme, members of "fringe" religious groups were ridiculed and shunned. They were often termed "holy rollers," "holy jumpers," or simply fanatics possessing what newspapers sometimes called "an excess of religion."

Into this setting emerged one of the most unique evangelists of all time: Maria Woodworth, later known as Woodworth-Etter. The story of her life can hardly be contained in a single volume.

By far, however, the most colorful, controversial, and intriguing period of her life is the early period of her ministry. This was the period that stretched from the time she first entered ministry around 1880 until her apparent nervous and physical collapse in 1899.

In this study, we will begin with her early call to ministry and will continue to examine her life through the rest of the century. We will examine an era in which literally any newspaper in the country might have included at least a brief mention of this unique woman. This was the woman whom the press loved to call the "trance evangelist."

A large percentage of her extensive press coverage was the result of persecution, or at least consternation. That was the typical response to manifestations of what was typically termed "the power" in her meetings. The story of her early ministry is a story of continual battles against persecution and criticism. This was because her ministry did not fit into the traditional denominational structures.

Her supporters saw these manifestations as the power of God. Her detractors, however, insisted they were merely the result of religious hysteria, and likely hypnotism. Mrs. Woodworth, on the other hand, insisted that her followers were simply experiencing what the Bible calls "signs following."

Her favorite song was one she referred to as "The Power." As she frequently sang in one of its many verses,[10]

Our fathers had this power, our fathers had this power,
Our father had this power, and we may have it too.
'Tis the power, the power,
'Tis the power that Jesus promised should come down.

At a time when conventional religion was highly predictable and nearly totally devoid of "signs and wonders," Mrs. Woodworth's meetings did not fit the mold. Even one of her biggest critics referred to her as "a revivalist of remarkable power."[11]

She was accused of being insane; she was accused of hypnotizing her followers. A 19th century observer wrote of her, however, that "She is the disease-healing and trance-working preacher, who from Indiana to California has produced great excitement."[12]

EARLY LIFE AND MARRIAGE

Maria Woodworth-Etter, originally Maria Underwood, was born into an Ohio farm family on July 22, 1844. Her first name was pronounced with a long "i" sound, which resulted in her name sometimes being spelled "Mariah."

Her father, Samuel Lewis Underwood, had married Matilda Brittain and settled onto an Ohio farm. They lived near Lisbon, a small town which in their day was known as New Lisbon.

In July of 1857, when Maria was just nine years old, her father Samuel was killed in a storm. This threw the family into desperate circumstances. Maria's mother Matilda, then age 44, was left to care for nine children.

Even before Maria was born, the area around New Lisbon had been visited by various revivals and revivalists. Lorenzo Dow, the eccentric evangelist of the early 19th century, visited New Lisbon in 1817.

There he preached to as vast a multitude as Columbiana County could muster. That crowd gathered under a grove of trees at the end of Market Street. During an even earlier era, pioneer Presbyterian missionaries held revival meetings in the same neighborhood.

Even at an early age, Maria seemed quiet and withdrawn, with a vaguely defined religious orientation. In later years she was to say that she earnestly sought after God from the time she was about eight years old.

Sometime around 1857, when she was 13, she was born again in a local church meeting. The 1860 census shows 16-year-old Maria Underwood still living at home, but shortly afterward she left to work as a domestic servant. She earned barely enough money to survive.

Shortly after his Civil War service, she met her first husband. This was in 1863, when he came into her hometown of New Lisbon, Ohio to visit friends. Philo Harris Woodworth, who sometimes simply went by the name Harris,[13] was being introduced locally as a "great hero"[14] who had just returned from the war.

One of Maria's closest friends decided to play the role of matchmaker. She invited the timid and spiritually-minded Maria Underwood over one evening. The two—Philo and Maria—were left in the room together while their hostess prepared the dinner.

As Philo impressed Maria by telling her of the hardships he had suffered and the dangers he had withstood in battle, he gained Maria's sympathy. At the same time, for Philo Woodworth it was love at first sight, as he often testified later. He decided he would marry this shy young woman no matter what it took.

By her own later admission, Maria had no idea how to respond to Philo's great fascination with her and his earnest interest in marriage. She was no social butterfly, and felt out of place in anything but a very private world. Friends who she highly trusted, however, urged her to consent to marriage.

As a result, against her own better judgment, she eventually complied. The two were married within a month. This would later prove, however, to be the biggest mistake of her life.

"I had not been in his company much," she later noted. Not only that, but Maria eventually came to realize that she had forgotten the Biblical injunction to be "not unequally yoked together with unbelievers" (2 Corinthians 6:14). "I thought I could easily lead him to Christ," she later observed, "but I came near being led away myself and losing my experience."[15]

On the other hand, she believed that her marriage to Philo Woodworth might present a solution to a pressing spiritual issue in her life: She knew she was called to ministry, but in her day women did not preach. By marrying Philo, she reasoned, perhaps she would be able to enter ministry on her husband's coattails. First, however, she would have to get him born again.

Not only was he not a Christian at the time, but, evidently unknown to Maria, there was another serious deficiency in Philo as a suitable husband: He appears to have been married just a short time before, although only very briefly. Documentation is sketchy, but his marriage to his first wife seems to have ended earlier that same year.

Marriage records show that Philo Woodworth had married Lucinda Callahan on November 7, 1857 in his native Mahoning County, Ohio. Lucinda, according to the county marriage record, was only about 16, while Philo, who is listed as Philo H. Woodworth of Mahoning County, was about 19. They were married by a justice of the peace.

The marriage license application, on the other hand, which is dated the same day, refers to him as Philo H. Woodworth, age 19, and she as Lucinda Callahan, age 18. The application is signed "Philo Woodworth" in an unusually large and confident hand.

They must have lived together only a short time, however, because she appears to be the same person who is listed as Lucinda Callahan—not Lucinda Woodworth—about three years later in the 1860 census. By that time, Philo Woodworth had moved on and had joined the army, perhaps to escape his marital situation.

There is no evidence, however, that Maria Underwood even suspected that Philo Woodworth had been previously married. Since she was obviously trepidatious about marriage in general, it would seem extremely unlikely that she would have married him if she had known that he was previously married.

Unverified family genealogical data asserts that he even had a child by Lucinda,[16] although no child appears with her in the 1860 census. Philo Woodworth applied for a divorce in Mahoning County, Ohio in October 1863 according to the same genealogical data. That was the same year in which he married Maria Underwood.

In addition, young and naïve Maria was unaware that the supposedly great war hero, Philo Harris Woodworth, had not reached the officer status that he often claimed. Many years later, Philo Woodworth would be remembered by some as "Colonel Woodworth." In reality, however, he never advanced beyond the lowest rank, that of private. Not only that, but he was referred to in official military records as a "deserter at large."[17] This is the man who Maria Woodworth unwittingly married.

Although he bragged of his military exploits, Woodworth's Civil War pension records seem to suggest a rather ordinary term of military service which terminated with desertion. He had been introduced to Maria Underwood as having returned from five years' service, when in fact he had only been in the army about three years.

Philo claimed to have received a blow to the head as a war wound. That supposed war injury would, in later years, be used as a justification for his ever-worsening mental condition. Some, however, suggested that the injury to his head was not war-related at all, but was the result of an accident while mining coal.

Philo Harris Woodworth was born about 1838 in Buffalo, New York, the son of Nelson H. and Hannah Woodworth. He had worked as a blacksmith, as his father before him, before enlisting in the army in Cleveland, Ohio. Cleveland was the closest big city, not far from his home in rural Mahoning County.

At the time of his enlistment in 1860, Philo was described as having sandy hair, hazel eyes, and a fair complexion that was described as "florid."[18] His height was five feet, eight and a half inches. He was 22 years old.

Woodworth was not a volunteer, but enlisted in the regular army on September 21, 1860, according to the official register of enlistments. He served as a lowly private, despite his later claims of officer status, in Company E of the 3rd U.S. Infantry.

After the war, handwritten pension records list a variety of ailments afflicting Philo Woodworth. These were apparently the result of harsh but not atypical conditions during his Civil War service. For 1861 alone, medical reports for Woodworth refer to diarrhea in July, what looks like "contrisis" in a handwritten notation for August, and rheumatism in September.[19]

These problems were followed by phlegmon in September of the same year and catarrh in October. Then, during 1862, he was reported to be suffering from colica in January and March, catarrh in April, colica in August, and diarrhea in December.

Severe diarrhea, which often resulted from poor quality drinking water, was a common ailment among Civil War soldiers. Among many, this was a serious issue that sometimes even resulted in death. Finally, typhoid fever was reported in Philo Woodworth's records in February 1863.

In June and July of 1863, Woodworth was reported absent. This was because he had become sick at a place called White House, which is a small unincorporated community in Page County, Virginia. He later claimed that this was around the time that he contracted what was described in a pension record as "fever resulting in disease of feet and head" while at Fredericksburg, Virginia.

According to his own testimony, Philo was treated at Norfolk, Virginia from June to August of 1862, and then at Stanton General Hospital in Washington in February of the following year. The Adjutant General's office, which was a part of the War Department, later noted that from that point on, he was "A deserter at large."[20]

To his credit, however, a great many in his shoes similarly deserted. The page listing Philo Woodworth in the official enlistment register shows a number of others who also left the service by unofficial means.[21] Later that same year, 1863, Woodworth married Maria Underwood in Pennsylvania.

EARLY LIFE AFTER MARRIAGE

After marriage, the two moved out into the country in Philo's native Mahoning County, Ohio. The couple settled far from most of the Christian fellowship that Maria had earlier taken for granted, and this became a severe hardship for her. By 1864, Philo Woodworth and his new wife Maria had moved to an adjacent county, Columbiana County, which was where Maria had been born.

Maria, now Maria Woodworth, took up the tasks of child rearing and housekeeping. In the process, the continual sense that she was called to ministry was increasingly pushed aside.

She sank into poor health, and then, among her children, one after another mysteriously died at early ages. Out of her six children, only one, her daughter Lizzie, would survive past childhood.

Elizabeth ("Lizzie") Cornelia Woodworth was the couple's first child. She was born during their first full year of married life, on March 11, 1864. Elizabeth eventually became Lizzie Ormsby, wife of John Frederick Ormsby. He was also born in Columbiana County.

An 1871 county birth record for Fredrick Woodworth, son of Philo and Maria, shows the couple as living at Salem in Columbiana County. An 1872 county birth record for another son William, shows the family as living at Alliance in Columbiana County. There, Philo's name is recorded as "Harris Woodworth." When daughter Nelly was born in 1876, the county birth record shows the couple as living in Elkrun Township.

The untimely death of all but one of the children was a major contributing factor toward Philo Woodworth's growing mental instability. Maria continued to believe that his mental condition began during the Civil War, the result of a blow to the head during battle. Whether this was the case or not, his military pension records do refer to a "contusion" to the head.

Not only did Philo Woodworth's mind begin to go, but, increasingly, his physical health as well. Eventually he was not always able to go to work. Whatever the cause of his mental condition, Philo, known in later years as "Pop" Woodworth, would eventually become one of his wife Maria's most bitter opponents and persecutors in ministry. This seemed to become increasingly the case, the more his mind became impaired.

In 1877, Maria Woodworth was battling gnawing internal demands that she enter ministry. Around the same time, revival meetings were being conducted in East Liverpool, Ohio, in her home territory of Columbiana County.

The message of evangelist Francis Murphy (1836–1907), who had formerly been a saloon keeper from New England, held sway over the crowds. Murphy had been born in Ireland but had served in the Union Army in the U.S. during the Civil War. Around 2,000 people who attended his Columbiana County meetings signed a temperance pledge as a result of Murphy's appeals.

Eventually, it was said, about 16 million people across the country signed his pledge. That pledge read,

With malice toward none, with charity for all, I hereby pledge my sacred honor that, God helping me, I will abstain from the use of all intoxicating liquors as a beverage, and that I will encourage others to abstain.[22]

Women committed to the temperance message held prayer meetings in front of Columbiana County saloons during the following year. Whether Maria Woodworth took part in this 1878 "Women's Crusade" is unknown. She may, however, have been influenced, either directly or indirectly, by this and other religious revival movements that swept through the area.

The sorrow connected with her repeated experience of the death of loved ones, first her father and then one after another of her children, began to drive her to listen more intently to the ever-present call to ministry. At the same time, she earnestly longed to see the same heaven in which her children were now residing.

Maria Woodworth began to see vision after vision. As Mrs. Woodworth would enter the "trance" state, she would typically see heaven. During the 1870s, as she witnessed one after another of her children passing on into heaven, she also saw visions of her children's new home.

She saw the New Jerusalem. She saw Jesus. She saw the angels. At times she would see her departed children, living happily in another realm.

The experience of seeing visions of heaven continued throughout her ministry. This was an experience that she firmly believed was intended for others as well. "Hold your head up, brother," she was heard to shout in one of her tent revivals, "and look right through the top of this tent into God's eternal kingdom."[23]

As the visions continued, at times heavenly things seemed far more real than earthly things. The visions began to be accompanied by a state of being that others described as a "trance." These trances sometimes lasted for hours.

Today the term "trance" may be more frequently associated with hypnotism or eastern religions. The phenomenon of trances accompanied by visions is certainly not, however, foreign to the Bible.

Balaam experienced a vision while in a trance, as recorded in Numbers 24:4. In Acts 10:10, when Peter prayed on a housetop, he entered into a trance in which he saw a vision. This experience is also recounted in Acts 11:5. While in the Jewish Temple in Jerusalem, as recorded in Acts 22:17–18, Paul saw Jesus in a trance.

As her visions continued, eventually Maria Woodworth's health returned and her husband was born again. Shortly after his conversion, Philo Woodworth began to experience what is commonly known as speaking in other tongues, although this was an era in which such an experience was evidently extremely uncommon. He seemed a different person.

Whenever difficulties came his way, however, he quickly became discouraged, evidently the result of his mental instability. His spiritual condition was characterized by his wife as up and down.

Before long, even Maria, who was still unable to come to grips with a pressing call to ministry, was experiencing emotional problems. She lapsed into a state described as "nervous affections,"[24] and was expected to die at any moment.

At this point, Maria Woodworth made a promise to God: If he would only heal her, she would serve him.

She immediately began to improve, but then, yet again, found herself making excuse after excuse as to why she could not possibly enter ministry. Her primary excuse was that she was a woman. This was, after all, an era in which very few women entered ministry on their own.

Then, in a vision, she saw the pit of hell. She saw people falling headlong into the pit, while she tried to warn them and to point them toward the dazzling brilliance of the heaven that she saw overhead. As a result, she felt that she must enter full-time itinerant evangelistic ministry, but her husband was opposed and so were her friends.

Then another child died, the fifth to go. She then was left with only one child, Lizzie. Maria's husband Philo was described as "completely deranged" for several months as a result of the fifth child's death.

HER MINISTRY BEGINS

In later years, Maria Woodworth would retrospectively trace her ministry beginnings to about 1880. In that year, Philo, Maria, and their sole surviving child, Lizzie, had moved back to Mahoning County. There Philo Woodworth tried to eke out a living as a peddler, while Maria's only occupation was that of housewife. She was 33 years old.

Finally, sometime around this point, Maria began with steeled determination to enter the work to which she believed God had called her. Her Bible then became her constant friend.

She later testified that, at this time, complex Bible truths became clear to her through a single vision. She began to speak to groups of people here and there on Saturday nights and on Sundays, and the crowds began to grow. The unique ministry of Maria Woodworth had finally begun.

Then as well as later in life, she would not prepare her messages. In this sense, her ministry was very similar to that of Evan Roberts (1878–1951), the best-known figure associated with the Welsh Revival of 1904 and 1905. Roberts was said to rarely, if ever, prepare sermons. Instead, he depended on the leading of the Holy Spirit.

One description of Maria Woodworth's early meetings suggests that she often started with obvious effort, as though not sure what to say and as though waiting for something.

Finally, however, that something would come. Then, according to the same description, "her manner changes, her eyes light up, and the words flow rapidly from her mouth."[25] This is also remarkably similar to accounts of the spoken ministry of 20th century Pentecostal figure Smith Wigglesworth (1859–1947).

Mrs. Woodworth often had no idea what to say until she faced her audience. Then a Biblical passage, oftentimes a very obscure one, would supernaturally be given to her along with the exact reference so that she could look it up.

Then the words would seem to just flow out of her mouth. According to one observer, it was undeniable that her words came from what he termed "some abundant fountain."[26]

As she spoke these words that were not her own, the Spirit of God would fall on congregations. Sinners cried out for mercy. Many shouted praises or fell to the ground.

At other times, after she had become well-established in ministry, Mrs. Woodworth would focus on recounting various manifestations of healing that she had seen in her ministry. She would follow this by asking for testimonies from those who had experienced healing, those who were, as she liked to put it, "healed soul and body."[27]

As was the case with Evan Roberts in Wales, however, some noted that after only a few years of ministry her face seemed to bear the marks of the strain of overwork. One writer commented that her face carried "many traces of fatigue and sleeplessness."[28] Her eyes would appear tired only until she began to minister, however. Then they would begin to sparkle.

Her critics were quick to point to her poor grammar, which they took as an indication of Maria Woodworth's lack of education. Her detractors suggested that if she had received more schooling, she would not have been so prone to experience the trances and other unusual manifestations that she allowed to accompany her ministry.

Alfred B. Sibert, a friend of the Woodworths from Rochester, Indiana, noted that she "had but little book learning, but she possessed native intelligence, commanded an easy and fluent use of appropriate words, and displayed a wonderfully pleasing and impressive manner."[29] Various newspapers referred to her speaking style as eloquent.

According to the *Boston Globe*, Mrs. Woodworth appeared "comely," with "a fine physique."[30] While not cultured or refined, she was said to be an "impressive speaker," words that were echoed by the *New York Evangelist*.[31] Both publications said she was of "commanding appearance." The *Evangelist* added that while she spoke, she kept her hands "in constant motion."

Mrs. Woodworth often dressed in black, other times entirely in white. In 1885, she was described as having braided hair, which was kept in place with a tortoise shell comb.

She appeared to be obviously "earnest and entirely confident" while ministering, according to the *Chicago Tribune*. The same source pointed out that while she was not educated, she was "a fluent speaker" with "more than ordinary native talent."[32]

What her ministry lacked in formal training seemed to have been amply compensated for by supernatural manifestations. Wherever she went, controversy invariably followed her. This was precisely because the denominational church world did not know what to make of what was commonly termed "the power" evident in her meetings.

Philo Woodworth found himself faced with his wife's overwhelming desire to travel and preach. At first he was reluctant to even consider accommodating her calling. Eventually, however, he sided in with her desire to minister. Once that was settled, they entered ministry as a team.

According to Maria Woodworth, churches offered her ministry positions with substantial salaries, but she refused. She aligned herself first with the United Brethren Church, then became a traveling evangelist with one of the several denominations known as the "Church of God." In her case, she affiliated with the "Church of God, General Conference," also known as the "Winebrennerians."

The "Church of God (Winebrenner)" grew out of a movement associated with reformer John Winebrenner (1797–1860), who had come out of the German Reformed Church. Winebrenner organized his own group in Dauphin County, Pennsylvania in 1828. Then around 1880, he reorganized the movement, attempting to bring it further in line with what he envisioned to be the Biblical pattern.

Shortly afterward, the Winebrennerians began to hold what were termed "Pentecostal meetings." The term "Pentecostal," as it was used in those days, simply referred to a focus on the Spirit of God. Those who were affiliated with the Winebrenner movement developed a close fascination with anything associated with the Holy Spirit.

The movement's primary historian was a writer by the name of Christian Henry ("C.H.") Forney. Forney referred to what he called a "tenacious interest" in the "person, functions, and offices" of the Holy Spirit, as well as the Spirit's "inworking and outworking."[33] Perhaps this intense concern with the Spirit of God is what attracted Maria Woodworth to the denomination.

During these so-called "Pentecostal meetings," the primary agenda was to get to know the Spirit of God. Meetings were designed specifically to find out how the Holy Spirit functions. Adherents also wanted to know what it is that the Spirit wants to accomplish within the body of Christ.

Without elaborating, historian C.H. Forney said that they encountered so many "obstacles" to this mission, as he termed them, that such meetings were finally abandoned. Still, in his words, "Most persistent efforts" were still being made to "keep burning the camp meeting fires."

Even their camp meetings had to be eventually abandoned, however. This was because of what Forney admitted was, as he put it, the "growing indifference of the churches."[34]

In spite of acknowledged and growing spiritual coldness, the Winebrenner movement was based on the 1844 doctrinal statement of its founder, John Winebrenner. That statement refers to the Bible as constituting the denomination's "only rule of faith and practice."[35]

Not only that, but as the doctrinal statement was interpreted in 1899, "the individual is free to interpret it," meaning the Bible, "in the light of his own conscience."[36] This stance would seem quite amenable to Maria Woodworth's unorthodox ministry methods.

Once she began to work among the Winebrennerians as an evangelist, however, many of the movement's ministers began to criticize Mrs. Woodworth. They found issue with her stand on healing, trances, and visions. This was the case in spite of their avowed respect for one's "own conscience."

As long as she simply preached, no one found fault with her. Once healing, trances, and visions entered into the picture, however, it was another story. Some years later, an observer noted that

> When Maria confined herself to pulpit exhortations, punctuated with an occasional trance, she was regarded as a most marvelous woman by the generality of people. But her new specialty of healing the sick, raising the dead and so on has made her fame and reputation that she had never hoped to gain.[37]

This did not, however, keep her husband from becoming what was known as an "exhorting evangelist"[38] among the Church of God adherents. As Philo Woodworth entered ministry, one must wonder what his relationship was, if any, to an earlier minister of the same name. A certain Philo Woodworth, who died in 1871, had been a presiding Methodist Episcopal elder in Maria's husband's home state of New York. The earlier man was born there in 1801 or 1802.

This revival pioneer first appears in Methodist records in 1826. He became the leading figure in a powerful revival at the Niagara Street Church in Buffalo, New York. Buffalo was the same city in which Philo Harris Woodworth, who married Maria, was born about twelve years later.

Following in the footsteps of the great revival led by Charles G. Finney in New York State, the earlier Philo Woodworth led about four hundred persons to conversion during the winter of 1840 and 1841.

According to one historical account, this earlier Woodworth's revival methods appear to have worked "even better than those of Finney."[39] "At any rate," according to the same writer, the results of that revival firmly established the Methodists as a formidable force in Buffalo.

One account of the revival led by the earlier Philo Woodworth declared that,

Brother Woodworth was very successful in winning souls to Christ. The most powerful and extensive revival ever witnessed in the city of Buffalo took place under his ministration as Pastor of the Niagara-street Methodist Episcopal Church. His preaching was emphatically in the demonstration of the Spirit and of power.[40]

As already noted, Maria Woodworth's ministry began around 1880. One of the earliest known news items pertaining to her ministry appeared in the *Woman's Evangel* of June 1883. A local branch of the Women's Missionary Association, it was reported, met April 24th in Lima, Ohio, and "Mrs. Woodworth of Columbiana County spoke in the evening."[41]

The name of Maria Woodworth began to appear among lists of Indiana Winebrenner Church of God elders by 1884. In July and August of that year, Maria and her husband Philo Woodworth held a memorable revival at a place in Indiana with the unlikely name of Buzzard's Schoolhouse. This may possibly have been near Pleasant Mills, southeast of Decatur.

A church with 90 members was the result. In that year, 1884, Maria was licensed to preach by the Indiana Eldership of the Winebrennerians. At the same time, they made her what was termed the "eldership general evangelist." She was reappointed the following year.

THE TRANCE STATE AND OTHER "SIGNS AND WONDERS"

Already by the early 1880s, reports of most unusual supernatural manifestations accompanying her ministry were beginning to surface in press reports. The most prominent of these manifestations was what was described as the "trance" state.

This condition appears similar to a phenomenon that had surfaced in rural camp meetings about 80 years earlier. Then, however, something akin to the "trance" experience was in evidence, and was often termed the "falling exercise."

As the 19th century began, powerful revivals broke out in the rural wilderness in the form of camp meetings. Camp meetings were called that because those who attended, who were primarily farm families, came from near and far, bringing their farm wagons and camping in the woods.

The sheltering branches protected them from rain. The abundant trees allowed for the construction of rough benches and what were called "preacher's stands."

At the Cane Ridge camp meeting at a place known by that name in Kentucky, perhaps as many as 20,000—maybe more—camped under trees in a remote location. This was to hear fiery preaching and to praise God day and night. Many of those who attended Cane Ridge became subject to the "falling exercise."

The phenomenon was nothing new. Countless individuals fell to the ground under the powerful preaching of John Wesley and George Whitefield during the previous century.

Falling might be compared to the modern experience of becoming what is called "slain in the Spirit," a common experience in "charismatic" Christian meetings, were it not for some pronounced differences. The experience was often not at all the same.

Those who fall in modern Christian meetings are typically back on their feet within a few short moments. They tend to be easily brought out of their "slain in the Spirit" state and moved back to their seats when convenience so dictates.

The prostration experiences associated with Mrs. Woodworth's ministry, however, were often radically different and far more powerful. Frequently, they were more akin to what was experienced in some of the early camp meetings, such as at Cane Ridge.

There, it is said, some of the fallen individuals did not even appear to breathe. They could be picked up and stacked up like logs without disturbing them.

In fact, those who had succumbed to the "falling exercise" were often picked up and carried off to a more convenient location where they would be out of the way. In the process they remained undisturbed and did not emerge from their trance for many hours or perhaps even several days.

In Mrs. Woodworth's meetings, some individuals were so affected that they could be pricked by a pin or picked up and carried, without disturbing them at all. Those attending Woodworth's meetings sometimes remained in the trance state for as long as eight days.

In some cases they did not fall at all, but simply became frozen in their tracks. Then they might resist all attempts to bring them out of that condition. Oftentimes their eyes were wide open, while not a single muscle of their body moved.

Observers tried to concoct all sorts of explanations for these phenomena. Some claimed that she drugged her followers, others that she hypnotized them. Occasionally someone would attempt to construct scientific-sounding analyses of the trance phenomenon, but they only sounded silly at best.

One newspaper reporter, as an example of a scientific-sounding but nonsensical explanation, commented that it was a matter of "ecstasy which is produced by a concentration of the mind through one set of faculties to the exclusion of all others."[42] The same writer claimed that similar trance states were said to result in ancient times from the worship of the goddess Venus.

The reporter commented that although opinions differed about the trance state, "one thing is sure, it is real." Real or not, people just did not know what to make of it. Another newspaper asked, "Is it contagious or infectious, epidemic or endemic, good or evil?"[43]

By the time of Maria Woodworth's early ministry, the "falling exercise" and trance-like states associated with early 19th century camp meetings had become all but forgotten by most Christians. Mrs. Woodworth, however, caused public attention to once again be riveted on these types of manifestations.

As Mrs. Woodworth ministered, evangelistic movements led by such big-name evangelists as Dwight L. Moody (1837–1899) and Thomas Harrison (1854-) (the "boy evangelist") were in their heyday. In their meetings, such phenomena as falling, trances, and visions were strangely absent.

A correspondent for the *Herald of Gospel Liberty* noted in 1885, however, that Maria Woodworth's meetings did not fit the late 19th-century norm:

> I attended one meeting at New Corner, [Indiana,] conducted by the lady evangelist, Mrs. Woodworth, and saw some in trances. I talked to different ones who had been in trances and had beheld visions of the better land. One was in a trance sixteen hours. I count it a manifestation of the power of God, similar to the manifestations at the Cane Ridge revival in 1801.[44]

When such experiences began surfacing in Mrs. Woodworth's meetings, the sheer novelty resulted in extensive press coverage. Her crowds and the press were both perplexed: What was the cause of these experiences? Was it God, the devil, hypnotism, mesmerism, or simply religious hysteria?

Even as early as February 1881, a Pennsylvania newspaper reported that an Indiana woman fell into a trance at a revival meeting.[45] She remained in that state for six days.

While the article does not mention Maria Woodworth or any minister in particular, she was very likely associated with the meeting, either directly or indirectly. Newspapers quickly began to pick up on the trances associated with Mrs. Woodworth. Literally countless articles (certainly not all of which have ever been found in modern times) in newspapers across the country commented on the strange woman evangelist and the trances in her meetings.

Once she had entered ministry, the experience of entering into trances accompanied by visions seemed to rub off onto others. As an 1885 newspaper account expressed it, not only did Maria Woodworth enter into trances herself, but she "so influences her congregations that they also go into a trance state."[46]

As prostrations and trances became more common in her meetings, her reputation continued to grow. Of course, attendance swelled as the curious crowded into her services.

An 1884 newspaper mentioned that she was personally entering a trance in "almost every meeting."[47] Before long, she was being referred to as Mrs. Woodworth, the "trance evangelist." Occasionally, she was given other nicknames: the "shouting evangelist,"[48] and even the "electric evangelist."[49] After her second marriage, when she became known as Maria Woodworth-Etter, she was also called "the hyphenated evangelist."

Some saw the phenomena associated with her ministry as genuine manifestations of the power of God, while others saw them as simply the result of hypnotism, hysteria, or what was commonly called "religious enthusiasm." When a newspaper reported that she had "fallen over in a heap" during a revival meeting in Sheldon, Indiana in 1884, the paper attributed this to "an excess of religious fervor."[50]

Some claimed that she possessed mysterious occult powers that were the result of carrying powerful lucky charms with her. On one occasion, a reporter told her, "Some say that you have a rabbit's paw, taken from a graveyard at midnight, and that it is studded with turtle eyes." "Well, I never heard that before," Mrs. Woodworth replied, "but I suppose some foolish ones talk that way." She continued,

> You would be surprised at the foolish ideas that some people have. Why, they say I wear an electric belt. Well, so I do, please God! It reaches to the heavenly throne and the Lord sends down shocks to the sinners.[51]

As the press increasingly picked up on the goings-on of this unconventional woman evangelist, sensational reports of phenomena at her meetings continued to fill columns of papers, especially in the Midwest. As often as not, she was simply made the object of ridicule.

A Fort Wayne, Indiana newspaper complained in 1884 that she had "failed to do her great emotional flop-over act"[52] while holding a meeting in a small town near the city. The same paper had announced in a tongue-in-cheek manner that, at those meetings, special seating would be reserved for "ungodly newspaper men." Another article claimed that she had worked what the paper called the "trance racket" to "perfection."[53]

On the other hand, many of those early reports also noted that sinners were coming to Christ in droves in her meetings. An 1884 account referred to her as the "sensational" evangelist who had converted the Indiana towns of Monroeville, Hoagland, and Sheldon.[54]

A bit later, while ministering in the tiny hamlet of Zanesville, Indiana, she was said to be "yanking Zanesville sinners by the dozen."[55] Five days later the same paper reported that she had "succeeded in converting every person in town but one."[56] A couple weeks after that, she was said to have "converted all the people in Markle,"[57] another small Indiana town.

By the mid-1880s, much of the Midwest had heard of Mrs. Woodworth, and whole towns appear to have been thrown into a frenzy whenever she arrived. One of her 1885 meetings in Indianapolis, held in a Methodist church, was reported by no less than the *New York Times* and the *Boston Globe*.

Both papers quoted a letter from Indiana that noted the unusual manifestations accompanying her meetings:

> Scores have been stricken down at these meetings, and whatever form the limbs or body chance to assume in that position, immovable as a statue, they remained— sometimes the hands were uplifted far above the head,

the eyes open wide, and not a muscle of the entire body moved; they were as immovable as in death. Many have gone to these meetings in a spirit of jest, and were the first to be under the influence pervading the assembly. The people are wonderfully excited, and neighbor asks neighbor, "What is it?"[58]

The reference to those who attended her meetings in "a spirit of jest" sometimes being among the first to succumb to the manifestations was echoed in various later articles. One man, who interrupted one of Maria Woodworth's meetings to hurl profane accusations at her, suddenly found himself incapable of speaking.

When asked by others what happened to him, he answered, "Go up yourself and find out."[59] Others who came to mock the trances found themselves among the first to fall under what became termed "the power."

In a much earlier era, similar experiences had met those who came to ridicule the early camp meetings. There, it was said, individuals who were deriding the camp meeting phenomena often suddenly fell to the ground, in many cases in mid-sentence, as though shot by a gun. On other occasions, they were seized by another early 19th century phenomenon, the "jerks."

Although Mrs. Woodworth's meetings were known for common occurrences of the "falling exercise," or prostrations, she appears to have not inherited the other manifestation for which the early camp meetings were known, that of the "jerks." Anyone in the early 19th century who knew anything about the camp meetings was familiar with this experience.

Individuals taken with the jerks suddenly found themselves being jerked rapidly back and forth. This strange occurrence seemed to especially affect those who were sinners and were not born again. Oftentimes those who came to ridicule found themselves hit with the jerks while right in the middle of deriding the experience.

The jerks do not seem to have surfaced in Mrs. Woodworth's meetings, but crowds of the curious flocked to every meeting in hopes of witnessing what were termed the "trances." This term seems to have been applied loosely to both prostrations and another experience common in Woodworth's meetings, that of standing rigidly in one position, like a statue, for extended periods of time.

In fact, the latter experience came to be viewed as Mrs. Woodworth's trademark, so to speak. She even posed for photos with one finger pointing upward, since that was her common posture while in the trance state. The *New York Times* and *Boston Globe* both described the experience known as the trance state in identical terms, as it manifested itself in her Indianapolis meetings:

> . . . the body becomes stilled as though dead—naught but circulation and the act of respiration remain to signify life. The features are as pale as marble, the pulse weak and feeble. This morning a young lady was found in a trance or ecstasy in bed and could not be aroused for hours. The eyes were lifted to the ceiling and the hand pointed to heaven. When she was restored to consciousness, she shouted, clapped her hands, and sang 'hallelujah' for an hour, and said she was perfectly oblivious and totally unconscious to all about her.[60]

Mrs. Woodworth's ardent fans and admirers saw the trances as manifestations of the power of God. Others insisted that the trance state must be the result of mesmerism or hypnotism.

Some thought that perhaps the monotonous nature of the songs that were sung in her meetings, the waving of the arms in praise, or the gentle whisper of instructions to those seeking physical healing were all factors causing individuals to enter a state of hypnosis. No one could explain, however, why the trance state would so profoundly affect even those who opposed it. Some did not enter the trance state until sometime after leaving the meeting, perhaps not until the next day.

Further, even professional hypnotists or mesmerists confessed that they were baffled by the phenomenon. They insisted it was anything but hypnosis or mesmerism.

In addition, hypnosis does not ordinarily produce visions of heaven. Once individuals emerged from their trances, as a Fort Wayne, Indiana newspaper pointed out, they often immediately spoke of the glories of heaven that they had seen:

> . . . upon recovering, all attempted to describe the sublime spectacle of the New Jerusalem. They claimed to have seen visions of such grandeur and sublimity that the language of earth would utterly fail to describe; and heard such songs of angelic sweetness that compared with which the grandest music of earth is but blatant discord.[61]

A reporter in 1886 asked Maria Woodworth how she could account for the trances that accompanied her ministry. She replied,

> In the manner that I account for the same manifestations described in the Bible. A score or more of them are there set forth. It is the Spirit of God. I preach the word as it was preached by the apostles. I believe in no changes, in no alterations, in no revisions. These are the work of the devil. At the services that I conduct you can witness the very scenes described in God's book. The righteous are blessed, the converted are carried away in trances or

shout the praises of God, and scoffers are stricken down. Scores of times have I seen those who have come to ridicule the meetings felled to the earth and robbed of their power of speech for hours. This is the way God has of convicting and converting. This is the way Saul of Tarsus was brought into the fold.[62]

Many who experienced becoming "entranced" in Mrs. Woodworth's meetings were found to emerge from the trance state shouting praises to God. On the other hand, she was met with forceful opposition when individuals who did not understand the trances found their close friends and family members so affected.

While in Pendleton, Indiana in 1885, Maria Woodworth laid on the platform in a trance for six hours. After she emerged from that condition during her evening meeting, a daughter of a local man likewise fell into a trance.

By this time the evening was late. Her father, John Malone, was awakened from sleep and was told that Mrs. Woodworth had put his daughter into a trance.

In a rage, Malone entered the church and threatened violence. Within ten minutes, however, he was said to have become "the noisiest convert in town,"[63] jubilantly shouting praises to God because he had found salvation.

By this time, Maria Woodworth was becoming recognized, as Winebrenner Church of God historian C.H. Forney put it, as an evangelist of "more than ordinary power."[64] As a result, she was frequently asked to work with groups other than the Winebrenner Church of God. While this greatly furthered the scope of her work, it also caused a great rift and growing resentment among many of the leaders of her denomination.

This initiated an ongoing squabble that would continue for a number of years. In the mid-1880s, some of the denominational leadership had great confidence in her ministry abilities. Others, however, were already standing in opposition against her. Some of that opposition was, no doubt, the result of jealousy. Much of it, however, was simply due to an unwillingness to accept supernatural manifestations as being of God.

Mrs. Woodworth and her husband Philo, who were both a part of the denomination's Indiana Eldership, were made advisory members of the 57th session of the East Pennsylvania Eldership in 1885. This seems to have been largely because of the fame Maria Woodworth was acquiring as an evangelist.

At the same time, Forney noted that "some restraint" was "thrown around" her, as he put it. Regardless of the fact that her ministry had outgrown her denomination, Mrs. Woodworth was told to make sure that her ministry was being conducted, as it was expressed, "in the interest of the Church of God."[65]

On the Fourth of July in 1885, Maria Woodworth began revival meetings on the shores of Lake Manitou, a popular vacation attraction just outside the town of Rochester, Indiana. These meetings, which evidently were held in Talley's Grove on the eastern shore of the lake, likely were her first in the area.

Just before this, a variety of speakers had been lecturing or preaching on the same side of the lake on Sunday afternoons. The Woodworths circulated handbills announcing tent meetings featuring Maria as "trance evangelist" and Philo as "exhorting evangelist." They were accompanied by a third individual, Joe Salors, who was described as "the singing evangelist."[66]

Those meetings closed on the 14th with what Mrs. Woodworth thought was poor attendance, but which the local press called good attendance:

Mrs. W. B. [i.e. M.B.] Woodworth, who is well known through Ohio and Indiana as the trance Evangelist, commenced a series of religous [i.e. religious] services at Tally's Landing, on the east bank of Lake Manitou, last Saturday. There was a good attendance on Saturday and Sunday, many going by conveyance and many by steam boat from Skinner's Landing. . . . The lady is assisted by three male divines who are zealous workers, and it is probable that by another Sabbath the fires will be burning on the altar and many sinners will be inquiring what they shall do to be saved.[67]

The same paper continued by describing Maria Woodworth's personal characteristics and beliefs as they related to her ministry:

Mrs. Woodworth is well fitted by nature to soften the hearts of hardened sinners, and during the past year or two hundred[s] of men, women and children have been redeemed from the thralldom of sin through the inducements she has presented. She is of sanguine nervous temperament, and with a heart overflowing with sympathy which constantly illuminates a happy countenance her hearers are unconsciously drawn unto her and unite with her in songs and praises. Her power is not magnetic as some have said, but consists solely of a divine-like sympathy which takes hold of every one who will remain for a time in her presence. She is fully persuaded that no person will ever enjoy the society of the blest in the spirit world unless effectually converted while sojourning upon the mundane sphere.

Maria and Philo Woodworth were impressed with Lake Manitou. The following year, the couple decided to buy land on the lake and to make it their home and ministry headquarters. Part of the reason for their decision was that Mrs. Woodworth thought the lake would make an excellent location for an annual camp meeting.

The couple purchased a 12-acre resort known as Manitou Park from a local man, Alfred B. Sibert, in June of 1886. Around this time, Maria Woodworth explained to a newspaper reporter, "It is a lovely place and we frequently go there."[68] After they bought lakefront property from Sibert, the Woodworths announced plans to minister at the lake for a month that summer, beginning August 27.

In 1887, the Woodworths bought even more land at Lake Manitou and erected a large hotel at their location on the eastern lakefront. At that time, Maria Woodworth reiterated her plans to eventually use the property as a camp meeting ground, plans that appear to have materialized later that year.

The local press noted in 1887 that "A 400 dollar piano will be placed in the parlor of the Woodworth hotel." The same newspaper page observed that "The Woodworth hotel has ten 10W boats just completed for the use of guests. A landing for the steamer will be constructed in front of it."[69]

Another 1887 issue of the same paper announced that Maria Woodworth was expected to "commence a campmeeting" near what was described as "her new boarding house" in May. In addition, "Her new steamboat and other improvements" were said to be certain to "add much to the attraction of Lake Manitou."[70]

By July of 1887, the Rochester newspaper was running ads for the Woodworth Hotel. At the time, a certain K.G. Owen managed the hotel while the Woodworths were away:

WOODWORTH HOTEL.

The new Woodworth hotel is located on the east bank of Lake Manitou, at one of the most attractive points to be found at this Lake. It is now accessible to teams, and hitching posts have been conveniently placed to accommodate. The boats and fishing tackle are all new. Mr. K. G. Owen has charge of the Hotel and entertains satisfactorily and at reasonable rates. He desires a share of your patronage and is justly entitled to it.[71]

A few years earlier, in 1879, a Rochester newspaper had observed that Sibert had just sold his bakery and confectionery stand. At the time, Sibert was, as that source phrased it, "about to start another boat landing and pleasure resort on the east bank of the lake."[72] Presumably this is the land that he later sold the Woodworths.

A local newspaper declared in that same year that "A good place to spend a portion of today will be over in Sibert's grove, on the east bank of the lake." The paper added, "There will be good music, dancing, etc."[73]

Sibert's grove seems to have been a grove just south of what was known as Manitou Park. The Woodworths' property holdings, however, came to include Manitou Park plus additional land. The Woodworths renamed the property Woodworth Place. There, they operated a hotel and owned several cottages.

This property remained the home of both Philo and Maria Woodworth until they separated in 1890. Before that time, they lived there whenever they were not traveling and holding evangelistic meetings. Woodworth Place, later known as the Woodworth Mineral Springs Sanitarium, was described in 1887 as "a pleasant resort for Chicago and Indiana families."[74]

As what was likely a typical testimony from 1888, a newspaper noted that a Peru, Indiana man and his sister "have been occupying Woodworth Place Hotel, on the east bank of the lake[,] for the past two months." As a result, they left "much improved in spirits and delighted with Manitou as a summer resort."[75]

The land was deeded jointly to Philo and Maria Woodworth. Sibert later recalled that the money to buy the property came, as he put it, "wholly from the proceeds of the sale of Mrs. Woodworth's books and the other receipts of her meetings."[76]

Sibert continued to live next door and to watch over the property whenever Philo and Maria Woodworth left town to hold tent campaigns, which took place primarily in the summer months. On at least one occasion, however, the Woodworths leased the property out to another individual while they were traveling.

In spite of their close friendship, Albert Sibert declared even as late as 1891, "I am an utter disbeliever in many of the doctrines that Mrs. Woodworth is teaching, and do not approve of some methods she is using to convert the heathen." He continued to say, however,

> but I believe her to be honest and sincere, and when I see churches arising on every hand and thousands being turned from their evil ways through her, I cannot help but feel an admiration for the zeal and will-power that enables her to overcome difficulties not one woman in a million would grapple with.[77]

During one of Sibert's frequent visits to Woodworth Place, he was invited by one of Mrs. Woodworth's coworkers to observe a couple of individuals in a trance.

"Did you ever see anyone in a trance, Mr. Sibert?" he was asked. "No," he answered, "but I have a great curiosity to do so."[78] He was then shown two women in trances. They had both entered that state following a time of singing, praying, and exhorting after dinner.

Sibert was convinced that the trance condition associated with Mrs. Woodworth was a fraud. When he was shown a middle-aged woman in the house who appeared to be in a trance, he promptly removed a pin from his coat lapel and pricked her with it. He was surprised to find that there was no response whatsoever.

Another of those in a trance that same evening was a woman named Emma Posther, about 20 years old. She was one of Maria Woodworth's ministry assistants. Emma Posther, along with Emma Isenberg and Alice Daggett, accompanied Maria Woodworth in meetings across the country.

Sibert described Miss Posther as standing at the foot of the stairs with her eyes closed and with one arm raised. With that arm, she pointed upward toward heaven. According to Sibert, she was

breathing lightly through her nose, her lips being closed and her heartbeats even. There was still considerable rigidity in the muscles of her arms, but her temperature, so far as I was able to judge, was about normal.

A bit later Sibert heard one of Woodworth's tent revival songs coming from far across the lake. He declared that he had "never heard sweeter human melody."

He was startled, however, to find that the voice was not actually coming from across the lake at all, but from directly behind him indoors. The voice was that of young Emma Posther, who was still in her trance.

According to Sibert,

You may talk of your heavenly choirs and heavenly harmonies, but I do not believe that heaven above or earth beneath ever will or ever can produce sweeter music than came from the throat of that little trance subject in the Woodworth home that night.[79]

By this time, Philo Woodworth was not only accompanying his wife on her ministry journeys, but was himself licensed as what was termed an exhorter with her denomination, the Church of God (Winebrenner). The Winebrennerians gave an organizational home to the Woodworths' ministry, but their relationship with the denomination was always tenuous at best. The manifestations accompanying her meetings increasingly became a source of contention and criticism.

Maria Woodworth had also affiliated with the United Brethren. A U.B. newspaper, the *Christian Conservator,* commented in 1886 that although she appeared to be "divinely anointed" for ministry, "many objectionable things occur in her meetings," which the paper declared to be the result of "misguided zeal."[80]

Her stance against denominational traditions that were not Biblically based could only bring her into criticism by the established church world. When asked in 1886 to define her position in relationship to denominations, Maria Woodworth explained:

I am an ordained minister of the Church of God. I work for God. I preach the truth as it was in the Bible originally taught. There is no form or ceremony in our services. Form and ceremony are the curse of the church. The most powerful enemies I have are certain denominational ministers. They would do anything in the world to break me down. They have resorted to the basest ends, but have never been successful. Those outside of the church are the ones who have stood by me. I have carried the truth to them. [81]

She added that, in her opinion, "They never would have found the truth" as long as they were limited by "denominational form and ceremony."

Around the same time that the United Brethren and the Winebrennerians were actively engaged in criticism of Mrs. Woodworth and her methods, her husband Philo was frequently criticized by the press and public. Even as early as 1885, severe issues regarding bizarre conduct on the part of Philo were beginning to surface, and were becoming an embarrassment to Maria.

The press, however, tended to recognize that she was not to blame. A reporter for the *Rochester Republican* in their hometown of Rochester, Indiana felt compelled to note on July 23, 1885 that Mrs. Woodworth had temporarily left town, but "she has left behind some very erronious [sic] impressions that should be dispelled."

The writer continued by noting that she was "certainly a good woman," a woman who was being forced to cope with what he termed "circumstances beyond her control."[82] These "circumstances" centered around her husband, Philo Woodworth. According to that writer, "The evangelist's husband was injured in the army and has been under treatment in an asylum where he was partially cured of the aberrations of mind that frequently attack him."

That writer further explained,

On one occasion at the Kokomo meeting he created a scene by taking his wife out of the pulpit, and it was with the utmost difficulty that he was prevented from striking several gentlemen who tried to quiet him. At this place he spent his time fishing or loafing in the shade, except on one occasion when he stayed in the tent long enough to tell us that he was in the life boat, and to berate those who loafed outside in the shade, after which he quietly dodged out, and, lighting a cigar, threw himself down to rest.

The same reporter said that Philo made it clear that he disapproved of the small amount of money gathered in the collection, saying that if he knew who had given such paltry amounts, "he would give it right back to them." The reporter described Philo as "a large, square-built man," someone who was "deserving of pity rather than censure." Still, the writer noted, this was "a heavy load for his wife to carry in the mission [in] which she is engaged."

Philo Woodworth looked far older than his wife, and many wondered how the "comely" evangelist ever ended up with such a much-less-than-handsome mutton-chopped husband. The press derided him as both ugly and avaricious, as a money-hungry individual intent on cashing in on his wife's meetings any way he could.

While he left more spiritual pursuits to his wife, Philo Woodworth set up multiple tents at her meetings where he was observed to sell everything imaginable: beverages, peanuts and candy, watermelon, photos of his wife, her autobiography and song books, and occasionally even tobacco products. He was also not known to be above charging a small admission charge for her meetings or a parking charge for horse-drawn buggies.

While Maria Woodworth was exhorting sinners to repent in her revival tent at Xenia, Ohio, her husband was outside cranking an ice cream freezer to supply refreshments for sale. He was sometimes called "Watermelon," apparently because of his refreshment business. An 1885 newspaper noted that:

> . . . while the meetings are in progress, he and two assistants operate a peanut, candy, and lemonade stand within sixty feet of the pulpit. The other day, as men and women

were shouting and going into trances, old Woodworth sat beside an ice cream freezer and cranked away unconcernedly, preparing a supply of this popular refreshment for the weary, sin-sick crowd. Sunday morning he was selling cigars and plugging watermelons for the million, and the nickels, dimes, and quarters flowed into his till in a steady stream while his wife was laboring with care-burdened sinners.[83]

When Maria Woodworth pitched a tent in Madison County, Indiana in June 1886, it was said of her and her husband that:

At that time she and her husband were living together, he doing the business for the firm, and she did the preaching. He had nothing to do with her large tent in which she held these religious services. He took charge of the eating stands and establishments for the sale of merchandise and luxuries that was dispensed to the hungry multitude.[84]

Adjacent to her revival tent, he would erect multiple additional tents. There Philo Woodworth sold food and evidently anything else he thought might entice the crowd, including peanuts, lemonade, and books about his wife. The books were displayed alongside pictures of her that he sold for 40 cents a piece. During the 1887 Boiling Springs camp meetings in Illinois, it was said of the Woodworths that:

They have a refreshment stand where pies, cakes, peanuts, candies and lemonade are sold, and further away is another stand where meals are provided by a man from Warrensburg who bought the privilege. Photographs of Mrs. Woodworth, song books and little books detailing the life, trials and triumphs of the evangelist are sold . . . .[85]

When Maria Woodworth made plans to leave the Oakland Park meetings, which were also in 1887 in Illinois, again the press made note of the money-making activities of her husband. In this case, he was referred to as "Elder Woodworth:"

> The Elder is the financial manager of the combination. He has great faith in the power of the dimes, and while he is liberal in expenditures and lives well, he has an eye to business at all times.[86]

While Philo Woodworth expressed disinterest in the spiritual aspects of his wife's ministry, his wife expressed disinterest in its financial aspects. She seemed ambivalent about Philo's activities. In 1886, she noted that it was the only way they could stay afloat financially:

> It is all for the love of God. We demand no money from the people. You would be surprised to see the letters I have received from men who want to use me as a speculation. Were I willing to hire myself out to these men as a traveling hippodrome, I could make thousands and thousands of dollars. All I would have to do would be to state my price. I cannot conscientiously do this, and the only money we receive is from the refreshment stand Mr. Woodworth runs on the ground. Here we board. He also serves meals to anyone who desires them. This has been characterized as a money-making scheme, but it is the only means in the world we have of keeping up expenses. If we were in the work for the money there is in it, we could make ten times as much by other ways.[87]

Just the year before, however, she appeared to take a far more negative stance toward Philo's business interests:

> Mrs. Woodworth, the trance evangelist, denounces her husband's avaricious proclivities, and offered him $100

if he would fold his tents and quit the business of selling melons and red lemonade at her meetings. He saw a bigger speculation ahead and wouldn't accept. Mrs. Woodworth is in an embarrassing situation. She denounces her husband's conduct, but strange to say, has no influence over him. She threatened to bring suit for divorce.[88]

While his wife was preaching to crowds as large as 25,000, Philo Woodworth was criticized as showing no apparent interest in the spiritual aspects of his wife's ministry. On one occasion during one of her meetings, a newspaper reporter found two individuals sitting near the pulpit.

One of them, the reporter said, seemed to be experiencing "the most excruciating agonies of boredom." This was Mrs. Woodworth's husband, Philo. The other was his business manager, Thomas W. Dempsey, who was described as possessing a "smug, self-satisfied air."[89]

Dempsey is presumably the same individual who had been tagged earlier, in the Rochester, Indiana *Republican* of July 23, 1885, as "Dempsy, 'the dude evangelist,'" acting as "a sort of Second Lieutenant."[90] According to the same article, Dempsey's general demeanor and way of life did nothing to encourage respect for Mrs. Woodworth's ministry:

> Dempsy's daily "walk and conversation" stirred up the especial aversion of the young men and inspired no confidence in his Christian sincerity among the older ones. Dempsy has talents for higher things. He is being hampered and kept down. Some of the good brethren should buy him a block, cleaver, saw and butcher knife and set him up in a field more suited to his talents.

At the same time that Philo and his "Second Lieutenant" Dempsey seemed to be doing little, if anything, to instill public confidence in Mrs. Woodworth's ministry, even her daughter Lizzie was coming under fire. The Rochester, Indiana paper complained in 1885 that:

> We are not prepared to say what sort of an evangelist Mrs. Woodworth's married daughter is, but some of the boys suggest that in view of her usual costume and style, "slouch evangelist" would be very appropriate.[91]

The primary issue appears to have been that Lizzie and her husband were letting their two children more or less run wild during Mrs. Woodworth's meetings. They had, in the words of the Rochester newspaper, "turn[ed] the pulpit into a nursery and gymnasium."[92]

Chapter

2

LIGHTNING ACROSS THE MIDWEST

Maria Woodworth had already been drawing intense fire from critics who did not accept the trances. Increasingly though, individuals claimed physical healings as a result of attendance at Maria Woodworth's meetings. This, naturally, drew even further criticism on the part of the press and the established churches.

When a newspaper reporter asked her in 1886 whether she had the power to heal, she replied,

> I have not, but through me God has. I know such is a fact because instance after instance has come under my own immediate observation. Scores of people have been healed of their physical ailments, and have given testimony to this effect.[93]

Of course, in many cases, it was easy to doubt whether the healings were genuine or would last. Whenever individuals did not receive their healing, the blame tended to be placed not on their lack of faith, but on Mrs. Woodworth. In spite of the criticism, however, Maria Woodworth kept encouraging the crowds to trust in God for their healing.

After one individual testified of healing, Maria Woodworth noted that, in her words, "every other person can feel the same way, if they'll just get the glory in their soul."[94] A woman healed in a Woodworth service was heard to remark, "I just felt the disease going out and the holy power coming in."

Trusting in medicine was, in her view, antithetical to trusting in God. "Throw physic to the dogs," she proclaimed, "and take the standard prescription which comes down with the power and the Holy Ghost."[95] As she was known to sing,

> While on earth, Christ freely healed
> Divers plagues and evils,
> And delivered those possessed
> Of tormenting devils.[96]

Mrs. Woodworth was not only criticized for the trances and healings. Her denunciation of cold, dead religion certainly did nothing to endear her to established denominational churches. Even the United Brethren, however, had to admit in its paper the *Christian Conservator* in response to 1886 meetings that:

> Sister Woodworth is a very inviting and interesting preacher. She lives hourly in the Spirit. She handles the Gospel without gloves. She showed very plainly why the churches have no power. She argued well the point that the ministry of today was depending on their education for success. She showed very conclusively that the people were fed on the husks today, and were starving for the bread of life.[97]

In 1886, while talking with a newspaper reporter, Maria Woodworth summed up the work in ministry she had performed up to that point. She first explained that she had been in ministry for five years:

> I was converted when fourteen years of age, and ever since that time there has been something within me telling me that I was called to preach the gospel. I fought against this until I was thirty-five, when I could no longer withstand it. I entered the work and God has blessed me. In the last eighteen months 30,000 people have professed conversion in my meetings. I have no idea how many have come to the Savior through the humble work I have performed. They would make an army, were they marshaled together. My work has been, for the most part, confined to Indiana, although I have been more or less in eight states. In the summer the meetings are held in the open air. We carry a tent that will hold 5,000 people, which we use when it rains. This tent will not begin to hold the people attending. There are acres of people, ordinarily.[98]

HARTFORD CITY AND ADDITIONAL MIDWESTERN CAMPAIGNS

One of Mrs. Woodworth's most noteworthy series of meetings took place very early in her ministry, in 1885. In that year she ministered in a small town in Indiana, Hartford City in Blackford County.

By this time, she was already holding racially integrated meetings, a feature that would continue throughout her ministry. At Hartford City, she was assisted by a black barber, Ananias Frazier. He was said to sing "with a fervor that awakens enthusiasm to its highest tension."[99]

A visitor to Mrs. Woodworth's church in St. Louis in 1891, by the way, wrote that he believed that the trances present in her meetings were no different from those which accompanied early Methodism. He noted that these experiences still sometimes occur among those he termed "the colored people."[100] Still others, however, saw the manifestations as being reminiscent of the predominantly white camp meetings of the early part of the century.

Many (a Boston newspaper[101] said "scores") fell prostrate in Hartford City, Indiana as a result of the trances that by this time had become closely associated with her services.

Often those affected appeared frozen like a statue, with wide open eyes and perhaps with uplifted arms. Sometimes those who were deriding the proceedings were among the first to fall.

Those who tended to be more set in their religious ways were said to be "amazed and startled"[102] at the goings-on in Mrs. Woodworth's meetings in Hartford City. As a result, one newspaper noted the presence of what its writer called "mutterings of discontent."[103] Still, the crowds kept coming and the manifestations kept occurring.

One young woman who attended a Woodworth meeting at Hartford City then returned home to spend the entire night in a trance. Others found her the next morning sitting up in bed. Her eyes were wide open, but she was speechless.

The woman was motionless and appeared to be barely breathing. She emerged from the trance about two or three hours later.

In all, this woman entered into trances around five times by the time she gave her story to the press. She said that sometimes the trance state came on her without her expecting it, while other times it came as the result of praying for the salvation of some lost individual.

The woman was Viola McDermot, a Hartford City, Indiana resident. She was about 18 years old when she attended Woodworth meetings there in 1885. Miss McDermot described what it was like to go into a trance:

> I know as well as anything when the trance is coming on, for I have been in one now five times. My hands get cold as ice, and I feel my arms stiffening. My eyes get hard, and the inside of the church or room gets smaller. The darkness begins at the outer edges of the room, and comes toward me from all sides. I get more icy and stiff, and then the sight is gone. I can't talk, and don't want to talk. I am in both worlds—in this, because I can hear everything that is said around me, and in the other, because I can see the great white throne.[104]

Miss McDermot said that she had also seen the heavenly angels and the streets of gold. This was in addition to what she called "habitations, or paradises," which she said were glorious to behold. She also commented on the light of heaven, which she found to be remarkably radiant.

By the time of her Hartford City meetings, Mrs. Woodworth was said to be well-known all over Indiana. The Muncie area in Delaware County then became another of Mrs. Woodworth's 1885 campaign locations.

There she ministered for a couple weeks in a ten-acre grove of trees at a place called Madison, 12 or 13 miles northwest of the city. The crowd was estimated at 20,000 to 25,000.

There were so many wagons filling half the grove that the only way to walk through the area was to climb over them. She also held meetings in a Methodist church at a place called New Corner. New Corner is now known as Gaston, and was probably not far from the grove.

In that grove, the vast crowd stood up on Sunday and shouted in unison, "The devil is mad and I am glad. Oh, my soul, praise the Lord! Glory to God!"[105]

In order to minister, Mrs. Woodworth was stationed on a two-foot high platform in a tent in the woods. The tent was about forty by sixty feet in size. On the platform, she stood atop two chairs. The chairs were held by two men, while those around her sat on crude benches.

Many came under conviction of sin when she preached. Although the singing was described as "deafening,"[106] afterward one could hear the faint moan of those concerned about their lost and sinful condition. Some shouted until they fell to the ground under the power of God.

According to a contemporary account of her outdoor meetings near Muncie, "The woods rang with the shouts of the new converts, while here and there men and women by scores lay in trances, apparently dead."[107] The same source noted that observers were "unable to account for what they saw."

A correspondent for the *Herald of Gospel Liberty*, a mainstream religious periodical of the time, held the Woodworth meetings in high esteem.[108] The paper's correspondent, Albert Godley, first submitted a glowing report of other revivals in Delaware County, Indiana, claiming that almost all of the churches in the county were experiencing revival.

He believed that the reason was that the effects of Maria Woodworth's ministry had spread to outlying areas. Godley was impressed with the "enthusiasm," as he put it, that accompanied the various revival moves around the county. He then went on to explain, however, that he was singularly impressed with the trances in the Woodworth meetings at the Methodist church at New Corner.

He observed trances lasting as long as 16 hours and declared them to be, in his opinion, manifestations of the very power of Almighty God. He said that the trances were similar to those experienced over eight decades earlier at the Cane Ridge camp meeting.

Godley hinted that the trance phenomenon had spread from the Woodworth meetings to other locations in Delaware County. Someone was in the trance state for two hours at the nearby Corinth Christian Church.

On the final day of Mrs. Woodworth's Muncie area meetings, "dozens"[109] were said to lay immobile on the ground in the inevitable trance condition. One man, however, stood upright like a statue, oblivious to this world.

So that he would not be a distraction, some decided to stash him away somewhere out of the way, but found there was no room to lay him. As a result, three men found they were able to fold his body into a seated position so that they could place him on one of the benches.

There were so many people present that when Mrs. Woodworth ministered on an open-air platform later in the day, people filed by her two or three abreast for about 40 minutes.

After leaving Muncie, Mrs. Woodworth spent a few days in late September of 1885 resting in Louisville, Kentucky. This was at that city's Louisville Hotel. Papers in St. Louis and Chicago picked up on her meetings around this time and declared her to be "an entire Salvation Army in the person of one woman."[110]

Although described as recuperating in Louisville, Mrs. Woodworth was already scouting out a place to hold new meetings. Because of her nonsectarian and nondenominational stance, she was said to prefer halls rather than churches. Where halls were unavailable, she would erect a tent.

In 1886, another woman evangelist appeared, also ministering under what was commonly called "the power." This was Mary Mershon of Pendleton, Madison County, Indiana. She was, however, described as a "disciple and convert"[111] of Mrs. Woodworth. She had found salvation around 1884 in one of Woodworth's meetings.

Mary Mershon was about 60 years old, of medium height with black hair and what was said to be "a broad forehead."[112] When she found God in a Woodworth meeting, she was immediately called to preach as an evangelist.

Although Mershon was an invalid, she obeyed the call. Not only did she find healing, but the press described her as "strong, vigorous, and energetic."[113] Her preaching was said to be plain and unpretentious, yet powerful in its impact.

Manifestations similar to those prevalent in Mrs. Woodworth's ministry also showed up in Mershon's meetings. Her meetings at Flinn's Grove near Marion, Indiana were not her first, but she said that she had never before encountered such initial opposition.

Although the Flinn's Grove meetings seemed uneventful at first, Mrs. Mershon was determined to not give up. Eventually walls erected in hearers' hearts were dissolved. Then the floodgates were opened. Sinners cried out with loud shrieks.

Others sang and shouted, while some jumped up and down for joy. The press described the scene as "wild, weird, and unearthly."[114] The same reporter was largely at a loss for words. That writer used the term "wild" four times in a three-paragraph article in a largely vain attempt to describe the meetings.

At one point in Flinn's Grove, many began to fall to the ground. They were described as rigid, with "wide-open staring eyes."[115]

Those who had not previously known salvation saw visions of hell. Some saw themselves hanging by a thread over sulphurous pits or being nibbled by fiery serpents, while some saw themselves being saved from hell by the hand of God.

A bit later, a church with 168 members came out of her meetings in Indianapolis. Those meetings were first held at the Meridian Skating Rink, and then in a hall capable of seating 5,000. Trances and healings were commonplace.

The choice of skating rinks as venues for revival meetings might seem a bit inappropriate. They tended, however to be the largest and most convenient buildings available at the time. The rink in Muncie was described as the city's largest building.

Maria Woodworth was not the only evangelist around who was making use of skating rinks. In 1891, a well-known Michigan evangelist, Major James H. Cole, held crowded revival meetings in a skating rink. That was in East Liverpool in Maria's native Columbiana County, Ohio.

Maria Woodworth held successful meetings in a variety of places during the latter half of the 1880s, primarily in both Indiana and Illinois. These included a ten-day camp meeting in 1886 on the fairgrounds in Anderson, Madison County, Indiana. This was at a time when camp meetings elsewhere were clearly dying out.

Many saw the Anderson meetings as a success, pointing out that immediately following the revival, over a hundred were baptized. Others, however, were just as quick to criticize, calling the camp meeting "not any better than a fair."[116]

One of those healed at Anderson was Elizabeth Farrow, who had been an invalid for fifteen years. Her healing was so pronounced and dramatic that people gathered around her home in hopes of catching a glimpse of her.

A Mrs. Speize, wife of the local blacksmith, found instant relief from cancer of the stomach once she decided to stop using medicine and start trusting God. Before that time, she was unable to get out of bed and was expected to die at any moment. Now, however, she was up and attending church.

In November of 1886, Maria Woodworth was back in Muncie. She was met, however, with a petition from the established churches in town, urging her to abandon her plans to once again invade Muncie.

The petition, according to an Indiana paper, alleged that her Muncie meetings had resulted in "a ten thousand dollar libel suit, an abduction, a lady brought to the brink of a suicide's grave, a woman rendered insane and other similar occurrences."[117]

She forged ahead anyway, with meetings at the Royal Skating Rink in that city. The building could not hold the crowds. Trances accompanied every meeting.

A doctor examined one of those in a trance and diagnosed the condition as a case of "jimmery fits"[118] yet the phenomenon continued, and the crowds continued to grow.

A church with 150 members resulted from her 1886 campaign in Muncie, Indiana. By this time she had fully given herself to the work of a traveling evangelist and was seeing great results across much of the Midwest.

THE ILLINOIS CAMPAIGNS

Other Woodworth meetings were held in 1887 in Greensburg, Indiana and Urbana, Illinois. The Greensburg meetings were held in the local opera house. About 28 years later, those meetings were still remembered, and were the subject of comments in a county history published in 1915:

Mammoth crowds attended the services. People went into trances and walked the floor in a frenzy or seemingly lost consciousness and became stiff and rigid. The utmost excitement prevailed.[119]

A new Church of God resulted, using a building at West North and Anderson in Greensburg. When interest would begin to die, Mrs. Woodworth would make one of her periodic visits to the town. Eventually, however, the church died out:

> At last the doors were locked and the church stands empty, vacant reminder of an emotional storm that once shook a city.[120]

On the outskirts of Urbana she erected a tent where the excitement created by her meetings continued for some time after she left. There, it was said at the time, her most noteworthy conversions were among those who showed up just to make fun of the trances. Those converts included such local notables as two lawyers, a man who was not only a railroad conductor but a "confirmed skeptic," and a man described as a "millionaire banker."[121]

A newspaper account of one of the Urbana meetings published in the *St. Louis Globe-Democrat*[122] described Woodworth's ministry style when it came time to pray for the sick. That description is certainly vivid, although colored by prejudice and misunderstanding:

> When the excitement was at its whitest heat Mrs. Woodworth seemed ubiquitous. One moment she would face her shrieking auditors from the platform, wringing her hands, screaming to God for mercy in a voice that sounded high and shrill above the wailings of her congregation; the next, prostrate upon her face, tearing her hair, . . . ; then flying about among the people, encouraging,

arguing, commanding them to help her drive the fiend from their midst, again upon the stage, stamping her feet tragically upon the imaginary form of the 'Old Boy' himself, and then, as the great climax to her exhausting efforts, shrieking 'Victory!' at the full power of her lungs.

In the midst of pandemonium thus engendered she would call upon the afflicted to come forward and be healed, and with each demonstration of her certainly inexplicable power, the enthusiasm would break out anew, and men and women, overcome by their overwrought emotions, would hurl themselves upon the ground, bewailing their sins, and invoking God to spare them from the endless torments of hell.

When a man in Urbana was healed of deafness and of pain in his back, he let out a yell that released a storm of spontaneous praise from the congregation. "Don't imagine I did it," Mrs. Woodworth shouted to the crowd. "It was the Lord's work and you must give all the glory to him!"

In the next meeting a paralytic was brought to her on a stretcher. "The success of this crucial test should convince you all that God's power is present among you," she declared. Then she turned to the individual in need of healing, a local woman named Harris.

"Do you believe in God?" Mrs. Woodworth asked. "I do," she replied. "And if God assumes your malady, will you devote your remaining years of life to his holy service?" "I will," Mrs. Harris answered.

"Then," announced Maria Woodworth, "in God's name get up and walk!" Mrs. Woodworth dropped to her knees and raised her hands heavenward. Mrs. Harris laid there a few moments, then raised her head a bit off the pillow.

Then she lowered her head back onto the pillow in apparent resignation. Although she had evidently given up, Mrs. Woodworth had not. "The Lord of heaven commands you to rise!" she shouted.

This time Mrs. Harris grabbed onto the sides of the cot and raised herself to a seated position. Before she knew what she was doing, Mrs. Harris was standing erect.

Maria Woodworth brought her to the platform. There Mrs. Harris stood with tears streaming down her cheeks. Shortly afterward, it was reported that she had spent the day washing and ironing.

Mrs. Woodworth also prayed boldly for a woman with cancer. "Will you promise me," she asked the woman, "never to take any more medicine except what the Lord is about to give you?"

When the woman answered in the affirmative, Mrs. Woodworth boldly placed her hand directly on the grotesque cancer sore. "God be praised!" she shouted. "I feel it going!"[123] The entire cancer totally disappeared. Her doctor later testified that it was a miracle.

After the Urbana, Illinois meetings, residents of nearby Champaign were said to have all but literally begged her to come and hold meetings in their town. Some of the more affluent residents told her they would build a church just for her if she would come and minister in their midst. Mrs. Woodworth believed, however, that she was needed elsewhere.

She held a camp meeting in 1887 in Boiling Springs, Illinois, seven miles from Decatur. There the press noted that, in their estimation, "the faith-cure business is overshadowing all other things in the meeting."[124] As a result of the meetings at Boiling Springs, Mrs. Woodworth baptized a hundred new converts in nearby Stevens Creek.

Sometime around mid-September, the services were transferred to a place near Decatur called Oakland Park. This spot was described as "a pleasant picnic ground"[125] not far from the city limits.

The press reported that many were expected to join Mrs. Woodworth there after coming by train. Of those, many expected to receive healing.

Although a number did indeed claim to have received healing, others left disappointed. Evidently many came with the desire to be healed, but did not necessarily possess much faith. Still, a reporter noted that there were enough cases of healing present to "astonish and bewilder the skeptics."[126]

At Oakland Park, Mrs. Woodworth erected six tents, one of them capable of holding about 1,500 people. That was a brand new circular tent, complete with folding entrance, provided to her by some of those who appreciated her ministry.

It was while ministering in the Decatur, Illinois area that Maria Woodworth first allowed her ministry to become what one paper called "thoroughly systematized."[127] This was when she assembled around her a small ministry staff consisting of, most prominently, three women. By this time, she was typically accompanied in her meetings by Emma Posther, Emma Isenberg, and Alice Daggett. Miss Daggett was called "Allie" (also sometimes spelled "Ollie" in newspaper accounts).

A reporter described the three as "good singers" and "mighty in prayer." Of these three women, as the press expressed it, one had been saved from blindness through Mrs. Woodworth's ministry, another from tuberculosis, and "all three from the bottomless pit."[128]

Allie Daggett was formerly from Perkinsville, Madison County, Indiana. She not only helped with the tent meetings, but also cooked for the ministry team.

Emma Posther had been healed of advanced tuberculosis, then known as consumption. She was said to be an attractive "snub-nosed" young woman.

Emma Isenberg was only about 18 at the time. Her hair was short and parted on one side. She was a small woman who frequently smiled with what was termed a "comical"[129] expression.

In addition, the young man named Thomas ("T.W.") Dempsey, mentioned earlier, acted as Mrs. Woodworth's business manager. He was responsible for promotion of the meetings, as well as the sale of her books and photographs.

Some scandals erupted when accusations flew regarding Dempsey's marriage and the possibility of extramarital affairs. The accusations may have been nothing but lies, but they certainly did nothing to bolster Maria Woodworth's already controversial image.

Business manager Dempsey was likely appointed by Mrs. Woodworth's husband, Philo Woodworth. During her meetings, as has already been noted, sales of such items as refreshments, photos, and literature seemed to have been a particular forte of Mrs. Woodworth's husband Philo.

Despite the hiring of Dempsey, Philo Woodworth was still said to be acting as "doorkeeper, assistant treasurer, and general factotum"[130] at Decatur.

Word eventually got out about the miracle healings present in Mrs. Woodworth's Decatur area meetings. Over a thousand showed up for the camp meeting at the new location.

There, a certain Mrs. Sea of Clinton, Illinois urged others to yield to divine healing. Mrs. Sea had been freed from being a helpless invalid after thirteen doctors had said her condition was incurable.

Another woman seeking healing suddenly caught a vision of heaven: "Blessed Jesus! Oh, God!" she cried. "See their robes and crowns! . . . Oh, them beautiful angels!"[131]

A reporter visiting one afternoon noted that the tent was filled with the well-dressed elite of the city. That writer found the meeting to be characterized by "intense fervor," and the singing to be "most vociferous."[132]

By this time, one song in particular had become closely associated with Mrs. Woodworth's meetings, so much so that some erroneously thought she wrote it. Actually, however, it was her own adaptation of an old 19th century hymn called "Pentecostal Power." Mrs. Woodworth retitled it "The Power."

She compiled and published a little booklet of songs, titled *Revival Songs*,[133] that she then sold at her meetings. In that booklet, "The Power" appears as song number one.

A newspaper reporter estimated that this song had around 50 verses, and commented that the chorus seemed almost endlessly repeated.[134] The lyrics included the following words:[135]

'Tis the very same power,
The very same power;
'Tis the very same power
That they had at Pentecost.
'Tis the power, the power,
'Tis the power that Jesus promised should come down.

While with one accord assembled,
All in an upper room,
Came the power,
The very same power,
That they had at Pentecost.
'Tis the power, the power,
'Tis the power that Jesus promised should come down.

With cloven tongues of fire,
And a rushing mighty wind,
Came the power . . . .

'Twas while they were praying
And believing it would come,
Came the power . . . .

Some thought they were fanatic
Or were drunken with new wine.
'Twas the power . . . .

Some of the song's verses aptly describe Maria Woodworth's method of ministry: praying and waiting on God until the fire falls. She became known for manifestations of what the public increasingly termed "the power," although people differed in their opinions as to just what that power was.

Many saw it as the power of God, while others insisted it was the result of hypnotism or what was often termed an "excess of religion." Again, however, as the song "The Power" expresses it,

With cloven tongues of fire,
And a rushing mighty wind,
Came the power, etc.
'Twas while they were praying,
And believing it would come,
Came the power, etc.

This principle—that of praying and "believing it would come"—is also in evidence in a list of "Rules of the Church of God" that Maria Woodworth drafted in January of 1889. That was when she set up a Church of God in Springfield, Illinois. That church resulted from pioneering meetings she had conducted in the Springfield area.

Most of her rules concerned practical business matters. Part of Rule 11, however, says that "The Church shall meet once a week to pray for and talk about the power, and tarry till it comes."[136] The idea of "tarrying until it comes" seems to have become a vital part of the fledgling holiness/Pentecostal movement which was beginning to develop around this time.

That movement was initially termed "Pentecostal," but in a different sense from the manner in which the term would later be used. In the late 19th century, "Pentecostal" often signified an intense focus on what was loosely termed "holiness." Holiness, for holiness movement adherents, in turn entailed an intense focus on a sanctification experience.

Sanctification was commonly regarded as a definite separate experience subsequent to salvation. Countless individuals testified to an experience of "entire sanctification." Once the experience of the baptism of the Holy Spirit began to become defined in terms that associated it with the experience of speaking in tongues, however, use of the term "Pentecostal" began to be largely dropped from the ranks of those who clung to the sanctification experience but who rejected the tongues phenomenon.

Throughout both movements prior to World War I, however, tarrying for the power to be manifested was a common practice. This was a practice that even continues today among some. To what extent its practice may have originated, or at least was largely encouraged, by Mrs. Woodworth and her followers is unclear.

Part of the practice of tarrying for the power to be in manifestation in Mrs. Woodworth oftentimes involved singing her favorite song, "The Power." Although, again, some thought the song which Mrs. Woodworth called "The Power" was written by her, it actually predates her ministry by several decades. The song was quoted by various sources throughout much of the 19th century, and at least as early as 1873.

In that year, for example, a reference to the song appeared in an account of the 16th National Campmeeting for the Promotion of Holiness. That event was held in Landisville, Pennsylvania.

The account was edited by Adam Wallace and released in book form as *A Modern Pentecost*. In reference to a particularly anointed meeting, Wallace noted that

> . . . in the midst of Jacob-like wrestling, waves of power rolled over the place and scores of souls were endowed with the unction of the Holy One; the whole company broke out in the rapturous song, "'Tis the very same power that they had at Pentecost."[137]

The renowned 19th century African-American evangelist Amanda Smith quotes from this same song in her 1893 book, *An Autobiography: The Story of the Lord's Dealings with Mrs. Amanda Smith, the Colored Evangelist*. "Those were wonderful days," wrote Amanda Smith about early meetings. She continued,

> One does not see it in that fashion now. Oh, how we need the mighty Holy Ghost that they had at Pentecost!
>
> It was while they all were praying
> It was while they all were praying
> It was while they all were praying
> And believing it would come.
> Came the power, the power,
> Came the power that Jesus promised should come down.[138]

Further, legendary Holiness Movement author Beverly Carradine quotes from the same song in his 1899 book *Heart Talks*:

> Our fathers had this power,
> And we may have it too!

'Tis the power, the power!
'Tis the very same power!
'Tis the power, the power!
'Tis the power which Jesus
Promised should come down.[139]

By the time Amanda Smith and Beverly Carradine quoted from the song, however, it had become closely associated with Mrs. Woodworth's ministry. The notion that they learned of it from her is not impossible. The lyrics of the song also appear under the title "Pentecostal Power" in an 1886 songbook called *Songs of Joy and Gladness*.[140]

Another song had become frequently associated with Maria Woodworth's Midwestern tent meetings by the time she came to Decatur. The song was also included in her published collection of *Revival Songs*. This was a variant of "Palms of Victory," a song still widely sung today. Maria Woodworth retitled it "Happy Pilgrim."[141]

"Palms of Victory" is also known as "Deliverance Will Come." As sung in the Woodworth meetings, the song began by clearly delineating Maria Woodworth's stand on loud and expressive worship:

I am a happy Christian,
One of the noisy crew;
I shout when I am happy,
And that I mean to do.
Some say I am too noisy,
I know the reason why;
And if they felt the glory,
They'd shout as well as I.

According to the song's chorus, "Then palms of victory, crowns of glory, palms of victory, I shall bear!"

In one of Mrs. Woodworth's Decatur meetings, she eventually began to preach after a great deal of praying and singing. She chose as her text Isaiah 29:14: "Therefore, behold, I will proceed to do a marvelous work among this people, even a marvelous work and a wonder . . . ."[142] Mrs. Woodworth related the text to her present meeting, and that meeting did indeed become a marvel and a wonder in the hearts and minds of the people.

In commenting on the Decatur meetings, one reporter suggested that Mrs. Woodworth was likely to rise to even greater prominence as an evangelist. She could be expected, it was claimed, to assume the role formerly occupied by such 19th century ministry notables as Sam Jones, Thomas Harrison, and even Dwight L. Moody.[143]

All of them had their day, but now, in the reporter's words, they needed a rest. Mrs. Woodworth, it was pointed out, offered a distinct advantage over the others: There were supernatural healings present in her meetings.

This view of her ministry ignores the fact, however, that some fought her tooth and nail over the issue of healing. They presumed that the healings and other manifestations were of the devil, or at least certainly not from God.

One unusual feature of the Decatur meetings was evidently not deemed particularly controversial at the time, although it could have been if her detractors had chosen to focus on it: Mrs. Woodworth's ministry team charged 10 cents admission to her evening meetings at Overland Park.

This may have been the idea of her business manager, Thomas W. Dempsey, who was quoted as saying, "Of course, we cannot live on air."[144] At Oakland Park, Philo Woodworth and his agent-assistant Dempsey posted signs along one side of the road leading to the revival tent: "$5 fine for hitching here." A bit further, near the entrance to the meeting grounds, those attending were met by another sign: "10 cents to hitch inside. Will not be responsible for any damage."[145]

Eventually Philo Woodworth announced that he would only charge an admission fee at night and on Sundays. The local paper ran a notice which read,

> Ten cents admission to the camp-meeting at night hereafter. The charge is made to meet expenses and to bar out toughs and hoodlums.[146]

The cost of holding the meetings, it was said, was expensive, running as high as $14 to $20 a day.

Mrs. Woodworth and her ministry team finally closed the Decatur meetings after five weeks. She, her husband, and the three women who assisted her made plans to return to ministry headquarters on Lake Manitou near Rochester, Indiana for a few weeks of rest.

Then, on November 1, 1887, they expected to leave once more, this time for St. Louis. There they expected to minister indoors from November until March of the following year. Evidently, however, these St. Louis meetings never materialized. Mrs. Woodworth would not reach St. Louis until 1890.

After leaving the Decatur area, those profoundly affected by her services there continued to meet all winter in the form of two local societies. These were known as "Daniel's Bands." Daniel's Bands were formed in various cities as a result of Woodworth's meetings. Their purpose was to carry on her work after she moved on to new locations.

CENSURES AND SUCCESSES

In the 1887 session of the Southern Indiana Eldership of the Church of God, the Woodworths played a prominent role.

During that session, which met in Indianapolis, Maria and Philo Woodworth were made "general evangelists."

The fact that another couple were made what was termed "evangelists to labor within the bounds of our eldership" while the Woodworths were designated "general evangelists"[147] in the same session would inevitably lead to confusion.

The Woodworths were evidently led to believe that they were given permission by the denomination to labor wherever they wished. This would prove to not be the case. This mistaken impression would soon lead to controversy and rebuke directed against the Woodworths by their denomination.

Maria Woodworth's 1887 meetings in Illinois caused a stir among the Illinois Church of God leadership, primarily because of physical healings present in her meetings. The Church of God immediately appointed a committee to look into the matter of her ministry and methods.

The committee had some positive things to say about her. They admitted that she was "earnest" and "enthusiastic," and that many had been converted under her preaching. On the other hand, however, they were bothered by the supernatural manifestations in her meetings. According to church historian C.H. Forney, using wording copied in the *Chicago Tribune*, they

> condemned "her manner of practicing the healing art as unscriptural and deceptive," and on the whole "regarded her work, as at present conducted, as being more detrimental than beneficial to the cause of Christianity . . ."[148]

The committee members further said that they viewed her ministry with what they termed "alarm." They declared that "the Church of God in Illinois cannot endorse the work."[149]

Just to make sure that everyone knew where they stood, the Illinois Church of God elders decided to make their censure of

Mrs. Woodworth public. They published their attacks against her in the October 7, 1887 issue of the *Chicago Tribune*. This very public attack was signed by "W.I. Berkstresser, Clerk of the Eldership."

There they made it clear that they believed that her spiritual views were "misleading," as they put it, and "not in harmony" with those of her denomination. They saw her healings as "unscriptural and deceptive."[150]

The elders took issue with the sale of books and photos on Sundays. They were also bothered by the sale of tobacco at her meetings, which was another of her husband's money-making schemes.

Later, when one of the Illinois pastors asked that Maria Woodworth come and hold him a meeting, the Illinois eldership was adamant in its refusal to allow it. Their decision came out of the 48th session of the Illinois eldership, held in 1900 at Hildreth, Illinois.

In November of 1887, Woodworth meetings were conducted in Hannibal, Missouri. This is the small Mississippi River town that had been the home of Mark Twain. Those meetings were held at the WCTU (Women's Christian Temperance Union) Tabernacle. She also returned to Anderson, Indiana.

When a new "tabernacle," the result of her labors, was dedicated in Anderson on November 6, 1887, she and her husband ministered alongside Winebrenner Church of God pioneer R.H. Bolton.

He was likely the brother of Charles S. Bolton. He was the Church of God evangelist and missionary who later assisted with Mrs. Woodworth's renowned 1890 Mississippi River baptisms in St. Louis, Missouri. Henry H. Spiher, who would later pastor her St. Louis church, became pastor of the new Anderson church.

In February of 1888, the whole area in and around Chambersburg, Pennsylvania was said to be in a state of excitement about Woodworth meetings in that city. The *Chicago Tribune* covered the event, but believed the phenomena present to be the result of hypnosis. The paper referred to Mrs. Woodworth as "a revivalist and mesmerist."[151] (The same paper the following year called her a "faith cure medium,"[152] whatever that was intended to mean.)

Meetings were held in the Chambersburg Opera House, which was filled to capacity with 2,500 people nightly. Perhaps this was when she met Samuel Etter. Etter, who was from Chambersburg, would eventually become her second husband after the death of Philo Woodworth.

The evening meetings in Chambersburg often ran for about five hours, from 7 o'clock until after midnight. A newspaper reporter believed that Mrs. Woodworth was personally responsible for putting members of the congregation into the trance state, and reported that she would "every now and then" throw someone into a trance.

Various other reporters were investigating the healings that resulted from the meeting, and were apparently finding them to be genuine. One of those healed was a Church of God minister, D.W. Keefer of the Shepherdstown circuit. He had been forced to give up preaching because of his health. During one of Mrs. Woodworth's meetings, however, he received instantaneous healing for dyspepsia, rheumatism, and a bronchial infection.

Mrs. Woodworth returned to central Illinois in 1888. She ministered at Overland Park near Decatur. Then it was announced that she was coming to Springfield with her tent and about a half dozen coworkers. Because of the Church of God's resolution against her, she was now working with the United Brethren denomination.

After ministering at Overland Park near Decatur, Mrs. Woodworth moved her operations to Oak Ridge Park, just north of the Springfield city limits. There she set up her tent in June. She held two meetings daily except Sundays. On those days, she held three meetings.

United Brethren minister W.W. Knipple would use the same grounds for a camp meeting in 1890. This was when he and others broke away from their denomination over the issue of admitting members who belonged to secret societies.

Mrs. Woodworth ministered at Oak Ridge Park with two of those who had served with her in Decatur—Allie Daggett and Emma Isenberg. Philo Woodworth was also present. They stayed on the grounds in three tiny tents.

Maria Woodworth expressed gratitude for the monetary support friends had given them. At the same time, her assistant Emma Isenberg dismissed the suggestion that they needed more comfortable accommodations.

"Oh, bosh!" Isenberg insisted. "If we had a good house we should be tempted to waste our time in it, and who knows that we should not then miss the glorious mansion above and land somewhere else."[153]

Mrs. Woodworth did not complain about their living conditions, but her husband Philo certainly did. He said he could not get enough sleep. "It is midnight before we can clear the camp and retire," he said, "and then the flies wake us up about 4 in the morning."

That was not his only complaint. "You see," he explained, "that crowd about the altar makes it awful hot. It's enough to kill one. So many of them have bad breaths, too. That makes it worse."[154]

Philo saw the congregation's bad breath as not only unpleasant; he also believed his health was becoming impaired. That was because of breathing what he referred to as the noxious fumes emanating from people's mouths as they crowded around the altar.

He told the press exactly that on one occasion. At another time, he complained of "physical prostration" resulting from breathing "the terrible breaths of his wife's patients." A newspaper reporter suggested in response that he needed either "a summer vacation or more faith."[155]

Typically, some would crowd around the altar to see what was going on during services. When that would be the case, Philo Woodworth was known to force them back by beating them with a fan. He was increasingly becoming an embarrassment to his wife and the subject of ridicule by the press.

In 1889, during meetings in Springfield, he became offended at his wife and left town, taking her tents and all the money with him. He was removed from the train at Peru, Indiana in an apparently semiconscious condition. At the time, he was repeatedly shouting "Mama," the term he used to address his wife.

He then wrote a note to a newspaper back in Springfield, Illinois, where his wife was attempting to continue to minister. Philo Woodworth tried to make it appear that the note, which concerned himself, was written by a sympathetic stranger.

His wife, however, immediately recognized her husband's own handwriting when a reporter showed her the note. Considering his writing ability, a newspaper must have cleaned up Philo Woodworth's spelling before publishing a transcription of the note:

Editor of the Evening News. Sir. As the train arrived from Decatur at 3 p.m. an aged man was carried off the train in an unconscious condition. When he would recover consciousness, he would cry out, "Mama! Mama!" until he was exhausted. We learn it is the husband of Mrs. Woodworth, the evangelist who is holding meetings in your city. The old gentleman is in a dangerous condition and needs attention. He had his pocket picked while on the train. Please give us the facts, and oblige Reporter Evening Journal,

L.D.[156]

When shown the note by a reporter, Maria Woodworth declared, "Why, it is in his own handwriting. Why, it is from him."[157] She showed the reporter one of Philo's signed letters, which was written in obviously the same handwriting and which exhibited the same abysmal spelling.

Mrs. Woodworth told the reporter, "Friday night he left and was too sick to travel, so at first I supposed it was so, but now I see it is one of his old tricks to get money from me."[158]

Regarding Mrs. Woodworth's relationship with her husband, one paper declared that she was "deserving of great praise for standing the trouble alone and in silence as long as she has."[159]

The press openly alleged that he had been financially taking advantage of Maria. He had been living, as one paper put it, "by the sweat of his frau."[160] Although he clearly did suffer from a growing mental incapacity, he was known to frequently cry out for "Mama." Then he would proceed to have a "spell" whenever he wanted money or attention.

Meanwhile, Maria Woodworth's meetings in Springfield, Illinois were drawing tremendous interest. Only in July, however, did her meetings there achieve the sort of local notoriety that typically characterized her ministry.

By that time, various individuals began to spread the word that they had been healed, some instantaneously. Soon the tent was filled, often with some of the most respected names in the area. As the crowds swelled, the number of healings grew.

When one woman experienced healing, her mother declared, "Well now, the power of the Lord has come down right here in Sangamon County."[161] After hearing another woman's healing testimony, Mrs. Woodworth declared that "every other person can feel the same way, if they'll just get the glory in their soul."[162]

Her detractors, however, believed that the healings that were taking place must have been the result of anything but the Holy Ghost. The suggestion was made that she was a hypnotist, and that the cures were the result of hypnotism. The fact that no clear evidence of hypnotism could be found did not deter those who chose to believe the rumor.

Some who attended Mrs. Woodworth's services were said to come from adjacent states in hopes of receiving healing. Some of them were falling into trances.

A coal miner was carried home in a trance that lasted five hours. One young woman was forbidden to attend any more of Maria Woodworth's meetings. This was after she entered into a trance for nine hours and then experienced additional trances at home.

On another occasion, two women were laid out on the altar. They were described as "rigid in religious ecstacy and as speechless as the dead."[163] Mrs. Woodworth told their relatives not to worry about them.

Even if they had to lay there as long as four days, she said, they would be protected and the flies would be kept off of them. In an era in which revival tents were typically surrounded by carriages and their horses, which of course drew not only regular house flies but also horseflies in profusion, this was of particular concern.

One of the two women who were in trances was finally carried home the following night, still stiff and still in a trance. Obviously this was something beyond the sort of prostration experience, often termed "slain in the Spirit," that is common in "charismatic" churches today. In fact, one newspaper described those in trances as "rigid as a corpse."[164]

They showed no signs of life whatsoever, except for what a newspaper called "slow and weak pulsation and measured respiration."[165] The eyes of individuals in trances in Mrs. Woodworth's Springfield services were usually wide open. Some of those who went into trances did so while standing upright. They stood erect and perfectly motionless, like a statue.

When Mrs. Woodworth herself went into a trance at one point during those Springfield meetings, she held her arm up at a 45 degree angle. A reporter, while not stating how long her trance lasted, noted that no one could do this under ordinary circumstances.

Another feature sets these trances apart from probably the majority of ordinary falling as experienced today, and that was the presence of visions. Those who entered into trances very commonly saw visions of heaven, and sometimes of hell.

On one of the last days of the Springfield meetings, a woman who had been healed earlier came up on the platform to sing. Instantly she went into a trance and stood rigid, with her book in her hand.

That book was presumably her hymn book, perhaps a copy of Mrs. Woodworth's *Revival Songs*. The woman's mouth was left open, as though ready to sing.

Perhaps this was Mary Kittell. She was a young black woman, about twenty years old, who was healed although formerly bed-ridden. Kittell, who was described as "tall, graceful, and of elegantly cut features,"[166] helped lead the singing in at least one of Mrs. Woodworth's meetings at Oak Ridge Park near Springfield.

Kittell's style, said to be "irresistibly contagious,"[167] was described as essentially shouting. On one occasion she led the congregation as she sang:

There's a union in heaven where I belong
There's a union in heaven where I belong
There's a union in heaven where I belong
I belong to the blood-washed band.

Another time Mrs. Woodworth herself led the singing during the Springfield meetings. She had the congregation sing:

Look away over yonder, and what do I see?
A band of angels after me.
They're in my room and around my bed
To carry me home when I am dead.[168]

When a young man became apparently hysterical during one of Mrs. Woodworth's Springfield meetings, the blame was somehow placed on Mrs. Woodworth. A rumor circulated to the effect that she had been using some sort of magic powers on him to try to force him to marry one of her assistants.

One of Woodworth's converts at Springfield was A.G. Wood. At the time, everyone was familiar with Robert G. Ingersoll, the well-known advocate of the atheistic "infidel" philosophy.

Mrs. Woodworth's convert claimed to have been one of the first to instruct Ingersoll in atheism. He said he intended to go home and write Ingersoll, retracting his earlier views.

By the end of July, some were beginning to wonder how much longer Mrs. Woodworth would be in the Springfield area. The meetings had been going on for five weeks already.

"How should I know?" Mrs. Woodworth responded when asked. "I work where the good Lord calls me, and as long as the sin-sick and perishing come here, here is my field of labor and duty."[169]

Mrs. Woodworth and her assistants did announce, however, that they needed to clear the Oak Ridge area by August 2. That was when the Free Methodists had plans of setting up their own camp meeting in the same location.

Somehow, though, Mrs. Woodworth managed to continue in the same spot for another week. Some of the most outstanding healings took place within the last few days of the Springfield meetings.

Just before she left Springfield, Maria Woodworth set up a local Church of God with A.W. Baker as pastor. After the church had been in operation for a while, however, trouble began to brew. Members expressed dissatisfaction with Baker. While the trance state continued among the congregation, that appears to have been the case in spite of Baker's ministry.

The problem, they averred, was that he had no clue how to manifest "the power" on the same level as Mrs. Woodworth. He was not known to enter the trance state, and did not minister in such a way as to assist others to experience it.

As one paper put it, "The preacher has . . . lost his power, can't go into a trance himself, and can't assist others."[170] In addition, likely as a result, the church was experiencing financial problems.

The church held a business meeting in early July of 1890 to consider the question of getting rid of the pastor. Although members decided to keep him on, dissatisfaction continued.

Baker announced that he would join Mrs. Woodworth, assisting her with ministry elsewhere. Then, it was said, the congregation could perhaps find a new pastor better capable of maintaining what was commonly termed "the excitement."

By August of 1890, the situation in the church was no better. The congregation was waiting on Mrs. Woodworth to assign a new pastor. She announced that she was returning to Springfield to try to sort things out.

"We don't want Sister Woodworth to give us another Englishman," according to one member. "We want a native American who ain't queer and contrary. More than that we want a man who can handle the power."[171]

After Mrs. Woodworth had left the area, the *Chicago Tribune* reassessed the 1888 Springfield meetings. The paper noted that Mrs. Woodworth had drawn a large following in the area from those of "weaker minds" and "the humblest walks of life." Her ministry was condemned, however, according to the paper, by those of "the better class of people."[172]

This statement does not appear to have been accurate, however. According to other accounts, her meetings were sometimes attended by "the better class of people," complete with expensive clothes and professional titles.

After temporarily forfeiting her license in 1888, Maria Woodworth remained affiliated with the Winebrennerian Church of God, but only amid intense criticism. After the year closed, however, the denomination summed up the fruits of her labors in general in an 1889 report:

We have a membership of nearly 1,000 as a result of her work, representing about a dozen churches. Half a dozen church houses have been erected, a dozen or more preachers licensed, quite a number of Sunday-schools carried forward, and prospects for rapid church upbuilding.[173]

Still, Church of God historian C.H. Forney pointed out that once she began to defend healing, trances, visions, and what he called "other vagaries,"[174] Maria Woodworth encountered additional severe opposition. She was further criticized by the Church of God elderships for ministering outside of Indiana.

In spite of Maria Woodworth's still present but ever-weakening Winebrenner Church of God affiliation, some of the organization's ministers refused to cooperate with her. She declared that she was hit with, in her words, "opposition on every side."[175]

The denomination noted that her churches tended to quickly dwindle in size. This was seen as "proof," according to Forney, that she was spiritually building with what he called wood, hay, and other flammable materials.[176]

In fact, her view that God can heal today was bitterly opposed by a majority of the Winebrenner Church of God ministers. They insisted, instead, that the day of miracles had passed. Obviously they had no miracles in their own services to suggest otherwise.

Maria Woodworth evidently believed, however, that if her churches did not always survive, it was only because they were more heavily attacked. She continued to travel and to minister. Intense fasting and prayer for revival on the part of others appeared to accompany her meetings wherever she went by this time.

Despite opposition, impressive results did accompany her ministry. Even Forney, the Church of God historian, was forced to admit that:

An encouraging effect of Mrs. Woodworth's wonderful revivals was the inspiration to energetic endeavors felt by ministers and churches in the work of evangelism and church extension. Her work, with all its defects, was of a very serious character, and it suggested the propriety of "days of fasting and solemn prayer for revivals" in many localities. Gratifying results followed.[177]

In this era, the word "wonderful," it should be noted, had a different meaning than it holds today. Referring to "Mrs. Woodworth's wonderful revivals" did not suggest that the writer viewed them positively. Instead, he was simply suggesting that they were astonishing or that they evoked wonder.

The 1888 Indiana Eldership session was held in Anderson. Although the elders met in a large church building that came out of Maria Woodworth's labors there, they were quick to attack her. Forney later declared that:

Mrs. Woodworth's independent spirit manifested itself before she was a member of the Eldership a year. For in February 1888, the Standing Committee declared her license forfeited, as well as that of her husband, because "they could not conform to the laws of cooperation of the General Eldership, as found in Article 29 in the Constitution of said body."[178]

That article restricted Church of God ministers from ministering outside of the area in which they held membership. Exceptions were made for those with additional memberships in the elderships of other areas.

The East Pennsylvania Eldership complained to the Southern Indiana Eldership. This was because the Woodworths, who were Indiana members, ministered in Pennsylvania.

The fact was, however, that Mrs. Woodworth's ministry had developed a national reputation. Her ministry had become far too large to confine to just one of the Church of God's narrowly defined "elderships."

In establishing its "eldership" structure, the denomination had not foreseen the type of ministry conducted by Mrs. Woodworth. The requirement that evangelists remain restricted within an eldership might have worked fine for other Winebrennerian ministers, but it created a box that was simply too small to hold Mrs. Woodworth's growing ministry.

Decades later, a remarkably similar situation would arise with the tent revival ministry of evangelist A.A. Allen. In the 1950s and 1960s Allen quickly grew to prominence as one of America's foremost healing evangelists.

Originally an Assemblies of God minister, as A.A. Allen's ministry became nationally known he ran afoul of denominational controls. This was because his meetings had become too large to fit into the denomination's only existing church buildings.

His tent held 18,000 to 20,000 people while the largest Assembly of God churches at the time held 500. He was pressured to restrict his meetings to Assembly of God venues, but his ministry had clearly outgrown the denominational structure.

Although the Woodworths were advisory members of the East Pennsylvania Eldership, they ran into pronounced opposition when they tried to minister in Pennsylvania. This was because the Winebrennerian Church of God denomination saw the Woodworths as operating outside of their territory.

This was said to be because the couple were not full members of the Eldership there, only advisory members. In addition, they did not ask for permission from the local elders. As a result, the Church of God hierarchy protested against Mrs. Woodworth's plans to minister in Pennsylvania.

The real reason for the fuss, however, appears to have been because of a growing resentment on the part of some of the denomination's ministers against Maria Woodworth's ministry in general. According to Forney,

> The Standing Committee, believing that such meetings would prove seriously detrimental to the churches and the peace and harmony of the Eldership, through her advocacy of trances, faith-healing and other occult views, ordered her to desist from these labors and leave the territory of the Eldership.[179]

Not only that, but the tabernacle at Chambersburg, Pennsylvania where she and her husband had been made advisory members was declared "closed against her."[180] This was in 1888. After extended discussions, the Indiana Eldership agreed to a list of charges against her.

In response, she and her husband Philo wrote a letter of apology. As a result they were reinstated as ministers. This decision was made by the Southern Indiana Eldership by the end of the 1888 session.

The following year, 1889, the Southern Indiana Eldership met in Greene County, Indiana and celebrated the Woodworths' victories in Louisville, Kentucky. Since Louisville lies on the Indiana border and because the Winebrennerians did not yet have churches in Kentucky, evidently the city was not seen as outside Mrs. Woodworth's geographical bounds.

Rather than appearing in person at the Eldership's conference, Maria Woodworth reported in "by letter." The Indiana elders renewed her license, but her husband Philo Woodworth resigned his membership.

This seems to be around the time that tensions between the two, said to be the result of a growing mental instability on the part of Philo, were becoming a major crisis in their lives.

When a new church emerged from Mrs. Woodworth's labors in Muncie, Indiana, Henry H. Spiher became its initial pastor, just as he had done earlier in Anderson, Indiana and as he would do in the future in Louisville, Kentucky and in St. Louis, Missouri.

During the same year, 1889, a certain Pauline King decided, in a very public act, to ask God to turn water into wine. The fact that her ceremony was opened by someone described as one of Mrs. Woodworth's "disciples"[181] did nothing to enhance Maria Woodworth's credibility.

Pauline King, a Black woman, was a Woodworth convert from the Oak Ridge meetings near Springfield. After Mrs. King had fasted for 40 days, she announced that she would ask the Lord to perform a miracle on an eight gallon stoneware crock full of water from a neighbor's well.

She earnestly and fervently asked the Lord to turn the water into wine, so that he could display his power and convict the unbelievers. Although Mrs. King thought it was a great opportunity for the Lord, evidently he did not share her enthusiasm for the plan.

The water remained water, even after Mrs. King had prayed earnestly with tears. Then the congregation sang their hearts out—"until they nearly sang themselves hoarse" according to one newspaper account[182]—but still there was no wine.

Mrs. King then declared that she was not discouraged; she knew that God was capable of performing this miracle. A dipper was used in order to pass around samples of the water for everyone to taste, in hopes that some taste of wine might be detected. The desired miracle, however, was not to be.

Then, in the 1890 session, also held in Greene County, it was reported that "some purgings were necessary" in churches that came out of what were called "the Woodworth excitements."[183] Still, Church of God officials acknowledged that her Louisville church was the first church of their denomination in Kentucky and that members were "straight and sound."[184]

There, Henry H. Spiher was appointed pastor as well as "general evangelist." Spiher would later pastor the Church of God that came out of 1890 Woodworth meetings in St. Louis.

Chapter

3

A TIDAL WAVE OF CONTROVERSY

On September 15, 1889, Maria Woodworth closed her meetings at Gardner, Grundy County, Illinois and set out for Oakland, California. By this time a move of criticism against her, directed by churches, ministers, and much of the press, seemed to grow by the day.

Some of the specific accusations seem highly unlikely and appear to have made little sense, but still made the papers anyway. A certain Henry Gast, for example, was said to have been attracted to one of Mrs. Woodworth's assistants, Allie Daggett, during meetings in Louisville, Kentucky.

When he later refused to heed suggestions that he should marry Miss Daggett, Maria Woodworth was said to have given him a colorless liquid to drink, which was believed to have rendered him insane.

At the same time, she was viciously attacked because of the faith cures claimed by some of those who attended her meetings. Some alleged that the cures were fake.

Her denomination, the Winebrenner Church of God, vehemently denounced her after a man insisted on anointing her feet with oil during one of her meetings. She did not encourage the man. The fact that she did not prevent him, however, was seen as an act of sacrilege.

The meetings in Oakland, California, however, would prove to be disastrous to her already crumbling public image. While there, prophecies of doom directed toward Oakland and San Francisco would emerge from her meetings. A great tidal wave, it was said, was coming to wipe out the Bay cities.

To what extent, if any, Mrs. Woodworth was personally responsible for those prophecies is unclear. In the public mind, however, Maria Woodworth was guilty, at least by association with those who became labeled as "doom-sealers."

Maria Woodworth may have been alluding in part to this issue when she told reporters, "There are a great many things [that] occur in this tent that displeases me greatly, and that I have no power to control." She continued, "A great many of these manifestations are made by those who are possessed of the devil and have not the power of God, and to the unconverted all cases look alike."[185]

PROPHETS OF DOOM: PREDICTIONS OF DESTRUCTION OF THE BAY CITIES

As far as the prophecies of destruction were concerned, the primary culprit appears to have been a recent Swedish immigrant to the cities of the Bay, George Erickson. Because of his words of impending doom, Erickson was arrested on March 11, 1890. The charge was insanity.

He was described in records as 29 years old, having recently arrived in the city from Humboldt County, California. Humboldt County is known for its redwood forests, and there Erickson had found work in the local lumber industry.

Once he was arrested, Erickson told reporters that God would inflict divine punishment on his enemies. "I am not crazy," he insisted. "I am the messenger of the Lord."[186]

A tremendous earthquake was coming, he predicted, with a resultant tidal wave that would wipe out the cities of the San Francisco Bay. As a result, a number of individuals sold their homes and furniture at low prices and headed for higher elevations, hoping to avoid the doom to come.

Whether God had anything to do with any part of Erickson's visions, he was officially declared insane. He was confined to a mental institution in Stockton, California.

Erickson watched April 14, 1890, the predicted day of doom, come and go from within the confines of that institution. He is quoted as claiming that "God made a mistake with the date."[187]

Meanwhile, Maria Woodworth became a laughingstock. Whether she agreed with Erickson's predictions or not, the *Washington Post* referred to the words of gloom and doom as being those of "Mrs. Woodworth, George Erickson, and several other revivalists."[188]

Perhaps Erickson's views were not those of Maria Woodworth at all. On the other hand, the *Peoria Transcript* briefly noted in 1887 that Mrs. Woodworth had predicted the end of the world in four years.[189] Then again, another purported Woodworth prophecy about the end of the world surfaced in 1891.

In that year, a crowd gathered on the shores of Lake Michigan at Chicago when a man kneeled there to pray. He was near the spot where the 1893 World's Fair buildings were to be constructed.

The man announced that Mrs. Woodworth had sent him there to ensure that the fair would be dedicated to God's glory. She had also asked him, according to this individual, to ask the fair directors to build a small chapel in a corner of each of the fair's buildings.

This was Douglass Miller, a minister from Muncie, Indiana. He appeared to be around 50 years old. Miller was dressed in clerical garb and said he was with Mrs. Woodworth's denomination, the Church of God.

Miller believed he was to hold services in each of the corner chapels, where he would encourage the World's Fair visitors to repent. This, he said, was an especially urgent matter since the Lord had told Mrs. Woodworth that the world would come to an end with the close of the fair.

Miller said the fair's directors had been unsympathetic to his ideas. He thought, however, that he would try to work up public demand that would force their hand.[190] Of course, it is not clear to what extent, if any, his actions were actually commissioned by Maria Woodworth.

In the case of the 1890 Oakland predictions, the press focused on the tidal wave aspect while almost ignoring the fact that Erickson had also foreseen an earthquake coming to the San Francisco Bay area. Of course, that earthquake really did occur, just about 16 years later.

George A. Erickson, the man who predicted that Oakland would be swept away by a giant wave from the sea, was a young man who had been been working as a lumberjack. He had immigrated to the United States from his native Norway just a few years earlier, in 1881.

Now, during the Woodworth meetings, Erickson was claiming a variety of strange visions. At one point he said that he saw a vision of Jesus with five wounds in his body. Each wound was supposed to represent suffering for a specific part of the earth. Blood ran from the wounds to save each of the areas designated in the vision.

Erickson claimed that on January 25, 1890 he had a vision of the destruction of the cities in the San Francisco Bay area by an earthquake and a tidal wave. When destruction finally did come, it was 1906, and then it arrived only in the form of an earthquake and a resultant fire.

He was off by 16 years, but was remarkably close as to the month and day. Erickson said that the date had been given to him as April 14, 1890. Once the San Francisco Earthquake of 1906 did hit the Bay area, it came on April 18—just four days after Erickson's predicted date of April 14.

Erickson likely did not know that there had been a strong shock in the San Francisco area ten years earlier, on April 14, 1880. Then another quake came on April 14, 1894, cracking the lighthouse at Point Arena and causing extensive damage at Mendocino. Another quake hit on April 14, 1898, resulting in the collapse of some Mendocino buildings.

Erickson was not the only individual claiming to have had a vision of destruction in the Bay area, however. A Mrs. Boillot said she had a vision in which Oakland and San Francisco would be overtaken by a tidal wave.

Her daughter, who fell prostrate in Mrs. Woodworth's meetings on two occasions, claimed to have emerged frightened by the possibility of falling into water which she saw as surrounding her.

A certain John Kelly also claimed to have had a vision. He saw himself on Market Street in San Francisco as the city was hit by a powerful earthquake. Buildings were collapsing until finally the earth opened and swallowed up everything.

Eighteen-year-old Edward F. Maggart said that while in a trance he had a vision in which he saw not only the destruction of the Bay Area cities, but Milwaukee and Chicago as well.

Then George Erickson also reported a similar vision warning of the destruction of Chicago and Milwaukee:

> Then he showed me the great city of Chicago and its railways, and that it would sink in the earthquake, and the waters of Lake Michigan would flow over it. There should be heard no more whistle of the cars therein; no more voice of man; the name of Chicago even should be heard no more. The Lord then showed me the line of the Northwestern Railway from Chicago to Milwaukee. He showed me that Milwaukee would sink like Chicago, and in the same great earthquake and that Lake Michigan would cover it the same as Chicago.[191]

A Mrs. Gifford had a similar vision in which she saw the Bay Area sinking into the ocean. She claimed to have even been told the time that the disaster would occur, and it coincided with the date touted by Erickson: April 14, 1890.

There was a difference, however, in that Mrs. Gifford's prediction was more specific. She said that doom would come at 4:45 in the afternoon. Others said New York and Chicago would also perish on the same day. About 60 people associated with Mrs. Woodworth's meetings in Oakland had similar visions.

Maria Woodworth ministered for several months and moved several times, each time to larger quarters. This was in order to accommodate the ever-growing crowds. Eventually she erected a tent capable of holding 8,000 persons, the same tent that she later used for meetings in St. Louis, Missouri.

By December of 1889, Mrs. Woodworth had set up her tent at Twelfth and Webster Streets in Oakland. Philo Woodworth had rejoined her. This was in spite of the fact that she had declared back in Springfield, Illinois that she would have no more to do with him. When ordered to vacate the lot her tent occupied, she moved again, this time to Seventh and Market.

Among those who attended the Woodworth meetings in Oakland was Carrie Judd. She had become nationally known as a proponent of divine healing after she had been healed in 1879 from a serious injury, the result of a fall on ice.

Judd, a white woman, received her healing through the ministry of African- American healing evangelist Sarah Mix. Although she was skeptical of Maria Woodworth's ministry methods at first, Carrie Judd became impressed with the level of divine power that she found to be present in Woodworth's tent meetings.

Intense public criticism of Maria Woodworth erupted, however, when an eleven-year-old girl, Flora Briggs, entered a trance state and was left for five hours in the tent. Criticism focused on claims that the temperature in the tent was too chilly to leave the girl unattended. Actually, she might have remained there longer if her uncle did not arrive with police to forcibly take her from the tent that evening.

Mrs. Woodworth told reporters later that the girl did not enter her trance until after Mrs. Woodworth had already left the tent. She did not learn about the incident, she said, until she was told about it afterwards.

Physicians began to warn the public to stay away from Maria Woodworth's tent. One doctor insisted that attendance would, in his words, "undoubtedly lead to serious nervous and brain troubles in a great many cases."

He continued by alleging that:

Insanity will surely follow with some of her converts. I understand there have been several cases of religious mania already directly traceable to the excitement at her meetings. Children and women should keep away from her tent, especially the former.

In similar words, another doctor warned that:

The woman is doing a great and lasting injury to this community. Parents should keep away from these meetings, and, above all things, keep their children away. It is to the women and children she will do the most harm.[192]

The public debated whether the Woodworth meetings should be silenced by legal means. This threat would haunt her later in 1890 when she held meetings in St. Louis.

After allegations were made that "the power" caused insanity, complaints insisted that Mrs. Woodworth's "bouncers"[193] were too aggressive in attempting to maintain order at her tent. In addition, a tramp claimed that he had been paid 50 cents by Mrs. Woodworth each time he pretended to enter the trance state.

Mrs. Woodworth was forced out of Oakland by police, and relocated her tent at nearby Santa Rosa. That was when the prophecies of doom began to surface.

HEADING FOR THE HILLS:
ESCAPING THE COMING DELUGE

The expected deluge was to arrive on April 14th. Meanwhile, local businesses had a field day using the area-wide hysteria as a basis for advertising. Napa Soda Springs alerted the public that the resort known by that name was located a thousand feet above sea level. As a result, it would be a perfect location for luxuriating while avoiding otherwise certain doom.

Etna Hot Mineral Springs in Napa County used similar tactics. The springs' owners advertised that, "Those who are in fear of the grand predicted smash-up should flee to the Etna Hot Mineral Springs." The ad noted that "It's a grand place for invalids and nervous people, and perfectly safe."[194]

A railroad line also decided to attempt to cash in on the fear of impending destruction:

> The California Railway will run regular passenger trains from Fruit Vale to Leona station on Laundry Farm, commencing Saturday, April 12th, when the timid may gain any elevation required above the fatal tidal wave, as predicted by Mrs. Woodworth to take place April 14th. Come one, come all, and get a view of the fatal wave from a safe and elevated position.[195]

A certain Mrs. L.S. Silberberg, owner of the "Eastern Hair Store," also ran advertising with a deluge theme. She claimed that Mrs. Woodworth was setting a good example by insisting on having her hair done just prior to the deadly tidal wave:

> We are going into eternity on the 14th of this month, so says Mrs. Woodworth; but before solving the future she says that she must have her bangs trimmed, hair dressed and head shampooed by the leading artist on the Pacific coast, viz.: Mrs. Silberberg, who holds forth at the Eastern hair store, 405 Twelfth street, between Broadway and Franklin. Ladies would do well to follow the example of Mrs. Woodworth, so that they may enter the future state with a clean head.[196]

After the predictions were seen to not bear fruit, Mrs. Silberberg still found a way to capitalize on the non-event. She ran yet another ad:

April fourteenth is over, and still we have not been washed away by the tidal wave, and it would do some of the doom sealers good to get some new brains. The only way for them to get any, is to go to the Eastern Hair store, 405 Twelfth street, between Broadway and Franklin, and get Mrs. L. S. Silberberg to shampoo, dress and trim their hair, after which their heads will be lighter, and their brains will have a chance to expand.[197]

One night before the 14th, a woman was seen running through the streets of Oakland after midnight only partly dressed, crying "I'm coming, good Lord! I'm coming. Wait, only wait for me!"[198]

The activities of an evangelist named V.E. Bennett attracted far more attention, however. He was seen to ride up and down the streets of Oakland on a bicycle, warning residents of coming annihilation.

"Flee! Flee! Flee! Flee to the mountains!" he cried,[199] while others went door-to-door to spread the message of doom. Still others preached of imminent doom to travelers at the train station and at the ferry station.

Ezekiel Stone Wiggins, widely known at the time as the Canadian "weather prophet," similarly prophesied disaster for Oakland. Wiggins was already well-known for predictions of dire weather emergencies that never materialized. He agreed that a destructive tidal wave was, indeed, about to strike the Bay area.

Some heeded the warnings, selling their property for minimal prices and heading for higher elevations. Many camped out on the mountains around Santa Rosa, Vacaville, and St. Helena.

The resultant revival meetings at St. Helena were said to be especially lively as crowds awaited destruction in the valleys below them. More skeptical locals were greatly entertained at what they regarded as the comical antics of the frantic as they fled from the wrath to come.

Pets and furniture were left behind, as those looking for higher elevations expected a tidal wave forty feet high. Broadway retailers said they sold all of their packing crates, and still there was a demand for more.

As the day of doom approached, the newspapers printed names of individuals who were known to have deserted the cities of the Bay. One man moving out of the city asked a local merchant for items on credit.

"I thought the city was to be destroyed," the store owner responded. "True," came the response. "If it is destroyed and you perish, the money would do you no good. If you are saved by some miracle, I will pay you."[200] The items were provided on credit.

Many retreated to the interior of California, including a wealthy doctor who left his fashionable home to his sister. Others who vacated the area included some of the more elite of local society. Many of them declared that they were going out of town on business or that they suddenly decided they needed a vacation.

A group of African-Americans who expected disaster left the area and formed a colony of their own at a place called Cottonwood, which a newspaper reported as being near Sacramento. Many of those who left the Oakland area never returned.

The morning of the 14th finally arrived. The "doom-sealers," as locals termed them, gathered on nearby mountaintops for special services.

The sky, however, remained clear and the sea was calm. Not the slightest quake was felt. Over the following several days, a number of embarrassed individuals quietly sneaked back into town.

Sixteen years after Erickson's predictions, the best-remembered earthquake in American history hit the Bay Area. The great earthquake had been predicted by Erickson to arrive on April 14, 1890. On April 18, 1906, the Bay cities were indeed hit by a major quake, but, of course, without the predicted tidal wave.

Maria's husband Philo was present with her in Oakland, but was giving her plenty of trouble. The believers there insisted that he leave after he evidently threatened her with murder. He had been exhibiting ever-worsening mental problems for some time.

Alfred Sibert wrote that while it seemed that Maria was going "onward and upward," Philo was headed "downward and backward."[201] He had a tendency toward gross immorality, and at times abused and harassed his wife.

Others urged her to seek a divorce, but Maria was determined to avoid that step at all costs. She defended him by insisting that his mental condition was the result of a head injury.

As already noted, he claimed that the injury was the result of military duty during the Civil War. Others, however, believed that he was hurt when rock fell on his head while mining coal.

Alfred Sibert, who sold the Woodworths their lakefront property in Rochester, Indiana, wrote of Philo:

> When I saw Philo H. Woodworth last, I thought him the most striking example of moral degeneracy I had ever known, but in the light of more recent information I am satisfied that he was the victim of growing insanity and that it would have been a mercy to have confined him in an insane hospital.[202]

Chapter

4

HYPNOTISM AND HYSTERIA: THE ST. LOUIS MEETINGS OF 1890

B y April 19th, 1890, Maria Woodworth had left Oakland, California and was now in St. Louis. There she intended to open a new series of meetings. She and her husband Philo Woodworth evidently separated while in Oakland. The rift never healed, and eventually led to divorce.

After her arrival in St. Louis, Mrs. Woodworth rented a hall and immediately began to conduct a series of salvation and healing services. This hall was in a neighborhood now known as Laclede's Landing, near the Mississippi River.

Not that many city residents paid much attention when her St. Louis campaign began. Eventually, however, the entire city would take notice.

Maria Woodworth came to St. Louis as the result of a petition in which she was asked to come and rouse the city with her unique style of evangelism. Although St. Louis had been visited by countless well-known evangelists in years past, the city had developed a reputation as highly resistant to revivals.

A certain E.S. Greenwood had been working among the spiritually needy in St. Louis' inner city after the bigger churches began their migration west into the suburbs. He volunteered his assistance once he learned of the petition to bring Mrs. Woodworth to Greenwood's hometown. Once she arrived, he led prayer in at least some of her meetings.

He is presumably the Edward S. Greenwood who appears in city directories at the time, living at 3017 Dickson. Greenwood was associated with the Liberty Evangelical Mission at 719 Franklin Avenue. This mission, where E.T. Colman was the pastor, was evidently sufficiently in revival to schedule services every night.

Another individual whom Maria Woodworth called "one of my active assistants" in the St. Louis meetings was a man she referred to as "Mr. Douglas."[203] This was James Douglas, a laborer living at 1215 North 10th Street.

At first, her St. Louis meetings generated little publicity and certainly no controversy, with one exception. She was, of course, a victim of the widespread skepticism that typically surrounds anyone with faith healing claims, even today.

In her case, however, her spiritual stance invited even more persecution than was usually the case with tent revivalists, for not only were healings claimed, but Maria Woodworth also claimed to see visions and to hear the voice of the Lord. The ever-controversial trances encouraged the curious to pour into her meetings, which of course only added to her notoriety among skeptics.

The earliest mention in the local press of her arrival in the city seems to have been on April 19th. That was when the *St. Louis Globe-Democrat* noted that "the faith-cure evangelist" was in town.[204]

THE CALM BEFORE THE STORM: ST. LOUIS MEETINGS BEGIN

Mrs. Woodworth began her work in St. Louis with a service on Sunday evening, April 20, 1890. This was in the hall she had rented, the Union Church Hall at 940 North 3rd Street.

The meeting was only afforded scant notice by the local religious community, if the city's newspapers are any indication. The local secular press did not even spell her name correctly, with both of the major daily papers casually noting in passing that a certain "Mrs. Woodward" was to hold meetings.[205] Soon, however, the building was packed.

That hall has long since disappeared. Its location was near the east edge of present-day Interstate 70 in downtown St. Louis, just about directly across the freeway from the Edward Jones Dome.

When Mrs. Woodworth began her meetings, the hall had just been renovated. Edison's incandescent lightbulb was still years over the horizon, but newly devised electric arc lighting was installed. Once she erected her tent a few weeks later, it also boasted a similar electric light.

Her meetings were scheduled for 2 and 7 p.m. every day, with an extra meeting at 10 a.m. on Sundays. Today, someone ministering in a similar capacity might avoid scheduling meetings for Sunday morning, preferring instead to encourage the locals to pursue their own customary church habits.

In the case of Maria Woodworth's 1890 visit to St. Louis, however, her ministry was seen to fly directly in the face of much of what was then customary. The controversy that quickly ensued can scarcely be imagined. When she first began her St. Louis meetings, however, everything seemed calm. That calm atmosphere proved to only be the proverbial calm before the storm.

The local press continued for a time to misspell her name. Evidently all that local newspaper reporters knew about her was based on sensational accounts that had occasionally surfaced in Midwestern papers since the early 1880s, supplemented by word-of-mouth reports about the enigmatic "trance evangelist." By this time, all sorts of behavior viewed as wild and sensational—trances and supposedly worse—were associated with her.

"Mrs. Woodward Preaches an Orthodox Sermon to Christians," a small article's headline proclaimed, with her name prominently misspelled.[206] The title suggests that it came as a surprise that her sermon turned out to be "orthodox." After all, this was the very unorthodox "trance evangelist," as she was known. Skepticism would eventually boil over into outright animosity on the part of some St. Louis residents.

In her initial meeting, she took as her text a passage in Matthew 20:1–8. There, Jesus speaks of the husbandman's duty to gather laborers. Mrs. Woodworth said that the vineyard represented the kingdom of heaven and that this kingdom lives within believers.

If we expect to reach heaven, according to the evangelist, we should be laboring to save others. She emphasized the role of consecration, which, she said, results in a passionate desire to win the lost.

Two local newspapers paraphrased her. According to one of those paraphrases, Maria Woodworth noted that "Laboring in the vineyard means service to God, a consecration which has its reward, for there is nothing so ennobling as laboring to save souls."[207]

She compared negligence in soul winning to negligence in properly maintaining the vineyard. Maria Woodworth urged her hearers to go out and bring in the lost. She insisted that they needed to do this with urgency and zeal, and she encouraged her hearers to avoid lethargy in soul-winning.

Mrs. Woodworth began to hold meetings every night, beginning on Sunday, April 20th, with her fifth evening service being held on April 24th.[208] Local reporters in St. Louis were initially respectful and receptive, while Oakland, California newspapers continued to angrily denounce Mrs. Woodworth and the "doomsealers" even after she had left the area.

In addition, one Oakland paper published an irreverent retrospective view of Maria Woodworth's Bay Area meetings, quoting the *New York Sun*:[209]

. . . about four months ago a woman, known as Mother Woodworth, started a revival racket in a tent, and whooped up salvation and hysterics in such an eccentric fashion that she waked up the whole town and inoculated about a thousand people with her hallelujah jumps.

The same article went on to note that:

. . . She was a pretty good-looking lass, with a musical voice and a wild, inspired sort of style that caught the crowd, and when she had a full head of Gospel steam on, she sailed up and down the platform waving her arms and swaying her body like one of those Oriental dancing girls. . . . A lot of nervous, hysterical people got excited at her meetings, thought they had religion, and had fits in the tent. Some tumbled down cold as a wedge and lay on the floor unnoticed, while others had the St. Vitus style of piety and pranced all over them. It was a perfect bedlam.

Meanwhile, no such "perfect bedlam" had yet surfaced in St. Louis. There, the local press noted that Mrs. Woodworth's inaugural meetings were not at all characterized by the "unnatural frenzy" that had become associated with her in Oakland. Although only 80 persons attended her fifth meeting in St. Louis,[210] by the 29th of April attendance was said to be "very large."[211]

On the afternoon of Sunday, June 9, 1890, she held a one-time outdoor meeting under a covered pavilion at the Union Market. This was a public market that had been established in 1866, bounded at the time by 6th and Broadway and by Lucas and Morgan.

There she spoke to a crowd that was predominantly white, but which included some individuals described by a newspaper account as "well-dressed colored persons."[212] By this time she was on the lookout for a site appropriate for her 120- by 180-foot tent, a gift from her followers in California.[213] The tent had been in storage in Oakland ever since her meetings there had closed.

"THE POWER" AND PERSECUTION

Before that tent could be moved into place, however, Maria Woodworth began using a temporary tent, which went up in May 1890 at the corner of Jefferson Avenue and Gamble Street. This was in North St. Louis in a neighborhood universally regarded as rough.

After she had been in the tent only about six weeks, Mrs. Woodworth and her congregation were attacked by a local Irish gang of young men generally referred to as "hoodlums." They bombarded her tent with bricks and cobblestones.

Then, on June 17th, the gang tore down her tent. They busted up the chairs and forced the congregation to scatter. There were no serious injuries, but "many" of the women fainted, according to the *Washington Post*, which covered these St. Louis events.[214]

That paper used the term "mobbed" to describe the attack. About six years later, in 1896, the *Los Angeles Times* would publish a list of notable events in history, beginning with the assassination of the Caliph Othman at Medina in 655. One of the historic events listed, included along with the Battle of Waterloo and "anti-Popery" riots in England, was the following:

1890—Mrs. Woodworth, evangelist, mobbed in her tent at St. Louis, Mo.[215]

In one of her tent meetings during another evening, a disturbance broke out that was described as a race riot. Since Mrs. Woodworth's meetings were racially integrated, perhaps there was some objection by whites to the presence of "colored" believers.[216]

Mrs. Woodworth was not the sort of woman to shrink back from criticism, however. Even after her tent was moved, her meetings were, at times, mercilessly attacked by young men bent on causing trouble. These were young men the press consistently called "hoodlums."

Fortunately for Maria Woodworth, the tent that was torn down was merely a temporary tent, not the tent that had been stored in readiness for her in Oakland, California. Upon its arrival in St. Louis, the Oakland tent was set up on a vacant lot on the northeast corner of Jefferson and Cass Avenues. The replacement tent was erected and ready to go by June 28th.

The new location was presumably chosen because of the gang violence. The persecution was, according to Maria Woodworth, partly the result of accusations leveled against her from the pulpit by a local Catholic priest.[217] This was Father Jeremiah J. Harty at St. Bridget's Church, a structure which stood near her first tent.

This was an Irish Catholic church located in a predominantly Irish neighborhood, an area known for street gangs. Moving her tent a few blocks away, however, did not make that much difference. Her new location was just five and a half blocks from Harty's church.

This left Mrs. Woodworth still on the edge of the city's best-known Irish neighborhood. Sources vary as to the exact parameters of this neighborhood. Her new location at Jefferson and Cass, however, appears to have been just about at the western edge of a district known as "Kerry Patch."

Kerry Patch was a poor area, and was widely recognized as a dangerous environment. This was the case even though one of its streets, Mullanphy, was named after the city's first millionaire. Mullanphy had been an Irish immigrant who made his money by dabbling in real estate.

The Kerry Patch neighborhood was home to several Irish gangs. One of these was the Snare Gang, also known as the Push Gang.

Some had warned Mrs. Woodworth that this was not the best location for her revival tent, but she insisted that this was, indeed, the place. She would, however, not escape confrontation with the infamous Snare Gang.

Woodworth's tent, as already noted, had been erected at the northeast corner of Jefferson and Cass Avenues. This lot was bounded by Jefferson Avenue on the west, 25th Street on the East, Cass Avenue on the south, and Mullanphy Street on the north. This lot, which is once again vacant today, since buildings were removed, was popularly known as the old Union baseball grounds.

A third major baseball league, the Union Association, had been formed in 1883. The league's baseball team in St. Louis was called the Maroons. The Maroons' baseball grounds at Jefferson and Cass were also known as the Union Grounds, Union League Park, or probably more commonly, Union Park.

This is precisely where Maria Woodworth erected her tent. E.S. Greenwood, the local man who assisted Mrs. Woodworth with her tent meetings, noted that the grounds were notorious before her arrival for what he called "Sabbath desecration."[218]

One night, during one of Mrs. Woodworth's revival meetings, the gang members were joined by a group of baseball players. Together, both groups caused a ruckus. Perhaps the baseball players were offended by Mrs. Woodworth's evangelistic use of a vacant lot formerly dedicated to their favorite sport.

Estimates suggest that Maria Woodworth's summer tent meetings in the northern part of St. Louis drew crowds of perhaps as many as around 8,000. Not everyone could fit under the tent, so many stood around the perimeter outside. One source claimed 9,000.[219]

A number of those attending arrived by streetcar. One night, a news reporter noticed an unusually large number of passengers onboard the Cass Avenue cars. They were headed for the tent at the corner of Jefferson and Cass.

Newspaper reports referred to her tent as being extremely crowded. Often all the seats were taken while at least hundreds stood in the back. Even Dr. Theodore Diller, who became one of Mrs. Woodworth's most outspoken opponents, estimated the crowd one night to be around 5,000. He admitted that about an equal number were turned away due to lack of space.[220]

Lighting was provided by two flickering electric arc lights and two gasoline-powered lights. Newspapers usually referred to the tent as being situated simply at Jefferson and Cass, occasionally referred to as Jefferson and Mullanphy. Clues as to its more specific location, however, come from a city coroner's inquest.[221] That same inquest also provided details about what it was like to visit Mrs. Woodworth's tent.

One night a rowdy gang member, Louis Burg, died as the result of a blow to the head inflicted by one of Mrs. Woodworth's watchmen. Afterward, various eyewitnesses offered testimony that described the tent and its surroundings.

Josephine Walker, who was in the tent the night that the blow was struck to Burg's head, told the coroner what she did when trouble started brewing in the tent: "I started to run out of the back way, out towards 25th Street, instead of Jefferson Ave."[222] This suggests that the tent's entrance faced Jefferson Avenue, a major thoroughfare, which bounded the lot on the west, with a back exit at the east toward 25th. The lot's eastern boundary was flanked by 25th Street.

Other testimony refers to an east-west alleyway, with the tent situated just south of that alley. Apparently this so-called alley was actually Mullanphy Street. Watchman Henry Kaufmann, who was one of the witnesses, explained it: "You see, Mullanphy Street isn't exactly cut through yet where the tent is."[223]

Describing the tent's interior, a certain T. Eckhard mentioned that ". . . there is two posts, main posts that hold the tent where there is lights on. They are about 20 or 30 feet apart . . . ."[224] Away from the posts, toward the west, was a wide, flat platform for ministry. Those attending Mrs. Woodworth's meetings sat on simple wooden benches.

As was common with old-time gospel tents, the dirt floor was covered with sawdust. Sawdust seems to have been used primarily in order to minimize problems with mud in case of rain. In the case of Mrs. Woodworth's meetings, however, it also served as a relatively soft landing spot for those who succumbed to "the power." These were, of course, those who fell to the ground in a trance.

On the evening of July 21, 1890, a gang of young men entered the tent. According to several descriptions of the events that followed, they began ridiculing the young women at the altar. They nudged them under the chin, and derisively asked them whether they had been saved.

Then, when the leader of a gang of young Irish "hoodlums" caused trouble in the tent, one of the two night watchmen hired to maintain order struck the young man on the head. The watchman later expressed surprise that the blow had caused damage. He testified that he thought he had merely discouraged the gang leader from hanging around, but in fact the blow fractured his skull. By morning, the young man was dead.

This was Louis W. Burg, age 22, who had been a carpenter. As one might expect from the leader of the infamous "Snare Gang," he also went by several other names: Matt Burg, Charles King, Charlie King, and Louis King. The confident Burg preferred to be known by his primary nickname, "King." This athletic young gang leader was a local hero in amateur sports circles, being active in local football and baseball teams.

He was a star athlete in the Kensington soccer team. That team was known at the time as the Kensington Football Club. Kensington won the St. Louis league championship in the same year in which Burg was struck, 1890. He was also a prominent member of a local amateur baseball team, a team which also went by the Kensington name.

On Monday evening, July 21st, 1890, Burg, or "King," as his close friends called him, showed up at Mrs. Woodworth's tent with several associates. Members of his gang, Burg among them, lingered in the tent long after a meeting had ended. Around the end of the meeting, about 10:20 or 10:30 p.m., a woman realized that her baby had lost its gold breast pin. She began searching for it in the tent's sawdust floor.

Burg became involved in the hunt, but only to give himself an opportunity to further heckle Mrs. Woodworth's followers. As Burg helped in the search, he did so mockingly. He suggested that the night watchman was likely to find the pin and pawn it to buy whiskey.

Two private watchmen were present at the tent that night. One was Henry Kaufmann. Kaufmann boarded at the corner of Mullanphy and Cass, right next to the tent. The other was 35-year-old Henry Saunders, who was originally from Kentucky. Saunders lived close by, at 1517 Cass Avenue.

Eventually Saunders confronted Burg and his gang, insisting that they clear out. When Burg was told to leave, he refused and became indignant. Tension mounted between the gang and Saunders.

A verbal skirmish began. Burg evidently called Saunders "a dirty Salvation Army cur." Saunders then struck Burg on the head, wielding a homemade club.

Mrs. Woodworth was up at the front of the tent near the platform, but she said later that she thought she heard the blow. One person later testified that he thought it could have been heard a block away. Another witness, however, said it sounded more like a dull thud than a sharp crack.

Saunders did not think the blow was delivered with excessive force, and Burg did not fall to the ground. Burg and his gang tried to rush Saunders, but Saunders then pulled a revolver. This caused the gang members to quickly leave the tent, while cursing at the two watchmen.

Once he was outside, Burg insisted to his friends that he was fine. He told them that the head injury was nothing to be concerned about. After he left the tent, however, he found that he was having difficulty standing up.

His condition worsened and he was helped home by friends. A policeman later testified,

> I took his hat off and examined his head, and seeing there was no cut or anything else on it, I told him the best thing to do was to go home and leave here and he said yes, I will do it, and he commenced to vomit. I followed him over as far as Cass Ave. and he commenced to retch again, on the far side of Cass Ave. I asked him if he wanted a Dr. He said no, so the other young fellows took him home. That is all I know of it.[225]

Burg still insisted that the blow was minor. He lived with his widowed mother at 2411 Biddle Street, a short walking distance from the tent. When he arrived back home, he told her that a policeman had hit him on the head. Burg, who was single and a carpenter, was his mother's sole source of financial support.

By around three in the morning, his mother was beginning to get alarmed. Around four or five in the morning, she insisted on calling for a doctor. Dr. R.J. Hill was rushed to Burg's home. Although the skin was not broken, Dr. Hill declared, "Why, young man, your skull is fractured. You should go to the City Hospital."[226]

By this time, however, he was in spasms. Burg was rushed to the city hospital, and Dr. Hill reported the case to the police. By 10 o'clock the following morning, July 22nd, young Louis Burg was dead.

Police then showed up on the doorstep of watchman Henry Saunders, who was shocked to find that his blow to the head of

Burg had resulted in death. Saunders was arrested for murder and thrown in jail.

Maria Woodworth, along with several of her coworkers, including Emma Isenberg and local minister Alexander Douglass, testified at the coroner's inquest the next day. That was July 23, 1890.

When asked where she lived, Mrs. Woodworth answered, "On Cass and Jefferson Avenue at present." She explained the gang's invasion in her tent:[227]

> We have had characters come to the meeting to interfere two or three times. This night there was a couple of ministers from the city were preaching, and they were interrupted with loud laughing and noises, and they began a disturbance while we were singing. Our singing was broken down and we had to stop twice. Finally, we had to give up the singing. Some whistled and we had to stop the singing—couldn't finish the song—and then when we assembled around the altar for altar service, quite a number came around the altar. Some took seats on the altar and they were requested by some parties in the meeting to get back—not to go out—to get back from the altar, and the meeting dismissed and I believe all this party went out, clear out.

She also discussed a further "commotion:"

> We were dismissed and the whole congregation was gone except probably a dozen, and then about 15 or 20 men came in again. I wasn't paying any attention to them. I was engaged [in] talking to those around the altar—we had some special business—and suddenly I heard a commotion back there, and I looked back and saw Mr. Saunders

standing and I suppose 15 or 20 men had pushed right up to him and was close to him.

According to Maria Woodworth's own testimony, after the disturbance in her tent she became startled and afraid:

I was frightened. I didn't know what was going on. I thought someone was going to be killed, and just in a moment it seemed they disappeared—scattered—went out. I didn't see anyone struck. No one fell. I didn't think anyone was hurt, and they all passed [in other words, went] out.

When what was termed "the commotion" happened, Mrs. Woodworth said she looked up. This was in order to see, in her words, "someone killed or something terrible happen." When she was asked if she had any final words regarding the matter, she responded by saying that she had already told everything she knew about what transpired that evening.

She added, however, regarding Burg,

I have identified this young man as being the one who seemed to be the leader of all the trouble, or nearly so, and I have talked to him personally more than any man, I believe, in the building [obviously the tent was meant], talked to him there a half dozen or a dozen different times.

Maria Woodworth added that this was not the first incident involving Burg:

I might refer to another trouble. A week ago last evening there was quite a commotion in the back part of the tent. Our meeting was interrupted twice. That was the most serious trouble we have had since the commencement of our meeting. There was a crowd around. I looked back. I

115

saw Saunders surrounded by about probably fifty men. I heard them holler "cut him," "kill him," and such things as that . . . .

The matter involving Louis Burg was, in Mrs. Woodworth's words, "the greatest commotion we have had yet." She confessed that she did not see the knife in his hands that others had seen. She once again told the coroner, however, that she heard such words as "Kill him!" and "Cut him!"

Mrs. Woodworth further commented,

I couldn't say who it was, and I called the police half a dozen times to stop the noise. There was no police within hearing distance. If there had been, the noise would all have been stopped.

Maria Woodworth's assistant Emma Isenberg had worked extensively with her in revival meetings around the country. Miss Isenberg also testified.

She told the coroner that she lived in Huntington, Indiana. This was where the United Brethren Church had its headquarters, and Mrs. Woodworth lived there briefly. Isenberg testified,[228]

I was, at the time of this occurrence, standing on the pulpit, up on the altar about ten feet from where this happened, and I was talking to a lady friend and I heard a commotion. I didn't see anyone struck, or I didn't see anybody called, but I saw afterwards—afterwards I saw this crowd rush on the private watchman, Saunders. Them boys all made a rush and it wasn't but a moment or two till they all scattered . . . .

Emma Isenberg also told the coroner that she had heard the sound of the club when it was applied to Burg's head:

Q. Was it a sharp crack of a report or a dull thud of a report?
A. Well, it was rather dull.

Q. Wasn't it more like a crack, a sharp blow?
A. No, sir, I don't think it was. It was more of a dull thud than it was a sharp report.

Q. Nobody fell, you say?
A. Nobody fell.

Q. And immediately after that report you saw a rush towards him, as though they were going to do him some harm?
A. Yes, sir.

Q. Was there any harm done him?
A. Well, no, there was not, but they made a rush. It wasn't more than a moment or two until they were scattered.

Others testified that members of the gang used foul language and insulted believers at the meetings. Several suggested that if Saunders had not pulled out his revolver, he would have been killed by the gang.

Still, at first it appeared that Saunders would be held responsible for murder. Instead, he was, in the end, completely exonerated, a jury finally determining that Saunders was simply doing his job.

Eventually, attacks against the Woodworth meetings by local rowdies were brought more-or-less under control by the police. Later, Mrs. Woodworth publicly thanked the police chief, Major Lawrence Harrigan, for his efforts to stop the hoodlums' disruptions.[229]

Harrigan was a new police chief, having only filled the post since May. His actions on behalf of Mrs. Woodworth, however, incurred the ire of the local German press. In fact, a local German-language newspaper vehemently insisted that if

Harrigan had really been doing his job, he would have not only put the rowdies in their place, but Mrs. Woodworth as well.

According to the paper, the police should have forced Mrs. Woodworth out of town, instead of aiding her to continue her meetings. In addition, one of the city's two German papers, *Anzeiger des Westens* (literally, "Announcements of the West"), claimed that the healings that appeared to be manifested in Mrs. Woodworth's tent were simply the result of hypnotism.[230]

Christian meetings of today often tend to follow a set pattern: Several songs are sung, then announcements are made and an offering is taken, perhaps during a special musical number. Then someone speaks. Maria Woodworth, however, tended to do things quite differently.

For one thing, she typically began by preaching. Then her preaching was followed by a time of singing. During the singing, which did not commence until after she had already built up faith by preaching the word, the power of God was usually greatly in evidence.

As Maria Woodworth spoke to the crowds, she often focused on supernatural events as recorded in the Bible. At times she spoke about visions, especially those recounted in the book of Revelation or possibly those she had personally experienced. She also told of specific healings that she had seen in her ministry.

Mrs. Woodworth was always known to dress very plainly, sometimes in black, but often in white. According to a St. Louis newspaper, she spoke rapidly and with what the paper called "much force."[231] Other sources have noted, however, that her normal speaking style could have been described as calm and confident.

The fact is that although at times she spoke quietly and calmly, at other times she loudly shouted, perhaps while marching around the tent. In one of her meetings she told the assembled crowd, "Well, you may shout, my brothers! If ever we get to that glorious country beyond the river, we'll be a shouting people."[232]

She further explained, "But who has a better right to shout? The country is there for us, and the last mortgage has been canceled." St. Louis newspapers, however, sometimes criticized what they saw as religious frenzy exhibited in her meetings. As one of her favorite songs expressed it, however, "Some say I am too noisy; I know the reason why, and if they felt the glory, they'd shout as well as I."[233]

On at least one occasion, according to a newspaper's description, she "marched back and forth on the rostrum," while "beating time during songs." The same reporter found the music in her meetings, led by one man and two women, to be "quite entertaining."[234]

Typically, during her St. Louis meetings, Maria Woodworth would conclude her sermon by encouraging the crowd to look to God and to praise him. That is when many entered the trance state.

Even more were said to "succumb" during the singing which inevitably followed. In many cases, the same song was repeated a number of times. Some of her detractors took this as clear evidence of hypnotism.

Maria Woodworth said that when she first learned that she was called by God to minister, God told her so in an audible voice. After her first such experience, she began to frequently see visions. Those visions were most typically of heaven and angels, and occasionally of hell.

As late as 1890, while she was ministering in St. Louis, she still often heard God's word expressed audibly when she was alone. At other times, she would see visions. A coworker said that at times she would find Mrs. Woodworth standing alone in her room with her eyes fixed and her body immobile.

Evidently the same spiritual anointing that caused Mrs. Woodworth to enter into trances and see visions tended to rub off onto those who attended her meetings. Sometimes she would enter into a trance, seeing a vision while on the platform. At the same time, others around her would typically experience much the same thing.

The mother of a young girl attending the Woodworth meetings in St. Louis noted that her daughter had been in the tent about seven or eight times. As the mother termed it, "She sees angels and Jesus and everything in heaven." She added that her daughter "says she sees such pretty things that she wants to come every night."[235]

Ironically, one of the most moving accounts of the early life and ministry of Maria Woodworth was written by one of her most outspoken opponents in St. Louis. This was a medical doctor, Dr. Theodore Diller. Diller, writing in a decidedly anti-evangelistic magazine titled *The Medical News*, called her "a paranoic who posed as an evangelist."[236]

In an earlier article in the same publication, he attempted to "expose" her as a misguided woman suffering from an aberrant mental condition. In the process of explaining her condition, however, Diller himself admitted that she tended to minister with what he termed "a peculiar radiant expression."[237]

Even Dr. Diller had to admit that her appearance was obviously a pure expression of ecstasy, and that it appeared to be supernatural. That was so much the case, that, as he put it, her countenance certainly "would have impressed anyone." The doctor claimed, however, that this was merely the result of a psychotic state. He firmly believed that she was hypnotizing her audience.

In fact, in the same article in *The Medical News* he referred to the presence of hypnotism in the Woodworth meetings as though it was an established fact. Diller noted that some of her followers claimed to have actually seen a halo of light around her head. This he took as evidence of mass or collective hypnotism.

Theodore Diller wrote off her "peculiar radiant expression" that he believed, as he put it, "would have impressed anyone." He declared, however, that it was nothing more than the result of what he termed "religious monomania" or paranoia. He also remarked that the types of supernatural manifestations present in her meetings were nothing new.

Diller believed that the trances and prostrations in Woodworth's meetings were examples of misguided religious enthusiasm that had been at work in countless earlier revival meetings. He recounted various examples.

He cited what he termed the "dancing mania" that appeared in Germany and France in 1374, as well as manifestations of the "jerks." The experience known as the "jerks" was that enigmatic phenomenon that was extremely widespread during early 19th century camp meetings. He also mentioned the falling (prostration) that accompanied what he called the Kentucky revival of 1810. Presumably he actually meant the revival associated with the Cane Ridge camp meeting of 1801.

Dr. Diller ranked Maria Woodworth with members of two groups that he saw as despicable, misguided, and religiously paranoid dupes: The Salvation Army and the followers of Schweinfurth. Schweinfurth headed a community around this time that seems to have originally been influenced by the 19th century Mormon movement.

Georg Jacob Schweinfurth made national news when locals in and around Rockford, Illinois tried to tar and feather him. This was because Schweinfurth, head of a cult known as the Beekmanites, evidently maintained a harem at his commune called Heaven. There his followers—called apostles—worshiped him as the Christ.

A number of Schweinfurth's Beekmanites also lived in a community they called Jerusalem, located at St. Charles, Minnesota. Beekmanites were so bold as to infiltrate mainstream Christian churches across the Midwest, where they attempted to testify in support of Schweinfurth's claims.

Despite Diller's accusations against Mrs. Woodworth, however, she never claimed any special ability or power in and of herself. She was always quick to point out that she was merely a believer in God.

Maria Woodworth repeatedly emphasized that the healings and other manifestations that accompanied her meetings were not the result of any power that she possessed. Instead, they were initiated by God in response to faith.

Diller and Adams were not the only medical doctors to take issue with the healings present in Mrs. Woodworth's meetings, however. The *Medical and Surgical Reporter* insisted that claims of healing in the Woodworth meetings were "blasphemous in form and probably insane in motive."[238]

This was during an era in which members of the medical community, as a part of the new, modern scientific ethos, were often especially eager to denounce claims of divine healing as false. Just a few years later, Australian healing evangelist John Alexander Dowie, founder of Zion, Illinois, would face severe criticism and ridicule from medical students. This was the case, even to the point of becoming the target of rotten eggs.

In spite of the criticisms against Mrs. Woodworth in St. Louis, many who came to her services fell flat on their backs by the power of God. Others at least seemed overwhelmed by a sense of spiritual ecstasy. Still others professed healing. Typically, many of those attending wept as the power of God was manifested.

Even one of her most outspoken and most bitter persecutors admitted that many of those who were in trances in Woodworth's meetings undoubtedly saw visions of heaven and of angels. That same witness said that perhaps a hundred or so individuals might have been lying on the ground in a trance at one time.[239]

During the St. Louis meetings, hardly a night passed without at least several individuals entering into the trance state. One apparently typical St. Louis meeting ended around 11 p.m., with some waiting for their friends or family members to come out of trances. When they did, they spoke of the wonders of heaven that they had seen. That night around forty persons had entered into the trance state.

By the time Mrs. Woodworth had first arrived in St. Louis, as has already been mentioned, she had separated from her husband Philo. He was still suffering at the time from a variety of physical ailments, apparently brought on by Civil War service. In 1890, while his wife's ministry in St. Louis was attracting nationwide attention, he applied for a government military pension on the basis of those ailments.

At the time, Philo Woodworth was living at the couple's lakeside resort hotel at Lake Manitou in Rochester, Indiana. There he collected receipts from tourists visiting Woodworth Place, the Woodworths' resort, while his wife paid the property taxes. In addition, she covered the debts he ran up at a local store.

The pension board examined his claims. As an affidavit phrased it, he had fallen victim to "Fever resulting in disease of head & feet also Diarrhoea & Contusion Rheumatism & Catarrh Colisas [or colica and] Typhoid fever." A blank was filled in on the same document in such a way as to read, "he receives a pension of Nothing dollars per month."[240]

The board quoted Philo Woodworth as saying that, in his words, "Head feels as if there was a heavy weight on it, pain in feet goes to my head." He also complained of chronic diarrhea, a frequent ailment of Civil War veterans. "I have wandering pain in joints if I get wet," he added. The board noted his "abnormal prominence of Eye balls" as well as his "seeming loss of memory."

VISIONS AND HEALING IN THE TENT
IN ST. LOUIS

At almost the same time that Philo Woodworth was applying for a pension, his wife's meetings were exhibiting in great abundance the sorts of supernatural manifestations that had brought her fame and notoriety back in Indiana. "They cause the brain to whirl in wonder," declared a St. Louis newspaper.[241]

Individuals frequently entered the trance state and saw visions of heaven. At the same time, curious onlookers in the back of the tent, who desired to see a spectacle, would occasionally shout, "More light!" "Give us light!"[242]

A 13-year-old boy was asked what it was like to see heaven:

Oh, it was lovely. . . . I thought that I was taken away up in the air some place, where there was sweet music all the time. There were angels flying all around. They had big white wings, and had on long white gowns. Their faces shown bright and like gold and in the middle of them stood Jesus. His face and form were so bright that it would hurt your eyes to look at him. Way down below . . . there was a big crowd of people . . . and they seemed to be waiting for the world to come to an end.

They looked so bright and happy and the angels seemed to be so glad all the time, I want to see it again.[243]

"Did you know where you were all the time?" a reporter asked. "Oh, yes; people kept punching against me as I lay there, and of course that broke the thing once in a while, but it was just grand while it lasted."

Occasionally, individuals in the Woodworth tent in St. Louis would be seen to make climbing motions, as though trying to climb an invisible ladder. They were presumed to be seeing the Jacob's ladder of the Bible, extending upward into heaven.

E.S. Greenwood, who was Maria Woodworth's volunteer assistant in her St. Louis meetings, offered a comment about, as he termed them, "those who fall." He said that they "invariably seem to strain upwards, holding their hands aloft and sometimes even trying to climb up."[244]

Occasionally in Maria Woodworth's meetings, not just in St. Louis, individuals were known to see Jacob's ladder extending to heaven. Mrs. Woodworth herself had spoken a few years earlier in a meeting in Kokomo, Indiana about climbing a ladder to heaven. In 1885 she noted that,

If we are climbing Jacob's ladder, as we should, we will be happy Christians, and will be praising God, telling the good things he is doing for us continually. Shout and make a joyful noise to God.[245]

A child in one of the St. Louis meetings was pulled down after she had begun climbing the tent ropes. Then she continued to try to climb, by grabbing the canvas of the tent walls. The same girl later told a local newspaper reporter what she had seen in visions:[246]

The first vision I had . . . was the other night. I dreamt that I was going to heaven, and I climbed up a long ladder to get there. I saw Jesus leading the flocks of people around, and it was all so beautiful. I saw among those people there my sister, who has been dead several years, and also my little niece. They seemed so happy.

She added,

Tonight I had another beautiful vision. I dreamed that I saw heaven again. The roof of the tent seemed to whirl around and round and all of a sudden it seemed to whirl into a beautiful fountain with the water all the color of diamonds and other bright things. Then it seemed to change until it was all as red as blood, and a voice seemed to tell me that it was the blood of Christ washing away the sins of the people. It was a beautiful sight and I want to see it again.

Her meetings continued to draw crowds, who sometimes stood twelve deep outside the tent. Not only whites attended, but a smattering of blacks as well. Many were healed; many fell to the ground and experienced visions.

When she ministered in Oakland, California, Maria Woodworth was heavily criticized by local physicians. By the end of August of 1890, her ministry was again under attack from doctors, this time from local physicians Wellington Adams and Theodore Diller.

Adams and Diller led a crusade against Maria Woodworth. In the process, they managed to interview Mrs. Woodworth without her knowing that they were physicians, having masqueraded as newspaper reporters.

Mrs. Woodworth unwittingly explained to them about the process of entering trances:[247]

When you have a vision like the folks do at the meetings, you must give everything right up to God . . . You must look right up and stretch up your arms and you will see the vision. If you are stubborn and won't look up, then you will not be transported. You don't completely lose consciousness, but know everything that goes on all around you. If a person in this state is touched, the vision is broken for the instant, but it comes back again.

Other accounts of Mrs. Woodworth's meetings refer to individuals looking upward, in anticipation of seeing visions of heaven. After telling the doctors about seeing the light of God, the doctors posing as reporters asked her whether she had ever heard the voice of the Lord. "Yes," she told them. She added that when she was called to ministry,

He talked to me. I was afraid at first, but then I got over that. I obeyed his command. I have seen the Lord a number of times. Once I saw the Holy Ghost in the form of a dove. The Lord seemed like a great ball of fire. The Lord talks to me frequently the same as other persons do.

Maria Woodworth also told the doctors what it was like to enter the Lord's work. In addition, she explained to them how she overcame the belief that a woman could not possibly preach:

I'll tell you how I received the power first. I was commanded to preach, but I was afraid, because I had never heard a woman preach. The Lord came to me and ordered me to preach. I fought against it, but I heard his voice talking to me to do so. I felt so bad that I wanted to kill myself rather than to preach.

Of course, the doctors saw the remark about suicide as a clear indication of mental instability. She added, however, that her lack of education was one reason for her fears:

But the Lord came to me and persuaded me to go. I saw a bright light and saw angels flying all around me. They kept calling for me to go and preach. Finally I got married, and all through the sickness of death which followed in my family, the voice comforted me and finally won me to the work.

The fact that Maria Woodworth said that she conversed with God was regarded by the doctors as clear proof of insanity. They also asked her about seeing the Lord:

"Oh yes, he was on the cross. I am sure of that because I put my hand on his body."

"Did he look like the pictures you see of him?"

"Yes, a good deal like them, only his face was so bright that I couldn't see it plain. There was the crown of thorns at his feet just as it had fallen off his head. Oh, he looked beautiful."

"Were you under the power when you saw this?"

"No, I just saw it like I see you. He showed me that he was the Savior of the world. I put my hand on his body and he smiled and said he had saved my soul. That was eleven years ago. I also saw hell once, but that was horrible. I want the people to know all about this. I saw the Trinity once, the Father, the Son and the Holy Ghost. They were all the same thing. It was awfully queer and I can't describe it."

Once she realized that she would have to enter ministry, she was sitting in church when a bright light came toward her. As she explained it to the doctors,

The light came straight from heaven, right through the roof of the church to me. My body grew as light as a feather, and I felt myself beginning to rise straight up into the air. I was lifted right off my feet up into the air and I commenced shouting praises to the Lord. I was up in the air about half an hour. I could see right up into heaven, and there was a crowd of angels flying around in the air. They kept me in the air by the motion of their wings. I never expected to have that kind of an experience again, but I did, and lots of times I have been lifted right up in bed by the power.

Mrs. Woodworth's testimony to the two St. Louis doctors convinced them, of course, that she was both deranged and dangerous. As Dr. Adams put it, they saw her as "the innocent insane medium of dissemination for a highly contagious disease."[248] The doctors claimed that without her realizing it, Mrs. Woodworth was placing her congregations under a very powerful form of hypnosis.

Not only was the public intrigued by the trances and visions, but many wondered aloud about the healings that took place in her meetings. Were they of God? If so, why was no one getting healed in the established denominational churches? Did not those churches clearly represent God? If no one was getting healed in the traditional churches, did this not indicate that what was termed "the power" present in Mrs. Woodworth's meetings was not of God?

Further, a few years earlier America had been visited by a wave of massive evangelistic rallies led by such revival greats as Thomas Harrison ("the boy preacher"), Sam Jones, and Dwight L. Moody. No one was getting healed in these evangelistic rallies, yet these evangelists led many to salvation. Did this indicate that Mrs. Woodworth's ministry was not of God?

In the case of Maria Woodworth, faith in the word of God clearly played a vital role in the many healings that were evident in her meetings. One woman who was unable to walk, for example, was told by Mrs. Woodworth, "Now walk!" When she replied that she was unable to do so, Woodworth replied, "You must."[249] The woman complied, and then found that she was able to walk with no difficulty.

On another occasion, a St. Louis man who could not walk was brought to a Woodworth meeting in a furniture wagon. Maria Woodworth asked him if he believed that the Lord could perform miracles now as he did in the past.

The man replied that he did. After a time of praying and singing, she said to him, "Rise up and walk."[250] The man immediately did just that, leaving his cane behind. With his arms upraised, he walked out of the tent. He then sat on his wagon, continuing to praise God with his arms lifted.

Another person healed in St. Louis was Emma Yates, who lived on Market Street. When Mrs. Yates first entered the revival tent after dark, the tent's interior seemed to her as bright as day. This was the case even though the tent, which was lit with only a single lamp, seemed dim to others.

When Mrs. Woodworth entered with a group of coworkers, Mrs. Yates immediately knew who she was, even though she had never seen her before. "It all went over me in a wink that it was her when she came in," she said. "I hadn't thought that I could get cured, but when I knew it was her, it kind of gave me faith."[251]

Yates experienced healing for her severe rheumatism and other serious health problems. The healing power felt as though a bucket of water was being poured over her.

As Maria Woodworth moved her hand downward, Mrs. Yates felt the disease go down and out of her body. Skin problems immediately left. Swelling in her knees immediately went down.

Yates no longer had to use a cane to walk. Without further explanation, a St. Louis newspaper noted that she was "the woman who slept fourteen days at a time and narrowly escaped being buried."[252] This suggests that perhaps her maladies had already been the subject of local news.

Elizabeth Hammell or Hammill (spellings of her name differ) was also healed in the Woodworth meetings in 1890 in St. Louis. She was a poor widow woman living in a one-room apartment on South 13th Street.

Mrs. Hammell testified that she was healed of problems in her left arm "by divine power,"[253] as she put it, at one of the meetings. This was after doctors were unable to help her. She felt sudden and instantaneous healing in her arm. When the healing came, she heard a voice deep within her telling her to stand up and testify.

Eliza Hammell, apparently her daughter, was also set free from what had been diagnosed as St. Vitus' dance. The healing came right after Mrs. Woodworth demanded, "Evil spirit, get out of her."[254]

On the other hand, of course, some who could not believe did not get healed. Others, evidently because of their level of faith, only received temporary help. One woman complained that she felt better for a time as the result of prayer, but that the symptoms eventually returned.

The woman knelt in the sawdust with the others under the tent, and found that her pain had left. When she tried to walk, she found that she could. She felt fine as she started to walk home, but after a few blocks she felt her old symptoms returning.

Friends helped her the rest of the way, and then she began to feel even worse.

Because she was unable to respond to the healing anointing with faith, her healing did not last. She later remarked that it seemed as though she had been, in her words, "under a kind of stimulant and that it had all been worked out."[255]

When local policeman Thomas Farley experienced healing, he saw instant and dramatic improvement. After being brought into one of the services on his death bed, he rose up, was able to walk, and felt much better. Several days later, however, he suffered a relapse and the symptoms returned. He was not expected to survive.

On the other hand, others testified to lasting healing. In addition to incidences of healing, many found salvation in the Maria Woodworth meetings in 1890 in St. Louis. That is what caused her volunteer assistant E.S. Greenwood to help with her meetings there in the first place.

Greenwood testified that he did not understand the supernatural manifestations at all.[256] He did, however, possess an earnest desire to win the lost. He found himself working with Mrs. Woodworth simply because people were becoming born again in her meetings.

"Oh, why don't you come to the throne of grace?" asked Mrs. Woodworth in her tent during a meeting one night in August of 1890. "Come all of you. You want to be saved. Come and get salvation. Hallelujah!"[257]

This resulted in such cries as "God, help us!" Mrs. Woodworth continued,

> It doesn't say the murderers and robbers and such shall go to hell, but it says those whose names are not in the

book of life. The rich can be saved as well as the poor. I'd rather walk to heaven than ride to hell in a chariot.

That sermon lasted an hour and a half. Later in the evening she declared,

> Anyone who wants to be healed of any disease, just come right up, free of charge. Crowd around the throne. It don't make no difference if you are two or three deep. It'll reach you just the same.[258]

Some fell to the floor. One 18-year-old girl declared that she saw Jesus, as she gasped, "I see him; I see him."

Two rowdies who attended that meeting for amusement thought it would be fun to go forward and kneel in the sawdust, as though for prayer. As one of them looked around at what was happening, he began to laugh but then became horror-struck: He saw that his friend was not only succumbing to "the power," but soon he watched that friend fall onto the ground.

This was far from the only time that someone had attended one of Woodworth's meetings in jest, only to be overcome by the anointing. During earlier meetings in Hartford City, Indiana, spectators noticed that those who came to ridicule the meetings might be among the first to be affected by "the power."

In that sense, the meetings in St. Louis were not much different from those that took place during the old camp meetings, such as during the 1801 Cane Ridge revival. Then, such manifestations as "the jerks" often most profoundly affected those who had come to poke fun at the proceedings and to disrupt them.

MISSISSIPPI RIVER BAPTISMS

Although Maria Woodworth's initial efforts in St. Louis had been viewed by the local media as tame, this quickly changed.

Wild controversy surrounding her ministry had developed by the time she conducted a Mississippi River baptismal service in August.

The site of the baptisms was just a short walk away from the hall at 940 North Third where she had started out in St. Louis several months earlier. Estimates varied wildly as to the number of those who turned out to watch her baptisms of 54 converts. Some said there were 5,000, while others said there were over 10,000. At the time, the scene was said to have represented "one of the most remarkable events in the history of St. Louis."[259]

The obnoxious crowd, made up mostly of those who were clearly scoffers, gathered as close as they could to Mrs. Woodworth's chosen baptismal spot. A local paper referred to the spectators as a "raving, roaring, ungodly crowd" who had turned one of Christianity's basic sacraments into a "howling blasphemy."[260]

The location chosen by Mrs. Woodworth was just south of the monumental stone-and-steel Eads Bridge at the foot of Locust Street. Eads Bridge, considered a 19th century engineering marvel, still stands as an impressive and prominent feature along the St. Louis riverfront. The date was August 31, 1890.

This was during an era in which a large segment of the population thought of themselves as being, in one sense or another, Christians. The established denominations, however, did not generally teach immersion, and certainly not outdoors in a river.

In Mrs. Woodworth's era, baptisms usually consisted of tastefully performed sprinkling within the confines of a church building. As a result, river baptisms were regarded as quite a novelty. Any outdoor baptisms invariably drew a large crowd of spectators. In addition, St. Louisans had been avidly following the adventures in Mrs. Woodworth's tent through the pages of the city's two major daily papers.

Long before the ceremony was to begin, thousands gathered up and down the west side of the Mississippi River just south of Eads Bridge. More gathered on the bridge itself, and on nearby steamboats and barges. This was despite protests from boat captains and owners.

By this time, of course, Maria Woodworth had developed quite a reputation as what would be termed, at the time, a hypnotic "crank." Much of the population of St. Louis had no intention of staying away from what they expected to be a sensational event. They looked forward to being entertained, more so than would have been the case had a circus side show come to town.

In fact, the spectators directly compared the proceedings to those of a circus. The highly irreverent crowd hurled various disrespectful witticisms from time to time, such as "New museum [in other words, circus] in town" and "Here come the animals."[261] They also made loud references to the popular song of the era "Down Went McGinty," with its theme of suicide by drowning.

As one after another clever joke was shouted out by observers, the crowd howled with laughter. When one woman hesitated to enter her watery grave, someone shouted out, "The spirit is willin' but the flesh is weak,"[262] which led to yet more laughter.

The location of the baptisms could not have been too far from the location of a much earlier river baptism, which took place April 4th, 1818. That event is sometimes cited as probably the first baptism by immersion in St. Louis. In the case of Mrs. Woodworth's baptisms, a crude wooden pier was built specially for the purpose. The structure extended about 30 or 40 feet out into the river from a spot south of the foot of Locust Street, but north of the foot of St. Charles Street.

On this pier Mrs. Woodworth stood with a male assistant, Winebrenner Church of God minister C.H. Bolton from Clay City, Kansas. Bolton was State Missionary for Missouri in the

Winebrennerian movement. Later, after a successful campaign in Topeka, Kansas in 1891, Maria Woodworth would summon Bolton to take charge of her work there.

Together, Bolton and Mrs. Woodworth baptized the converts in the midst of a curious, mostly irreverent, and often outrageously derisive crowd. Spectators watched from atop nearby Eads Bridge, while others crowded the riverside just to the south.

Many waded out partway into the river, oblivious of damage to their leather shoes, in order to get a closer look. Still others watched from nearby steamboats, while yet more sought a closer vantage point from rowboats or anything else that would float.

The levee, from the foot of Olive Street north to Eads Bridge, was crowded long before the announced start time of two in the afternoon. Before the service began, many in the crowd sang along with what a local paper called "extremely secular"[263] tunes. These songs were being performed by a band onboard a nearby passenger steamboat.

The "ungodly crowd," as they were called by a local newspaper,[264] created an atmosphere that was more appropriate for a circus than for a baptism. Jokes and derisive comments filled the air.

Finally, an entourage of three extra-large horse-drawn furniture wagons arrived at the foot of Locust Street at 2:40 p.m. These were used as changing rooms. They were followed by what was termed the "hoodlum wagon," containing the police. Local police had their hands full trying to control the anything-but-reverent crowd.

At 3 p.m., Mrs. Woodworth led a group of believers down Locust Street and toward the river. Meanwhile, the cheers and jeers of the crowd were said to be deafening. Rev. Charles Bolton, who had a gray beard, measured the water depth with a rod at the makeshift pier.

Finally the first baptism took place at 3:18. Two little girls dressed in white were escorted to the river accompanied by loud cheers from the crowd. As Mrs. Woodworth raised her hands, a choir sang "Nearer My God to Thee," and the two were immersed.

The presence of the Mississippi River seems to have encouraged the choir to sing at least three songs with a water theme: "Shall We Gather at the River," "Let the Lower Lamps Be Burning" (a song about God's seashore lighthouse), and "Throw Out the Lifeline" (which a local paper mistitled "Pull for the Shore Sailor"[265]) as the baptisms continued.

The latter song, "Throw Out the Lifeline," advised all who were present to:

Trust in the lifeboat, sailor; all else will fail,
Stronger the surges dash and fiercer the gale.
Heed not the stormy winds, though loudly they roar;
Watch the "bright and morning star," and pull for the shore!

One of those who was immersed was a woman who began to excitedly thrash her arms about, while shouting praises. A local newspaper reporter derisively declared that she seemed to have received what he termed "the 'power.'"[266]

A bit later, a man who was baptized emerged from the water with what the same paper called "a violent case of the 'power,'" while another was said by to have experienced "a well-developed case of 'power.'"

Most of the new converts were ridiculed by the crowd. When a woman described by the local press as "exceedingly corpulent"[267] entered the water, she immediately became especially subjected to jeers and degrading shouts. Bravely, though, she too was taken under the waters.

When she proved too heavy to lift, however, a man placed his shoulder beneath her and, with great effort, managed to raise her out of her watery spiritual grave. At that moment, the crowd shouted in unison, "Saved! Saved! Saved!"[268] The choir then sang "Safe in the Arms of Jesus" after the crowd let out a cheer, the likes of which were said to have never before been heard on the St. Louis riverfront.

The baptism of a person described as a "dudish man"[269] in white shirt and baggy pants was accompanied by the rowdy crowd singing the popular secular tune, "Down Went McGinty." When Mrs. Woodworth tried to address the crowd after the baptisms, the rowdy masses paid but scant attention.

Maria Woodworth's 1890 meetings in St. Louis had attracted some media attention outside of the immediate area even before the Mississippi River baptisms. After the baptisms, however, the media began to focus more particularly on the attempt by local doctors to have her committed as insane. As a result, her St. Louis tent revival became the focus of a number of newspaper articles across the country.

The meetings in St. Louis were covered in such prominent papers as the *Los Angeles Times*, the *New York Sun*, the *New York Times*, the *Boston Globe*, and the *Chicago Tribune*. Those articles often presented her ministry as though there was no question that she was using hypnotism.

As a typical example of these articles, the *Washington Post* noted that St. Louis was visited by a "religious frenzy rarely matched among civilized people."[270] The same paper suggested that the events that were transpiring in Mrs. Woodworth's tent were such as had only been seen in "the wildest orgies of old-fashioned Southern negro camps."

Chapter

5

A NEW WAVE OF
PERSECUTION

Woodworth's St. Louis meetings in 1890 were frequented by huge numbers of unbelieving spectators. They tended to see the proceedings as a source of entertainment. After the *St. Louis Post-Dispatch* published a spectacular account of supernatural manifestations at one of her meetings, for example, the tent was especially crowded the next night.[271]

Many had come there wanting to see what had been termed "wonders." That night, between 20 and 25 persons were said to have "passed into the trance condition."[272] The manifestations brought much criticism from those who could not understand what they were witnessing. There was even concern at one point that perhaps Mrs. Woodworth's staff could have been administering drugs to her followers.

Evidently, it was common for some of those attending her meetings to sway forward and backward a bit before falling under the anointing. A local newspaper reported that a skeptical doctor placed his hand on the back of a man in such a state in order to steady him. He then helped him to his feet as soon as he had fallen.

Of course, this distraction brought the man out of his trance. This was said to have supposedly proven to the doctor that the manifestations were the result of what he called "hysteria" rather than the Spirit of God.[273] In another instance, a doctor noticed that a woman in a trance had not blinked for ten or fifteen minutes. When he attempted to place his finger on her eye, he was prevented by one of the altar workers.

Probably because of the presence of the curious in the meetings, their fingers often poked or jabbed or pinched those who fell under the power of God. This was often done, of course, in order to see what response they would get.

As Woodworth's 1890 meetings in St. Louis attracted huge numbers of those who were more curious than reverent, her meetings—not just the river baptisms—were seen as something closer to a circus side-show than a Christian service. Many came to her tent strictly out of curiosity. They especially wanted to see individuals enter into trances.

Some embraced the trance phenomenon as being of God, while others rejected it as the opposite. One person who attended one of Maria Woodworth's St. Louis tent meetings mentioned, as she put it, "those awful trances which . . . are revolting to see if they are not horrible to endure."

Perhaps she thought that the look of intensity on individuals' faces indicated that the trance state was unpleasant. According to the same observer, it was "evident to every thinking man that Mrs. Woodworth is using some power which produces peculiar, perhaps dreadful results."[274]

Several years earlier in Indiana, at Woodworth Place in Rochester, one individual remained in a trance state for hours with her hand pointed to heaven. She was exhibiting the same pose that had come to be equated with Maria Woodworth. Evidently her experience was not atypical. The frequency, however, with which individuals entered the trance state in the St. Louis revival meetings may have been beyond anything that had been experienced in Mrs. Woodworth's earlier meetings in Indiana and Ohio.

THE MEDICAL COMMUNITY VS. MARIA WOODWORTH

The most common interpretation of what was happening in Mrs. Woodworth's meetings, on the part of those who did not believe that such phenomena were of God, was that those who entered trances or were healed were being hypnotized. Even as late as 1903, D.O. Teasley expressed similar views when discussing her ministry in his book titled *The Holy Spirit and Other Spirits*:[275]

> It is not so much my intention to delineate the character of what is known as the Shaker church or community . . . as to give an exposition of the fanatic shaking and quaking known as "the power" among Shakers, Quakers, and the followers of Mrs. Woodworth. . . . They will often spend hours praying for "the power" to come upon them, and when it has come they are prostrated and unable to move or speak for some time. In this semi conscious state the muscles become rigid, and the symptoms in general very much resemble what is known in hypnotism as the cataleptic state. . . .

He went on to say that, regarding Maria Woodworth,

> Many who are uninformed in the Scriptures become entranced with her hypnotic devil powers and are led to believe in "the power," which is the mainspring of her

cult. . . . As nearly as I can comprehend, this "power" or shaking is a mixture of hypnotism, spiritualism, and nervous derangement. . . . Sometimes this "power" takes on more of a spiritualistic nature, and visions are received. Through these visions people are sometimes led into unhappy marriages, and many other snares of the devil.

During her 1890 St. Louis meetings, doctors insisted that even when there did seem to be healings, individuals were merely receiving temporary help through hypnosis. The symptoms, according to the doctors, were only the result of hysteria in the first place. In their view, Mrs. Woodworth was hypnotizing them, only giving the appearance of bettering their condition.

In fact, an attempt was made during her St. Louis crusade to have her committed as insane, while others charged that her supposed "hypnosis" must be stopped. Claims of hypnosis merely echoed criticisms of similar experiences in camp meetings and other revivals at various points much earlier in the 19th century. Those claims would be repeated a few decades later when the public was confronted with the healing ministry of popular evangelist Aimee Semple McPherson.

Some were insistent that Mrs. Woodworth's supposed hypnosis must be stopped and that the claims of healing in her meetings were fraudulent. Interestingly, however, little complaint appears to have been made about psychic healings which were available locally at the same time in St. Louis. As an example, psychic healings were being attributed to "Mrs. Ros. Sabine, fortune teller," who advertised in local papers around the same time as Mrs. Woodworth's meetings.

Mrs. Sabine publicized what she called her "wonderful cures," at least some of which she attributed to the wearing of her "magic belts."[276] She offered "4 Convincing Proofs" in local newspaper advertising that "The Magic Belt Works Miracles."

Aside from an attempt at one point to have Sabine and her accomplice, "Professor Laredo," arrested for obtaining money under false pretenses,[277] her activities seem to have stirred up little or no general public concern.

While the public wanted to know what power Mrs. Woodworth was using, Mrs. Sabine was off the public radar. Mrs. Sabine, however, was not challenging established religion.

Some of the criticisms directed against Mrs. Woodworth were so severe that the attacks seem to have backfired. Instead of discouraging attendance at her meetings, the relentless persecution seems to have actually encouraged support for her.

Drs. Adams and Diller, the two local medical doctors, called for what they termed a "public inquiry" into her methods. Soon one of them declared that he was startled to find a great deal of popular support for Mrs. Woodworth even as he went about the task of trying to have her committed.

Before the call for an investigation, most of the city newspapers were, in his estimation, "poking fun" at her meetings. But once he began his merciless and unrelenting criticisms of her, in his words, "lo and behold, there is a complete change of heart."[278]

He wondered aloud if those who seemed to have sided with her had all, as he put it, "received the 'power' and been attacked by the 'spells.'" One local view was that the doctors' criticisms of Mrs. Woodworth were being commonly viewed as persecution and that this had encouraged popular support for her ministry.

Wellington Adams, M.D., who was one of Maria Woodworth's primary antagonists, ranked her with the Salvation Army and others of what he called "this class." In his words, these were "the religious quacks who stand on the outside of the regular church and hold side shows."[279]

Of course, the implication was that only the "regular church" was deserving of respect. Adams said that he was making these charges because Mrs. Woodworth was unqualified to enter the "straight and narrow gate," as he put it, into what he called "true religion." For him, true religion was that which relies on official denominational theology, and, of course, adheres to the traditional denominational approach.

Dr. Adams, along with another local physician, Theodore Diller, M.D., called for a legal inquiry into what they called "the power she is using,"[280] whatever that power was. They made this demand in spite of the fact that even the local press had to admit that there were some "marvelous" accounts of healings that had taken place in the meetings.[281]

The intense persecution that came against Mrs. Woodworth in St. Louis was supported by a variety of people: medical doctors, clergy, "infidels" (as they were often termed in those days), and ordinary but hostile citizens. At the forefront of these attacks, however, stood the two physicians, Drs. Adams and Diller.

In much the same way, some of the most intense persecution against the healing ministry of John Alexander Dowie about a decade later would come from the medical profession. Dowie came from Australia to America, after developing a reputation as a healing evangelist, even seeing healings from bubonic plague.

He was subjected to what an observer termed "catcalls and sarcastic remarks"[282] from medical students when he attempted to speak in London in 1900. Around the same time, when he tried to lecture in Chicago, medical students filled the hall with a foul chemical odor and pelted him with eggs.

Dr. Adams was more fully known as Arthur Wellington Adams, M.D. Adams owned an electric company, was known for his experiments in "chained lightning," and was regarded as a well-known scientist.[283] He was the author of *Electricity: Its Application in Medicine and Surgery*, published in 1891.

Theodore Diller, who lived from 1863 to 1943, was a nationally-known medical author. Diller wrote on a wide variety of medical subjects, but was especially concerned with nervous conditions and hysteria, in addition to mental illnesses in general. Some of his published articles bear such titles as "Care of the Chronic Insane" and "What Shall Be Done With the 'Homicidal Crank'?"

He saw the Woodworth revival phenomena as dangerous. He viewed her meetings as yet further manifestation of the same sort of mental conditions with which he had already been dealing outside of any religious context. To Diller's credit, he probably sincerely believed that he was helping others by protecting them from simply another form of insanity.

Diller did hear at least something of Mrs. Woodworth's gospel message, but he rejected it. For one thing, although Maria Woodworth had no use for doctors, he believed that true religion left plenty of room for physicians. In one of his articles appearing in *The Medical News*,[284] he was quick to point out that the apocryphal book of Ecclesiasticus (appearing in Catholic Bibles and in the original 1611 King James Bible) states that physicians should be honored.

Diller quoted from Ecclesiasticus 38:1–15. In the original 1611 edition of the King James translation of the Bible, that verse reads, "Honor a physician with the honor due to him, for the uses which you may have of him, for the Lord has created him." Similarly, the fourth verse reads, "The Lord has created medicines out of the earth, and he who is wise will not abhor them."

Dr. Diller said he believed that this text would, as he put it, "make an excellent short tract" that could be distributed to

Christian Scientists, faith healers, and the like. In his suggestion, however, he glossed over the fact that the same passage also refers to the role of God's power in physical healing.

Verse 9 reads, "My son, in your sickness do not be negligent, but pray to the Lord and he will make you whole." Then, verse 10 makes it clear that sin can prevent health. Further, verse 14 says that the physician should pray to the Lord that he would make the physician's work successful.

There is no indication, however, that Diller personally took the advice offered in this last verse, and not everyone agreed with the assessments of Mrs. Woodworth's ministry by Drs. Adams and Diller. In fact, one newspaper editorial writer was so incensed at the antics of Drs. Adams and Diller in their campaign against Mrs. Woodworth that he referred to the two as Drs. Clyster and Jalap.[285]

The terms "clyster" and "jalap" would not mean anything to the average 21st century reader. Use of the terms, however, was meant as a derisive insult to the doctors and to their medical reputation. Many modern-day history buffs are familiar with the medical use of clysters and jalap from the 1804–1806 expedition of Lewis and Clark. In order to optimize their health condition on the trip, those on the expedition took along a clyster syringe—to administer enemas—along with a good supply of jalap.

Jalap is a purgative medicine taken from a type of Mexican morning glory. It was often used because of its laxative qualities. Clearly, the writer of the 1890 editorial had but little regard for the medical ability of Drs. Adams and Diller, AKA Drs. Clyster and Jalap, whose expertise was associated in the editorial with enemas and laxatives.

The same writer complained that the battle to have Mrs. Woodworth committed, which was to involve the city's Health

Department, would cost the taxpayers a considerable sum. The editorial alleged that the move was only designed to fill the newspapers with free publicity for Adams and Diller, during an era when doctors were not allowed to advertise.

Further, the editorial claimed, so-called trances have always accompanied Holy Ghost revivals, so why be so concerned about them in the case of Mrs. Woodworth? Why should her tent revivals be the concern of the St. Louis Health Commissioner? Why not, instead, go after quack medical doctors with dubious medical credentials rather than bother someone who is trying to do some good?

The same editorial suggested that the interests of the Health Department might be far better served by examining the medical details behind area deaths. The implication was that in the case of burial certificates signed by Adams and Diller, those doctors might know about possible health risks that were far greater than any danger posed by Mrs. Woodworth.

The editorial writer also reasoned that if some of Adams' and Diller's patients died while entrusting themselves to the doctors' care, then they might be more potentially dangerous than Woodworth's tent revival meetings. The doctors were insisting on making what the writer declared to be "public nuisances" of themselves, while Mrs. Woodworth's only offense was that she was, in the writer's words, "ignorant and unconventional."

This editorial was not the only article in local newspapers to hint that perhaps Adams and Diller had little or no standing from which to criticize another individual. One local reporter asked why the doctors were not even listed in the city directory.

Evidently, however, this was only because both had recently moved. No mention of either doctor does appear, however, in the 1890–1891 edition of the St. Louis City Directory. Diller does not appear in the 1891–1892 edition either, although Wellington

Adams is listed as a physician at 500 North Jefferson Avenue, with his residence at 2741 Olive Street.

Even many of those who spoke highly of the ministry of Maria Woodworth, and who believed that no hypnotism was present, still could not explain the phenomenal power that was evident in her meetings. As already noted, E.S. Greenwood, a volunteer who led prayer in her tent meetings, said he did not understand the manifestations and could not explain them. As he put it, however, "I know no creed in evangelistic work, and being satisfied that Mrs. Woodworth is doing good work I am willing to help, but I can't explain what takes place."[286]

Even Drs. Adams and Diller could not deny that some sort of power was present. Although the doctors were convinced that they knew what the source of that power was, the public continued to debate the issue. To some extent, the purpose of the inquiry into Mrs. Woodworth's sanity appeared to be, as one person put it, "to know what that power is, that is all."[287] Oddly, it was apparently believed by some that this could be determined by the court system.

The big question in the public's mind was this: What was this power? Could it possibly be the power of God? As the press had reported earlier of her Indiana meetings, "The people are wonderfully excited, and neighbor asks neighbor, 'What is it?'" Further, "Is it contagious or infectious, epidemic or endemic, good or evil?"[288]

The physicians' complaint alleged that Mrs. Woodworth was, as it was termed, "of unsound mind and incapable of managing her affairs."[289] Dr. Diller insisted that her insanity and her supposed "hypnotic" influence over the masses was a clearly verifiable scientific fact. He was unrelenting in his vicious attacks against the Woodworth revival meetings, and seemed determined to stop them—and her—by any means possible.

Then, the attacks against her appeared to be suddenly intensified when another factor entered into the picture. A newly-arrived local Methodist minister, Dr. Boswell of the First Methodist Church, received a letter from Maria Woodworth's very recently estranged husband. In that letter, Philo Woodworth, who was himself clearly suffering from mental instability, claimed that his wife was not in her right mind.

Dr. Boswell insisted that it would be unethical for him to divulge the specific contents of the letter, saying that Mrs. Woodworth's husband requested that it not be made public. Although he would not release the letter's exact words, he made it clear, however, that he was eager to offer to the public a complete paraphrase.

The letter claimed that Mrs. Woodworth was a fraud and that she was mentally unsound. Although Boswell did not want to share the exact wording of the letter, he made it clear that he was putting it aside in case it would be needed as evidence at her trial.[290] He did not explain why he came to receive such a letter in the first place, and at such an opportune time for Maria Woodworth's antagonists.

Dr. Wellington Adams received a copy of the same letter and had no scruples about directly sharing its contents with the press.[291] As was the case with Boswell, Adams did not explain why he was a recipient of the letter. The doctors' campaign against her, however, had by now become national news.

The matter of why she was no longer living with her husband became the focus of yet more persecution against her. Her detractors paraded a series of allegations regarding her marriage before the public. Others pointed out, however, that she had much evidence and a number of witnesses in her favor.

In surviving (microfilm and digitized) copies of a local newspaper, part of the page duplicating Mr. Woodworth's letter is missing. Still, however, he appears to have alluded to accusations that he had threatened Maria Woodworth with murder.

In his letter, he complained that Mrs. Woodworth had abandoned him during the Oakland, California meetings while he was in poor health and unable to take care of himself. By his own admission, however, the letter appears to suggest that he was told by others at the camp to leave or he would be "arrested for threts [as he spelled it] of murder:"

ROCHESTER, Ind.,
Sept. 7, 1890.
I have seen your name in the Post-Dispatch about how you believe my wife is crazy. In regard as to me being in the asilum I will say at present I am at home. I was compelled to leave my wife Marria B Woodworth at Oakland Cal on the 15 day of last Dec by the request of Mrs. Woodworth . . . . My wife left me alone in the camp ground not able to be on my feet only part of the time. . . . After dark 2 of Mrs W friends came to me found me [unreadable] sick in my tent they said to me [unreadable] propostin to make to you; [unreadable] to-mory morning at 8 o'clock [unreadable] you arrested for threts of mur- [unreadable] my wife and after all sh [sic] [unreadable] have past through I would give [unreadable] last cent I have if She stood in need [unreadable] Laid all night in agny. I made up [unreadable] [?]nd before I would ezspose her i would [?mpt to start home. God only noes that I suffered on the way home and have suffered everything but death.

His letter continued with additional complaints, worded in such a way as to seemingly suggest that he was reduced to bread and water, and that his wife was to blame. The fact that she supported him financially after their separation is not mentioned. On the contrary, Philo claimed that, in his words,

I am broken down, total wreck amung strangers i need medical aid, but i hav not one cent of income. Often when i set down to a well filed tabel on money witch I should of had wheather iff she thinks of the person she promest God to nerish and cherish through sickness and death that sollem vow she has broken, yes she has. The Lord Have Mercy on her is my prayers. The only thing i desire is fer her to repent and make Heaven Her Home. God save my wife from a burning Hell is my prayers.

P. H. WOODWORTH.

At the same time that Drs. Adams and Diller were accusing Maria Woodworth of hypnotizing the crowds, a professional hypnotist challenged the physicians to prove that any hypnotism was actually transpiring in her meetings. During one meeting, Mrs. Woodworth produced a four-foot long green handbill advertising this "eminent mesmerist" or hypnotist as proof that he knew his business.

After much careful examination, the hypnotist declared that what was going on was, in his words, "strange and wonderful." He insisted, however, that it was definitely not a matter of hypnotism. He offered an impressive list of medical and academic credentials to support his assessment that not the faintest hint of hypnotism was occurring in the meetings.

In addition, a certain Dr. Troy, whose credentials are unknown, addressed Mrs. Woodworth's congregation in one of her meetings. He explained to them that the manifestations could not be the result of hypnotism. He pointed out that when individuals are hypnotized, they must be brought out of the hypnotic state by the hypnotist. By contrast, in Woodworth's meetings, individuals come out of their trance state without needing assistance by others.

In further support of Maria Woodworth and her methods, she told the press that a local physician who she identified as

"Dr. King" said that the trances were not harmful or debilitating. Mrs. Woodworth gave Dr. King's address as 2726 St. Louis Avenue. This identifies him as Dr. Henry R. King, whose address was actually 2720 St. Louis Avenue.

When Woodworth had first arrived in town, a local newspaper claimed that she had spoken in one of her meetings regarding what the paper termed "mesmerism and kindred things." The newspaper asserted that, in the paper's words, they "were of Christian origin."[292] Obviously she was misquoted.

By the time of the attacks on her ministry by Drs. Adams and Diller she made it clear that her ministry had nothing at all to do with mesmerism, also known as hypnotism. In addition, another local newspaper article (copied in Chicago) declared that "Mesmerism and hypnotism, says she, are devil's words and manifestations of the devil's power."

The same paper insisted that "Her strength owes nothing to either of these, but in faith pure and simple." Further, in the same reporter's words,

> Mrs. Woodworth maintains that her cures are strictly the work of faith in the power of God . . . In order to be cured of any bodily ailment, no matter how virulent or of how long standing, she claims all that is necessary to do is to come to her with one's heart ready to be converted. At the same instant the conversion is effected the worldly disease falls off like a useless garment and never returns as long as the heart is purged of sin and full of the belief in God and Christ.

Up until a few days before the court date in the effort to have Mrs. Woodworth committed, it appears that she was inviting individuals to come down front to the "altar" each evening during the meetings. Evidently this was done in order to pray for those who needed healing. Much of the time, however, the press assumed that when individuals came to the front they were inevitably acting under some sort of hypnotic power. This was certainly the allegation of the doctors.

They noted that Woodworth and her coworkers walked along the line of those who came to the platform, gently touching them and talking to them in a soft, soothing voice. The doctors believed this was evidence of hypnotism.

The practice of inviting individuals to come up front to the altar, however, seems to have been discontinued, at least temporarily, on the evening of Monday, September 1st. The court trial was scheduled for that Friday. On Monday night, what an observer termed "the excitement" began to be manifested. At that moment, however, some noticed that Mrs. Woodworth consulted with others by whispering, and no one was brought forward.

At the same time, the presence of newspaper reporters was publicly noted in the meeting. A local paper assumed that these developments indicated that the so-called "hypnotism" had been discontinued. One paper went so far as to claim that the supernatural manifestations in her meetings were "hypnotic seances" and that they had been "to a great extent abated." The same paper added that this had been the aim of the doctors, and that they considered their efforts successful.

According to Drs. Adams and Diller, a number of ministers and physicians contacted them to express their appreciation for the physicians' attacks on Mrs. Woodworth. Although they were unable to specify any specific wrong that she had done, they promised their enthusiastic support in "unearthing any wrongs which may exist." That may explain the sudden appearance of the letter from Mr. Woodworth.

At the same time that many were supportive of the doctors' actions, however, others were offended. In fact, the press reported that Dr. Adams had received "a number" of threatening letters as a result of his stand against Mrs. Woodworth. The local press and public alike looked forward to a long and sensational court fight. "The trial will probably be one of the most sensational ever held in the city," the *St. Louis Post-Dispatch* emphatically declared.

The print media outside of St. Louis picked up on the battle. The *Christian Union* misspelled Mrs. Woodworth's name and misplaced her hometown, but that did not stop the magazine from declaring that

> Two St. Louis physicians have appealed to the Mayor to stop the religious revival now in progress in a large tent on Jefferson Avenue, under the auspices of Mrs. Woodward, of San Francisco, on the ground that the woman is insane and hypnotizes her converts.

The publication continued by saying that, according to the doctors, her influence was "very injurious."[293]

Dr. Diller was asked by the local press why he believed Maria Woodworth was insane. He answered,

> Well, in the first place, she has had "visions," both when in the hypnotic state and during the waking state. She believes firmly in the reality of these "visions," and that she receives direct commands from the Deity. As is frequently the case in her type of insanity, she has diverse "visions." She has penetrated the depths of hell, and she has been exalted into the seventh heaven.

Diller added that "According to Mrs. Woodworth's own statements, she will sit in a room and talk aloud with the Deity." In his estimation, this served as clear evidence of insanity.

Meanwhile, the public appeared to hope that the legal battle would somehow determine whether Mrs. Woodworth's power was from God, from the devil, or was the result of hypnotism. A local newspaper pointed out that if the charges against her indicate insanity, then thousands are similarly insane. Further,

It will, of course, be interesting to learn whether this so-called "power" is hypnotism, whether it is harmful or not, if the investigation proceed so far, but if it be pronounced harmful the doctors who are experimenting in it as well as the revivalists should be stopped. Why not proceed first against the doctors who, according to themselves, are knowingly injuring people by hypnotic treatment?

Meanwhile, when asked how she would combat the legal threat against her, Mrs. Woodworth answered, "I shall do as the Lord directs me." She added that she had "no fear as to the result." In response to questions about manifestations of "the power" in her meetings, she replied,

I argue that "Jesus Christ is the same yesterday, to-day and forever." All Christians believe that, and I say that if he is the same now as he always was he can exert his power just as he did when Martin Luther, [John] Wesley, [George] Whit[e]field and [Peter] Cartwright preached. Hypnotism was never charged against any of these, and I don't suppose any of them knew anything whatever about it. I am quite sure I don't.

A reporter asked her whether the manifestations accompanying her ministry were akin to those evident in the ministries of such men as those she had named—Luther, Wesley, Whitefield, and Cartwright. "I do. It is just the same," she said.

During the height of the controversy in St. Louis over Mrs. Woodworth, a newspaper in that city published a lengthy description of trances and other supernatural manifestations during various historical religious movements. Referring to the 18th century preaching of George Whitefield, that article noted that:

> Under his preaching physical manifestations were exceedingly common. Men fell as though dead, and lay for hours unconscious, then rising, would make the welkin ring with shouts and songs. They had visions and told them with great freedom in their meetings, to the horror of formalists, who considered that sort of thing extremely demoralizing. Every effort was made by the ministers of the Established Church to suppress the excitement. There was talk of imprisoning John Wesley as a dangerous lunatic.

Meanwhile, some wondered whether the manifestations in Maria Woodworth's meetings could be explained by the administration of drugs to her followers. Regarding the more common accusations that the power present was simply hypnotism, she answered, "Nor more it is. It is simply the power of God exercised on the converts." She continued,

> But all the converts do not go into these trances by any means. Only a comparatively small number do so. The power of God is exercised in more ways than one. What I cannot understand is how these physicians can justify their position. First they said I was practicing hypnotism and doing injury to people even when I cured them, and now they want to say I am insane. Yet they admit there are cures, but they don't seem to have any explanation to adduce since abandoning the hypnotism theory. If this matter goes on there will be some very remarkable evidences of cure, thought I have never claimed to cure anybody. I merely pray, and unless the sick person has faith

in God's power, no cure can be effected, except in the case of little children who are too young to understand.

By late September of 1890, Mrs. Woodworth's followers were beginning to realize that she would not continue her tent meetings in North St. Louis forever. Discussion began about erecting a building in which they could continue to meet. They talked in terms of a brick or wooden building 80-by-120 feet in size, that would seat about 7,000 persons.

At the time, about that many were said to be attending her evening tent meetings, perhaps even more, although accounts differ as to her tent's capacity. Although one source claimed that the tent could shelter about 9,000, it appears more likely that the tent itself could only hold about three or four thousand.

The lot on which her tent stood, which is still a vacant lot today, could not have accommodated a tent much bigger than that. Many more, however, stood around outside, and yet others were turned away due to lack of space. Various individuals quickly pledged the needed funds for a new church building.

THE CASE AGAINST MARIA WOODWORTH

The day after Maria Woodworth's spectacular Mississippi River baptisms was Monday, September 1, 1890. On that day, Mrs. Woodworth's primary antagonists in St. Louis, Drs. Adams and Diller, consulted with the local health commissioner as to the best avenue to pursue in silencing Maria Woodworth.

Commissioner Dudley replied that he was glad they had contacted him. This was because even before he heard from the doctors, he had determined that Mrs. Woodworth was insane and needed to be, as a newspaper put it, "restrained." He suggested that they introduce charges of insanity before the Probate

Court. That court was then charged with administering the affairs of the mentally incompetent.

The following day, the two doctors submitted a complaint to the judge of the Probate Court. The case was brought to that court because this was considered a guardianship case. According to the law, if any county resident could be shown to be of an unsound mind, the Probate Court should determine whether the person was capable of managing his own affairs. The complaint read,

> To the Hon. J. C. Woerner, Judge of the Probate Court of the City of St. Louis:
> The undersigned hereby gives information, and alleges the fact to be, that one Maria B. Woodworth of the city of St. Louis aforesaid is a person of unsound mind and incapable of managing her affairs and prays that an inquiry thereinto be according to the statutes for such case made and provided.
> WELLINGTON ADAMS, M. D.
> THEODORE DILLER, M.D.

The press asserted that the basic reason the doctors had reached this conclusion was that Woodworth claimed to have, in the newspaper's words, "conversed with the Deity and descended into hades." [294] The doctors asked that an inquiry be made in accordance with any laws which might be found to be relevant.

Of course, the implication was that surely there must be a law that would require that she be institutionalized, incapable of further influencing impressionable members of the public. When Judge Woerner returned to St. Louis on September 5 from a trip out of town, he found that the doctors had filed their complaint on the 2nd.

One of Woerner's first actions on his return was to inform Dr. Adams that, as judge, he could not take action regarding Maria Woodworth without clear grounds on which to do so. Evidently Adams and Diller were able to convince him that such grounds existed. Mrs. Woodworth, who was completely engrossed in conducting one of the most historically significant series of revival meetings of the 19th century, was given five days in which to prepare her defense.

At the time, the Probate Court met in the east wing of what is today known as the Old Courthouse, on St. Louis' riverfront. That wing is the part of the building, still standing, which extends east toward the city's Gateway Arch.

The case was brought before Judge Woerner and "virtually dismissed" the same day, according to the local press.[295] Whatever "virtually" dismissed means is uncertain, however, since no records of the case have survived. A local newspaper said that "He did not absolutely dismiss the proceeding, but in effect did so."

In presenting the case against Mrs. Woodworth, Dr. Wellington Adams spoke of what a newspaper called the "motley" crowd that her meetings drew. He also pointed to what he termed the "bad effects produced upon the community." Adams also described the meetings as "sacrilegious." Woodworth was widely regarded as a nuisance, he insisted, and she was exerting a harmful influence over her deluded followers.

To a large extent, Judge Woerner agreed with Adams. In the words of a local newspaper, the judge believed that Woodworth's ministry "might be of a pernicious character—that is, if the published reports about her were true—and that it was damaging to religion." He did not, however, see any clear ground on which to have her declared insane.

"It was true," the paper continued, "she might be a regular nuisance." The judge, however, did not believe that the probate court was the proper place in which to try nuisance cases. Judge Woerner advised Dr. Adams to consult an attorney about bringing a new case against Mrs. Woodworth, a case alleging that she was a public nuisance.

The judge praised Adams in his attacks against Mrs. Woodworth. In a newspaper's words "he said the doctor was undoubtedly an intelligent gentleman with honest motives, but that he had undertaken a somewhat complicated task."

That was the end of the legal battle against Maria Woodworth, but this did not end the criticisms aimed at her. The German-language press, in particular, was adamant in its attacks on her and her ministry. The daily St. Louis *Westliche Post* insisted, despite Woerner's verdict, that she was "halbverrückte"—in other words, "half crazy."[296]

Dr. Arthur Wellington Adams, one of the two doctors who led the attempt to have Maria Woodworth committed, was born June 21, 1856 in Brooklyn, New York and died in December 19, 1898 in St. Louis. By that time, he had made an ill-fated attempt to form an electric elevated railway system and had become entangled in a patent suit with Thomas Edison over the matter of directly attaching electric motors to vehicle wheels.

Adams had married Suzanne ("Suzie") Slayback, daughter of well-known local figure Alonzo Slayback, who was one of the founders of St. Louis's deliberately enigmatic Veiled Prophet parade. Suzanne was, in fact, the first Veiled Prophet Queen. In 1882, her father Alonzo Slayback was murdered by John Cockerill, editor of the *St. Louis Post-Dispatch*.

By the time of Dr. Adams' death, his Adams Electric Company had gone bankrupt. In 1898 he became ill with double pneumonia, and testified during his patent suit with Edison while delirious. When he died that year, his virtually penniless widow was forced to place four of her six children in an orphanage.

The other doctor to come against Mrs. Woodworth, Dr. Theodore Diller, died in 1943 in Pittsburgh at the age of 80. His last position had been as a psychiatrist with the Army Induction Center at Altoona, Pennsylvania. His passing was noted in such prominent publications as *Science* and the *American Journal of Psychiatry.*

Supernatural manifestations in Woodworth's meetings were attributed by locals to what they called "the power." That term was, however, often meant in a derisive sense. Could "the power" have possibly been contagious? Could it possibly have even spread to another church?

On October 12th, 1890, Trinity Methodist Church at Tenth and North Market Streets in St. Louis held its regular staid, formal, and predictable Sunday evening services. Consternation hit the church when some who had attended Maria Woodworth's tent meetings brought "the power" to Trinity Methodist. The first to be affected were children who were meeting in Trinity's basement.

According to a local newspaper account, members were suddenly "taken with attacks" similar to those seen among those the paper termed "the enthusiasts" at Mrs. Woodworth's meetings. To borrow the words of an unsympathetic reporter, they "shrieked and prayed and yelled and sang . . . making a great deal of noise and confusion."

The young people met in the basement at 7:30, just before regular evening services upstairs. A young girl began to pray, but suddenly dropped to the floor as though she had been shot. Soon other children fell as well. About a dozen of them were said to be "taken."

Those in charge stopped the meeting immediately and ensured that what was termed "order" was restored. Some semblance of what was considered orderly may have been reached.

Then, however, came the service upstairs for the adults. Shortly after the pastor, Dr. Marlatt, began his sermon, someone rose and began to pray aloud. Others quickly began to do the same, about fifteen in all. All of them were said to be "violently attacked with the 'power.'"

Some began leaping and some fell to the floor, at the same time that loud cries were heard. Dr. Marlatt tried to stop the outburst. He finally decided to simply wait for them to come out of this so-called "attack." Nearly an hour passed before the service returned to what the pastor, Dr. Marlatt, considered normal. The meeting did not end until around 11 p.m.

Almost all those who had experienced these manifestations, which seemed similar to those common to Mrs. Woodworth's meetings, had been in her tent. Dr. Marlatt was certain that he had done nothing that could have elicited the effects.

In fact, the pastor was later at a loss to explain the next day what had happened. He said that up until that point there was nothing unusual in his services, nothing that would have caused what the newspaper called "excess of religious enthusiasm."

"I cannot explain the matter in any way," he said afterward. "I am sure I would not encourage anything of the kind, and am completely at a loss to understand why it should have occurred last night." To their credit, he had to admit that all of these were "good people" among his congregation. They were, as he put it, "undoubtedly honest" in their beliefs.

"They did not become rigid," he noted, "but some of them dropped as if they had been hit with an ax." Marlatt did say, however, that he did not think that the manifestations among his congregation were exactly like those seen in the Woodworth tent.

Although Dr. Marlett acknowledged that almost all of the people involved had been to Woodworth's meetings, he thought there must have been a different explanation for the manifestation. He realized that, as he put it, "the doings resembled very much of the old-fashioned Methodist meetings."

The next day, Monday, frazzled local Methodist Episcopal clergy met at the Methodist publishing house at 15th and Lucas Place. As they assembled for their usual Monday meeting, the topic of discussion was anything but usual.

They anxiously wanted to know what could have caused these experiences at Trinity Methodist Church. The agenda issue of primary importance was the matter of what Marlatt called the "excited condition" of some of his members.

None of the ministers, including Marlatt, could offer any explanation as to why these phenomena would suddenly occur for the first time in the entire history of Trinity Church. All agreed, however, that it was the result of what they termed "religious enthusiasm."

6

HOPE AND HARDSHIP

After Maria Woodworth left St. Louis, some of those who had participated in her revival meetings continued to meet at Sturgeon Market Hall, near Broadway and North Market Street. Those meetings appear to have been led by Frank Utt, described as an evangelist who a local paper claimed was personally responsible for individuals receiving what both the paper and Utt called "the power."[297]

The meetings became the subject of local controversy when, it was claimed by neighbors, some did not leave the hall until 2 or 3 in the morning. While some who fell under the power of God recovered shortly, others remained in a prostrated condition for hours, perhaps until the next morning.

Some who visited the meetings were afraid of touching Utt's hand or even getting near him, for fear that they would enter a trance and perhaps would not be able to ever come out of it.[298] A policeman was stationed at the door to keep out huge crowds of the curious.

In January of the following year, 1891, discord and division began to strike at the congregation that had grown out of Maria Woodworth's labors in St. Louis. Some accused those she had left in charge of church affairs of what was termed "gross mismanagement."

Evidently this was used as a basis for an attempted takeover of the church. When the press asked for details, a reporter was told, "This is not the proper time to speak. We are expecting Mrs. Woodworth here at the present and when she comes there will be a good old-fashioned shaking up of dry bones in the skeleton closet . . . ."

At the same time that spectacular healings were in evidence in meetings Maria Woodworth was holding in Indiana, she finally felt compelled to sue for divorce. Although she was no longer living with her husband Philo Woodworth, he continued to publicly denounce her and her ministry. In addition, by this time he had become, in the words of the couple's friend A.B. Sibert of Rochester, Indiana, "wild in his threats."

Maria Woodworth divorced her husband in 1891. She had hoped to avoid the necessity, but his attacks against her had grown increasingly severe. His adulterous affairs had become legendary. By this time, Maria Woodworth had as much of her husband's threats and affairs as she could stand. Evidently, as already noted, the couple separated by the end of Mrs. Woodworth's 1890 tent crusade in Oakland, California.

After the separation, Philo Woodworth returned to the Woodworth's resort at Manitou Park, just outside Rochester, Indiana. There he took in all the receipts from their hotel and lakeside resort park without sharing any of it with Maria. This was while she, for her part, was paying all the taxes on the property. As already noted, she also paid off Philo's store bill and other debts that he was unable to pay himself.

DIVORCE FROM PHILO WOODWORTH

In late December of 1890, Maria Woodworth indicated that she intended to divorce her husband Philo in the Fulton County, Indiana Circuit Court. The following appears to be a direct quote from Mrs. Woodworth's lawyer, a certain Judge West of Anderson, Indiana, directed to her husband. The reference to "such urgent need" would appear to be in reference to a plea from Philo for money:

> All attempts at reconciliation after what has occurred are useless. An application for divorce will be made in the Fulton Circuit Court. If you are in such urgent need, we will purchase your interest in the property, paying a sufficient sum down for immediate requirements and the remainder as you need it. If this suits you, make trustee's deed and payment will be made immediately.

Rochester, Indiana resident Alfred Sibert had sold the Lake Manitou property to the Woodworths in the first place. He said that Maria Woodworth's offer to pay her husband Philo for the property was probably $250 more than he could have received from any other source.

Philo Woodworth wrote to Maria, suggesting that they meet, but she did not respond to his letter. As a result, he then appears to have not believed that she intended to go through with her plans for a divorce. He then decided, however, to initiate divorce proceedings on his own, in order to make sure he received what he could of their property.

He hired a lawyer, Enoch Myers. Myers had only been practicing since 1880, even though an 1896 source said he had "long since been recognized as a lawyer of no mean ability." Myers and Philo Woodworth used the situation as an opportunity to further attack Mrs. Woodworth's ministry.

Regarding Maria Woodworth's divorce complaint, Myers made the following cryptic announcement to the press:

> Unless the allegations of that complaint are greatly modified, we will file a cross bill which will reveal the true inwardness of the Woodworth soul-saving aggregation in such a manner as to startle the whole religious world.

Before Maria's attorney knew that Philo was filing his own divorce application, however, Maria's lawyer had already made application for divorce. Philo Woodworth, with his attorney, met with Maria's lawyer at Anderson, Indiana. Philo was hoping to not only receive a substantial share of their property, but to eradicate or at least reduce the charges against him in the divorce application.

Philo later told Sibert,

> I did not see Mrs. Woodworth. All the business was transacted through Judge West. I sold on the terms offered in Judge West's letter, and the charges for divorce will be changed to abandonment and failure to provide. In addition to this I was told to continue using the property until it is needed, and will be given sufficient furniture to set up housekeeping. I could not ask Mrs. Woodworth to be more generous than she has been in this matter and I will say to you candidly that she is not to blame for the difficulties that have arisen between us.

That would seem to end the matter, but it did not. Sibert's letter was published in a local paper in mid-January of 1891. The following month, Mrs. Woodworth's application was finally pressed through in the Circuit Court of Fulton County, Indiana in Rochester. The charges certainly involved more than simply abandonment and failure to provide.

An Indiana paper observed that "sensational" divorce charges had been filed in Rochester:[299]

> Mrs. Woodworth, through her attorneys . . . alleges and charges . . . that Woodworth never properly supported her, and during the last five years has given her no support worth mentioning; that he has abused her by calling her vile names and applying indecent and offensive epithets to her, that he becomes furious and has pointed a revolver at her, threatening her life; that at various times and places with various persons he has committed adultery.

The same paper said on another occasion that she was often in "great fear that he would kill her." Further, he had "often threatened the life of the plaintiff, at times pointing a revolver at her."[300]

Regarding the accusations of adultery,

> On the latter specifications the complaint is specific, naming places, dates and persons. The Democrat [citing another paper, the *Anderson Democrat*] has been shown letters to and from Mr. Woodworth, from women not his wife, that are disgusting.

Without elaborating, it was claimed that "the attacks made on Mrs. Woodworth during her St. Louis meetings were inspired by her husband."[301] An Indiana paper said they had not lived together since June 1880. (Another article in the same paper, however, said they stopped cohabiting in June of 1889.[302])

In addition, they had property at Lake Manitou which was jointly owned. Even though Mrs. Woodworth said she is the one who paid for it, she was "willing to divide with her faithless spouse."[303]

After the judge heard about a few of Philo Woodworth's wild escapades with other women, described as "vile and disgusting orgies," he quickly terminated any further testimony and granted the divorce. Not only was the evidence overwhelmingly against Philo, but at one point the judge halted the spicy testimony, lest the older men on the jury, it was said, became too caught away with their imaginations. As Sibert phrased it,

> The evidence showed such vile and disgusting orgies in Columbus, Louisville and elsewhere that the judge, in consideration for several bald headed gentlemen on the front seats, shut off further testimony and granted the divorce.[304]

Evidently the "bald-headed old men" in the jury were listening intently to all the tantalizing details. Perhaps that is why surviving official records, some of which appear to have become permanently lost, are a bit skimpy.

Even so, the goings-on of Philo Woodworth as recorded in the county records were certainly scandalous, especially for their time. The Fulton County Circuit Court recorded for its February 1891 term that "The court further finds that the defendant did at divers times commit adultery with one Gertrude Smith during the year 1889, and with other abandon[e]d women. . . ."[305]

Maria Woodworth filed divorce papers stating that her husband had been guilty of adultery with several women on several occasions. Mrs. Woodworth was able to provide names, dates, and locations for acts of infidelity on her husband's part. These involved three different women, two of them described as "colored." The third was referred to as a "woman of bad repute."[306]

Records at the Fulton County, Indiana courthouse present a list of adulterous offenses with these three women. Philo Woodworth committed adultery with the first two while he and his wife were in Louisville, Kentucky. He took the third to the Railroad Hotel in Cincinnati. The complaint for divorce also mentions affairs with "other abandoned women." The press, at the national level, noted that the evidence had been "overwhelming" against Philo Woodworth.

The Rochester, Indiana newspaper noted that:

A colored gentleman, who was entirely familiar with the ins and outs of the Woodworth household, was brought here as a witness to substantiate the charges, and he soon demonstrated the fact that the guilt of the defendant was positive, excessive, numerous and abundant, and that many of the pollutions were practiced within the shadow of the sacred desk.[307]

Alfred Sibert, as has already been noted, assessed the relationship between Maria Woodworth and her husband Philo in the following terms:

Mrs. Woodworth was possessed of strong magnetic power, and it appears that at the height of her success in curing sin-sick souls, she was acquiring renown as a healer of physical ills. But it seems as she went onward and upward, her husband went downward and backward.

Sibert then elaborated:

Mrs. Woodworth excused these derelictions of duty by saying that his mind was affected from severe injury received years before, and she strongly refused, for a long time, to seek a divorce, as she was urged. Mr. Woodworth once told me that he had received severe injury to his head during service in the Civil War, but another and apparently reliable statement is to the effect that he had suffered from a fall of rock while mining coal. However this may be, it was certain that his escapades became so open and frequent and his abuse so continuous and unbearable that his wife felt forced to institute divorce proceedings in the circuit court at Rochester.[308]

In response to Philo's threats, Maria Woodworth and her friends raised $1,500 to be given to him in return for a pledge that he would do her no harm. This was after he apparently threatened to kill her in Oakland. As soon as he received the money, he wrote a pamphlet in which he spoke against his wife and the women who worked with her.

Since the pamphlet does not appear to have survived, the exact nature of his charges are not clear. Sibert said, however, that the pamphlet "attacked by innuendo the character of his wife, as well as the girls assisting her." He added that it was, in his words, "certainly as coarse, ignorant and unmanly a screed as I ever read."

Philo Woodworth came to St. Louis where he had the pamphlet printed. He tried to sell it on the streets there, until police gave him 24 hours to get out of town. He then returned to Rochester, Indiana, complaining that he had been a victim of persecution by his wife's supporters.

Woodworth then married for the third time. This time, he married a woman from Rochester, Indiana, only to run off to Cleveland shortly afterward.

The press in Maria's hometown of Rochester, Indiana announced on February 6, 1891, that:

A large photograph of Mrs. Maria Woodworth, the noted trance evangelist, yesterday divorced from her husband by the judge of the Fulton circuit court, can be seen in our office window.[309]

Not surprisingly, the same issue of the *Rochester Weekly Republican* also noted that:

> Those best acquainted with the parties to the suit justify Mrs. Woodworth, holding that she is personally pure, but the reverse is true of the old gentleman, whose career has been constantly evil.

NEW MINISTRY SUCCESSES AND STRUGGLES

Maria Woodworth's 1890 tent meetings in St. Louis resulted in the establishment of a permanent church in that city. A Church of God denominational account by C.H. Forney suggests that the congregation was "largely of persons of German extraction."[310] Perhaps this was largely because there was a strong German contingent in the Winebrennerian movement at this time. St. Louis was also known for its substantial German population.

Maria Woodworth resumed ministry in the spring of 1891 in her followers' permanent building in St. Louis. This structure had, at one time, been a Presbyterian church. Mrs. Woodworth's meetings in that building were characterized by what a newspaper called "strange scenes of hypnotic trances and mesmeric mummery." The same paper explained that what was termed "the power" had a "wild swing as long as it lasted."[311]

As was the case with her 1890 tent meetings, these manifestations brought opposition by yet another medical doctor. A local physician, E.W. Saunders, claimed to have treated three cases of what the *New York Times* and the *Chicago Tribune* called "violent insanity"[312] as a result of Woodworth's new series of meetings in St. Louis.

He declared that one of the individuals involved would never recover, a second might in time, while the third had been placed in a sanitarium because she had become overly enthusiastic about the Woodworth meetings.

Saunders claimed that if the three had not been "restrained," as he put it, they would have ended up in a state of what he called "incurable insanity." They were headed, according to the doctor, toward "religious monomania." Saunders said that this was one of insanity's "most dangerous phases."

He blamed the disposition of his three patients on what was termed "the Woodworth 'power.'" Saunders declared that the Woodworth meetings would have to be stopped, otherwise more insane asylums would have to be built.

In March of 1891 Mrs. Woodworth was in St. Louis, where an Indiana newspaper noted that she was publishing a newspaper called *Bible Truth*.[313] Saunders' attacks against Mrs. Woodworth came the following month, in April of 1891.

A bit later that month, newspapers announced that Mrs. Woodworth had "mysteriously" left St. Louis. One must wonder if that could possibly have been because of the accusations of Dr. Saunders. Perhaps she left town for a time in order to avoid another legal battle such as had occurred just the year before with Drs. Adams and Diller.

Naturally, rumors flew. One of those rumors asserted that Maria Woodworth had run off with church funds. F. Wheeldon, a man who had dropped out of her ministry organization, claimed that she had left because she had refused to submit the church finances to an investigation.

As a result, no one seemed clear at the time as to the future of the Church of God in St. Louis, the church that Mrs. Woodworth had established. The building was padlocked, Maria Woodworth and her coworkers were gone, and Wheeldon charged that she had taken $600 out of a church account at the Union Trust Company.

Once she was contacted, however, Mrs. Woodworth denied the allegations. She insisted that all the money was being held in a St. Louis bank. Nevertheless, the accusations made widespread headlines and the press tended to assume she was guilty.

The 1891–1892 edition of the St. Louis City Directory lists "Church of God (The Woodworth Temple)" on Lucas Place. This was at the northwest corner of 14th Street. Lucas Place is now known as Locust Avenue. Although the directory refers to the Woodworth Temple, once the church later moved it became known as the Woodworth Tabernacle.

Those who belonged to the Woodworth Temple were able to attend three separate Sunday meetings—morning, afternoon, and evening—at 10 a.m., 2:30 p.m., and 7:30 p.m.

The *Christian Advocate* published a letter in April 1891 that was said to have been written "some time ago" from a visitor to the Woodworth Temple in St. Louis. He noted that the building, which Mrs. Woodworth was renting, was in a "dilapidated" condition, as he described it. The Woodworth Temple could seat about 500 persons, "nine-tenths of them," he wrote, being from "the humblest walks of life."[314]

This observer found the meeting style to be characterized by prayer and singing that was, as he put it, "interspersed with various exhortations." The songs were, in his words, "very long." As the congregation sang them, Mrs. Woodworth was said to sway back and forth and wave her arms.

While in the building, the correspondent was able to buy a copy of her newspaper *Bible Truth*, five of her printed sermons, and a copy of her autobiography. While he was there, he watched as 19 persons entered the trance state. In this visitor's estimate,

As to the trances, I have no doubt that they are of the same nature as those which happened in early Methodism, and occur still among the colored people and among Baptists and Methodists in some parts of the world, Adventists, and other sects holding camp-meetings, and are precisely of the same nature as the jerks which occurred in the early part of the century. They result from continuous and contagious excitement, and take their peculiarly accidental type from the prevalent fashion.[315]

In spite of the negative assessment of this visitor, others noted the lasting good she had accomplished during her brief stay in the city. An opinion piece published in 1893 in the *Los Angeles Times* noted that St. Louis had been known as the "burial ground of the evangelist." There, the article claimed, "They come and preach to the church people, then go away in disgust, to return no more."[316]

The fact that Maria Woodworth had achieved anything there, the writer suggested, was grounds for praise. This writer, a Baptist minister named A.C. Crain, pointed out that:

Mrs. Woodworth has within the last three years and a half visited St. Louis several times, every time by invitation, every time a welcome visitor, every time her tent has been filled with thousands. The average daily attendance within the last two months has been 2000.

By this time, her St. Louis congregation had moved out of the old Presbyterian church building and had erected a new structure of their own. The same writer described their new headquarters:

They have built a beautiful church edifice at No. 2929 Montgomery street, the house costing $8000, and every dollar of this amount has been paid by these self-sacrificing, God-honoring people. The membership of this church is now 350.[317]

This was the new Woodworth Tabernacle, which also became known as the Montgomery Street Church of God. The new structure was dedicated August 14, 1892 by J.R.H. Latchshaw. He was president of Finley College in Ohio.

Elder H.H. Spiher became the pastor in the fall of 1891. Spiher had earlier pastored the Louisville, Kentucky church that came out of Maria Woodworth's revival meetings there in 1888. He was still pastoring the Church of God in St. Louis as late as 1899.

In 1916, the first congregation of the Assemblies of God denomination in St. Louis began meeting in the building that had earlier been the Woodworth Tabernacle. This was the building located at 2929 Montgomery.

By this time, the Assemblies of God had established its denominational headquarters in St. Louis. The facility then became known as Bethel Chapel. Bethel's first pastor was John William ("J.W.") Welch, one of the most significant early leaders of the Assemblies of God movement.

By December of 1890, Maria Woodworth had left St. Louis and was revisiting towns in Indiana that had earlier felt the impact of her itinerant ministry. One of her stops was the Church of God that sprang out of her earlier ministry in Muncie. Every night hundreds were unsuccessful at finding a seat inside the church. The sound of singing accompanied by hand claps could be heard for several blocks.

During Mrs. Woodworth's return visit to Muncie, a 17-year-old girl named Ruth Hughes became the talk of the town when she entered a trance for nearly 60 hours—about two and a half days. Then she went into another trance which lasted an additional 23 hours.

Ruth's mother also went into trances, but for shorter periods of time. During her longer trance, no part of Ruth Hughes' body moved except for one finger on her right hand. Presumably it was her right hand which was extended upward for the entire duration of the trance. She was kept in the church the entire time.

Several doctors stopped by to check on her, but they were not allowed to examine her. Once she showed signs of stirring, she was helped to a chair, but it still took her 45 minutes before Ruth Hughes was able to get up and resume normal activities. Then she entered another brief trance before finally being taken home.

The girl later declared that while in the trance, she saw heaven. There she saw Jesus, along with her brother and others she had known who had died. Although she saw the "pearly" gates,[318] she was not allowed to enter them. While describing what she saw of Jesus, she fell into her second trance, which lasted for about 23 hours.

In 1891, the Winebrennerian Church of God eldership of Ohio invited Maria Woodworth to come to their state to hold meetings. They unanimously decided at their 35th session that, as they expressed it,

> It is our duty to encourage the work of Mrs. Woodworth, and to invite and welcome her to Ohio to labor in her calling for the extension of the Church of God and the general good of all citizens.[319]

After the vote, two Ohio elders changed their minds and tried to have the matter reconsidered, but the resolution stood.

The same year, the Kansas eldership issued a statement to Mrs. Woodworth in which they commended her work and invited her to return to Kansas to minister. Although the measure passed by about a two-thirds vote, the invitation was seen as "objectionable" to a number of the Kansas ministers. At least part of that response seems to have been because of what C.H.

Forney called "the usual controversy" over meetings she had recently held in Topeka.[320]

Then yet another battle involving one of Maria Woodworth's churches erupted in the spring of 1892. A full-fledged court battle was waged over ownership of the building occupied by her Church of God in Springfield, Illinois. This was a battle that Mrs. Woodworth and her followers lost. Later that same year, her husband Philo Woodworth died.

THE DEATH OF PHILO WOODWORTH

Maria had offered Philo monthly payments to provide for his needs around the time of the divorce, but he refused. When he began to make wild threats against her, friends of Maria Woodworth helped her to raise a divorce settlement. This consisted of $700 in cash and $800 in secured notes. In addition, the Woodworths' Rochester, Indiana property on Lake Manitou was sold and the money was divided between them.

Philo Woodworth had tried in vain in 1890 and 1891 to receive a government pension based on his Civil War service. Since he was not a volunteer but was in the regular army, he does not appear to have necessarily been qualified to receive a pension. Even if he had been eligible, he forfeited the right by deserting from the army. Pension application records refer to his case as having been dismissed because he was still a "deserter at large."[321]

He claimed in his pension application that he was unable to support himself because of what was described on a pension form as "fever resulting in disease of feet and head." The form went on to say that "He also suffers from loss of vision, piles, and general disability."

In his own words he described his physical condition as follows:

> Head feels as if there was a heavy weight on it, pain in feet goes to my head. Diarrhoea comes on every 2 weeks. . . . I have wandering pain in joints if I get wet. Head stoped [stopped] up when I take cold . . . .

In addition he described a blood discharge that accompanied the diarrhea, along with what he termed "great pain."

Along with other problems, including severe hemorrhoids, a professional analysis of his condition revealed the following:

> Body well nourished. Skin florid. Tongue coated with a thick brown coat. Tonsils enlarged. Crepitation in left shoulder joint. Tender over region of kidneys, abnormal prominence of eye balls. Seeming loss of memory, ... Systatic murmur at mitral aricle [i.e. auricle].[322]

Philo Woodworth's health may have actually been noticeably deteriorating just during the time it took him to file the paperwork necessary to apply for a pension. When he signed a pension claim affidavit on June 18, 1890, his signature appears bold and clear. Letters are embellished by confident loops and flourishes.

When, however, he signed another affidavit just a few months later, on January 2, 1891, by comparison the lettering appears crabbed and constrained. He seems to have had difficulty wielding the pen, resulting in irregular bleeding of the ink.

One of the most insistent and troublesome attacks brought against 20th century evangelist Aimee Semple McPherson by her persecutors was criticism surrounding her divorced status. In the case of Maria Woodworth, however, she appears to have survived the divorce without stigma. Many, in fact, who knew about her husband, wondered why she had not divorced the scoundrel, with his bushy mutton-chop sideburns and his avaricious ways, much earlier.

As soon as he received the money from the divorce settlement, Philo Woodworth wrote what he claimed was the story of his life. This was included in the pamphlet he vainly attempted to sell on the streets of St. Louis.

After police ran him out of town, as already noted, he remarried shortly afterward in Rochester, Indiana. This was to Rose Lloyd. She was so young that the marriage was described as a "stunning combination of youth and old age."[323]

Then it was publicly learned and "reasonably well authenticated" that she was already married to a young man in Ohio. She had separated from her husband against not only his protests, but those of her parents.[324]

After remarriage, however, he almost immediately sneaked out of town when his new wife was out of the house. He ended up in Cleveland, Ohio, the city where he had enlisted in the army back in 1863.

A.B. Sibert, who had sold the Woodworths their Lake Manitou property, said that Philo Woodworth squandered the divorce settlement. He was then, according to Sibert, reduced to carrying coal through the streets of Cleveland on his back, selling a lump or two now and then for a few pennies.[325] This might have been something of an exaggeration, but evidently not much of one. Certainly Woodworth was in straitened financial circumstances.

After Woodworth died, his next-door neighbor James Driscoll told the coroner that a doctor had said that Woodworth "would be shoveling coal, but he was too weak."[326] When a doctor visited him in his home on the night of his death, Woodworth told the doctor that a man would be in shortly who could handle the doctor's written order to transfer Woodworth to a hospital. The doctor later testified to the coroner that this person who was to call on Woodworth "was delivering coal for him."

On June 21, 1892, Philo Harris Woodworth died, apparently from what was described as "privation." The more immediate cause was diagnosed as typhoid fever, because a doctor declared that he had "a typhoid tongue."[327]

Perhaps his life could have been spared, if he could have received medical attention within a reasonable period of time. On the night of his death, several individuals scrambled to try to find prompt and adequate medical attention for him. Concerted attempts were made to have the city transfer him to a hospital as a dying man with insufficient financial means. All of their efforts failed. Those efforts are detailed in the coroner's report.

Philo Woodworth was living at 408 Erie Street in Cleveland, having moved there from nearby Bolivar Street. This address no longer exists per se. Today, the site is in downtown Cleveland, between Cleveland State University and Jacobs Field.

At that address, Philo Woodworth rented a room from German immigrants, Fritz (Fred) and Anna Roever, also spelled Rover. Fritz Roever made combs for a living. Mrs. Roever testified on June 23, 1892, as paraphrased by the county coroner, "I knew Mr. Woodworth about 8 months. Been rooming my place since October, been living alone. He was sickly the whole time."

His next-door neighbor was James Driscoll, a produce dealer living at 406 Erie. According to the county coroner's transcription of remarks made by Driscoll, Woodworth "has been sick lately. His health was only fair when first met him. Complaining of bowel trouble and rheumatism for last three weeks."

Driscoll also revealed that Philo Woodworth's malady was not entirely physical. He was depressed, felt neglected, and was having suicidal thoughts. He wanted to end his life by taking arsenic. In Driscoll's words, as paraphrased by the county coroner,

Complaining of bowel trouble and rheumatism for last three weeks. There was doctor there June 12. Don't know doctor's name. It was on Sunday. He gave some powders. Took his temperature. He complained of cramps. Said no one to look after him and life was not worth living. Wanted boy to go after arsenic. Then sent for doctor. Gave him some hot lemonade and relieved him. In morning was around. Doctor said he would be shoveling coal but he was too weak.[328]

Calling for a wagon to take him to the hospital should have been a simple and straightforward affair. Instead, records of the coroner's office detail in page after page how all attempts to get Woodworth to the hospital were thwarted.

Attempt after attempt was made to get Philo to the hospital over a twelve-hour period. Normally, this would have been easily and quickly accomplished. In the case of Philo Woodworth, however, each such attempt was stopped in its tracks by unusual errors and confusion.

Anna Roever, Woodworth's landlady, said that she tried to see a certain Dr. Cole on the evening of Thursday, June 16. She wanted to ask him to transfer Woodworth to a hospital. While unable to see Dr. Cole, in her words a "man at Cole's marked it down."

Dr. George S. Parker came on Monday morning and found Woodworth in bed and wanting to go to the hospital. He was delirious and, as Parker later testified, "I was suspicious of typhoid fever." Parker wrote out an order for Mellen, the city's Infirmary Department Superintendent, to have Woodworth transported to the hospital.

Woodworth said that someone would be in soon to check on him, and told the doctor that he would give that person the doctor's written order for Mellen. Dr. Parker later said that he would have taken the order to Mellen himself, but was "pressed for time" and assumed the matter would be taken care of.

Later that evening a city patrolman, Leonard Cummisky, stopped by Woodworth's house. He was told that Mellen had been notified and promised to have him transferred to the hospital.

A policeman came by and told Mrs. Roever to return to Dr. Cole. Cole told her that Woodworth was outside his district. He stopped by and saw Woodworth briefly, then left. Then Dr. Parker was consulted. He said he would come and send Woodworth to a hospital but, as she put it, "He did not come."

Dr. Parker did arrive, however, the next morning. Then he found that Woodworth was sitting up but was suffering from a high fever and acute diarrhea. Parker advised going to a hospital, but Woodworth said he preferred to stay at home a few days to see if he would recover. The doctor gave him some medicine and returned again on Saturday, the 18th. Both the fever and diarrhea had left.

By Sunday, next-door neighbor James Driscoll found Woodworth "groaning and complaining of the pains he had." On Monday night he was laying completely nude with the front door and windows open. A neighbor, E. Thomas, said "He seemed out of mind and breathing very heavy." Thomas telephoned the city infirmary, apparently between 7 and 8 in the evening, asking that they send a wagon for him. They responded that they would do so as soon as possible.

When it became clear that no wagon was going to arrive, Thomas again called the infirmary around 10 p.m. He was then told that the infirmary could not send a wagon without a doctor's certificate. "I went up again and found his condition bad," Thomas later testified. "I was referred from one person to another till tired out." He added, "It looked to me as though they were neglectful."

At around 10:30 or 11 on Monday night, June 20th, Driscoll went to the home of Mellen, the superintendent of the city's Infirmary Department, to inform him that there was a dying man next door who lacked funds to put himself in the hospital.

Driscoll rang the doorbell. Eventually two men came up to the door where Driscoll was standing. When he told them his business, one of them went inside and consulted Mellen. Driscoll heard Mellen say that there was nothing he could do then, but that he would investigate the situation in the morning.

When Driscoll insisted that the condition was too serious to wait until morning, he was sent to Dr. Cole. Driscoll arrived at Cole's home about five minutes after midnight. After Cole came to the door, he told Driscoll that Woodworth was outside of his district. Cole complained that Mellen knew that, and that Driscoll should have been sent instead to Dr. Parker.

Cole wrote a letter to Mellen and handed it to Driscoll, asking him to take it to Mellen's house. Driscoll spent about a half hour ringing Mellen's doorbell, but to no avail. Mellen refused to respond.

Driscoll then returned to check on Woodworth. "He was moaning and incoherent," according to Driscoll. He was given some medicine that he already had on hand and Driscoll left about 2 a.m. Shortly afterward, around 3 in the morning, Philo Woodworth died. The date was June 21, 1892.

Philo Harris Woodworth was only 54, although the coroner's report of his death estimated his age to be 60. At the time of his death he was described as five feet, eight and a half inches tall with gray gray hair, a dark complexion, and "of spare habit."

The Cuyahoga County Coroner visited the morgue of Koerbler's Funeral Home on June 21st to view the body of Philo Woodworth. He then called for twelve individuals, including doctors, close friends, and relatives, to come to his office on the 23rd to testify as to what they knew about the case of Woodworth's death.

One of those who testified for the coroner was John Frederick Ormsby, Maria Woodworth's son-in-law. He was the husband of Lizzie (Woodworth) Ormsby, the daughter of Philo and Maria Woodworth. Ormsby, who was living in Columbiana County, Ohio, declared that he viewed the body and identified it as that of Philo Woodworth.

Philo's brother E. Woodworth also testified that he recognized the body. This apparently was Elisha V. Woodworth (although referred to as "E.W. Woodworth"), who was born about 1847 or 1848 in Ohio. He appears in the 1880 census in the village of Salem as a laborer. "I reside in Salem, Ohio," he said. "Saw him last alive about a year ago last month. His health was only fair at that time."[329]

Philo Woodworth was buried on June 23rd, two days after his death and the same day that the coroner concluded his assessment of the case. He was buried in Woodland Cemetery, located at 6901 Woodland Avenue in Cleveland.

Two days after he was buried, a letter left the Bureau of Pensions in Washington, addressed to "Mr. Philo H. Woodworth, Rochester, Fulton Co., Ind." The letter was returned stamped "unclaimed," with a handwritten note on the back of the envelope reading "Left City No address." That envelope apparently contained a form filled out by hand on the very day he died. The form read:

Sir:

You are advised the claim . . . is rejected on the ground that the claimant was not honorably discharged from the service, but is now a deserter at large.[330]

Philo Woodworth had applied for an honorable discharge in order to further pursue his military pension application. On October 17, 1893, the U.S. Pension Office noted that "no action will be taken until cert. [certificate] of discharge is furnished." By that time, however, he had been dead for over a year and his claim was eventually stamped "abandoned."[331]

He had been living in abject poverty. As Sibert put it,

I learned that the police of Cleveland, Ohio, had found him dead of privation in a bare back room, in the lowest quarter of the city. He had squandered his $1,500 inside of a year and been sustaining himself during the past few weeks by carrying coal around on his back and selling a cent's worth or more to any who would buy.

As noted earlier, Sibert saw Philo Woodworth's problems as largely the result of growing mental instability:

When I saw Philo H. Woodworth last, I thought him the most striking example of moral degeneracy I had ever known, but in the light of more recent information I am satisfied that he was the victim of growing insanity and that it would have been a mercy to have confined him an insane hospital.[332]

Chapter

7

BREAKDOWN
AND A NEW START

Despite constant criticisms and battles, Maria Woodworth moved on from the Midwest to the west coast. Ads in the *Los Angeles Times* in November and December of 1893 announced that she had pitched her tent in Los Angeles, at the corner of 8th and Hope Streets.[333] There she held meetings at her customary pace of twice a day, three times on Sunday.

When Maria Woodworth had first arrived in St. Louis from the Bay Area of California in 1890, she was referred to as an evangelist from San Francisco. When she was in Los Angeles in 1893, she was billed in local newspapers, in what were probably paid announcements, as the evangelist "from St. Louis."[334] Her Los Angeles meetings began on the evening of November 20th.

By December, she had moved her tent to the corner of Boyd and Los Angeles Streets. By March of the following year, critics were complaining that she was causing insanity in Los Angeles. In April she was still ministering, now at 4th and Wall Streets.

Then, later in the year, she was back in the Midwest. Newspaper accounts picked up her activities in Muscatine, Iowa in July of 1894, in Cedar Rapids in August of that year, in Canton, Ohio in November.

By this time, John Alexander Dowie, who was building his own healing ministry in the Chicago area, was denouncing her as promoting a false substitute for divine healing. "Divine healing is opposed by diabolical counterfeits," he wrote in his publication *Leaves of Healing* in 1894.[335] In another issue, he insisted that:

> Divine Healing is diametrically opposed to these dia-
> bolical counterfeits, which are utterly anti-Christian.
> These impostures are only seductive forms of Spiritual-
> ism. Trance Evangelism is also a more recent form of this
> delusion, and it deceives many.[336]

While not mentioning Maria Woodworth, the reference to "trance evangelism" was clearly made with her in mind. Although by this time she was not the only "trance evangelist" around, she certainly remained, by far, the best known.

By the time of the March 8, 1895 issue of *Leaves of Healing*, Dowie was no longer willing to mince words. He referred specif-ically to Mrs. Woodworth as he published a "public confession" of an individual who had not heeded Dowie's warnings about her. "He has made a public confession of his error," wrote Dowie, "in following Mrs. Woodworth . . . and others in this diabolical path of delusion."[337]

Mrs. Woodworth, for her part, denounced Dowie as a fraud when she was interviewed by the press in 1904. By that time, Dowie had been styling himself as the new prophet Elijah. "Dowie is a fraud," she told reporters. "He is no more an Elijah than you are or I am. The less said about him the better."[338]

THE END OF DENOMINATIONAL TIES

A group of Winebrenner Church of God ministers, meeting in Iowa in 1893, considered a motion to invite Mrs. Woodworth to their state to do evangelistic work. The motion was turned down. The following year the matter was reconsidered when the suggestion was made that she be invited to attend the Iowa Eldership.

An unnamed source quoted by denomination historian C.H. Forney said that she was unable to attend "owing to so long and continued labor, and tired physical condition."[339] This "tired physical condition" would seem to become an increasingly important issue in her life over the next several years, resulting in a reduced ministry schedule shortly after the turn of the century.

Mrs. Woodworth returned to St. Louis in 1893 to visit the church she had started. At the time, the Church of God was still meeting at 2929 Montgomery Street, at the corner of Slattery Street. A local paper reported that she had just finished "successful" meetings in the states of Oregon and Washington.[340] She had also just visited a church in Topeka that had sprung out of her efforts there a couple of years earlier.

Likely because of growing denominational sentiment against Maria Woodworth's ministry, a certain Rev. A.C. Crain wrote a letter on her behalf that he managed to have published in the *Los Angeles Times* in 1893.[341] Crain, who identified himself as a "Baptist clergyman," wrote his letter from St. Louis. He asserted that Mrs. Woodworth was the greatest of all living evangelists. Crain offered three reasons for this claim.

The first reason, according to Crain, was what he called "her great acceptability." He pointed out that St. Louis has been called the "burial ground of evangelists," from where evangelists would typically leave in disgust, never to return. Crain said that Maria Woodworth, on the other hand, visited several times in the past three and a half years, and always by invitation. Her average daily attendance at the time of Crain's letter was 2,000.

Of course, this is, however, a gross oversimplification of the history of Mrs. Woodworth's relationship with St. Louis. Her meetings were mobbed, her tent was torn down, her congregation had been attacked with bricks, and she suffered through an attempt to have her committed as insane. This does not sound like an evangelist who experienced "great acceptability" with everyone.

The second reason, however, why Crain believed that Mrs. Woodworth was the greatest living evangelist was because she was getting people healed while others were not. There were, said Crain, far too many clearly indisputable cases of divine healing in Mrs. Woodworth's ministry in St. Louis for anyone to deny that actual healings were taking place.

One of those healed, he pointed out, was a woman unconscious, suffering from what was described as "congestion of the brain." She was near death's door, but the prayers of Mrs. Woodworth saved her from death. The next day she was up out of bed and walking around her house.

Crain's third reason was that Mrs. Woodworth was, as he put it, "reaching the masses." Denominational ministers had talked for years about needing to establish rapport with common, ordinary people on a mass basis, he said, but Mrs. Woodworth had done it. Crain said such ministers could learn much from her if they would take the time to visit her tent meetings.

A little over a month after Crain's letter was published in the *Los Angeles Times*, another letter was published in the same paper, this one by Crain and four others. One of those who signed the letter is referred to as "Rev. N.N. Spiker."[342] This was presumably a misreading of a handwritten signature of H.H. Spiher, pastor of the Church of God that Maria Woodworth had founded in St. Louis.

In this bold public relations piece, the five declared that the ministry of Maria Woodworth was worthy of consideration as one of the most significant ministries of all time. Her proclamation of the "apostolic doctrine," they said, was accompanied by "signs and wonders." She did not resort to "side shows," according to the letter, but her "drawing power" came from being filled with the Holy Ghost.

They said that even though she had suffered intense persecution for a time in St. Louis, God used it for good. These problems provided an abundance of publicity for her meetings, publicity that caused the curious to come and be saved.

Spiher, they continued, was doing a fine job as pastor. He was described as abounding in "energy" and "executive ability," and was a "fine preacher." He was said to be "the right man in the right place." Spiher had directed the congregation, the letter continued, to build a fine church building at 2929 Montgomery, costing $8,000. Membership stood at 350.

Mrs. Woodworth, according to the letter, excelled in ministry because she was not answerable to anyone as she traveled. Instead, she was free to follow the promptings of the Holy Spirit, and was not sent out by any organization or committee.

Meanwhile, the church that resulted from Maria Woodworth's 1890 meetings in St. Louis continued to meet, and, in fact, was still thriving as late as 1895. Even C.H. Forney, who was occasionally antagonistic toward her in his 1914 Church of God history, offered some guarded praise for her work there:

> The success of Mrs. Woodworth in St. Louis gave quite a degree of inspiration to the brotherhood in the State.

She had organized a church which by January, 1895, numbered five hundred, with a fine house of worship.[343]

During the same year, although some of the Winebrenner Church of God elderships had barred Mrs. Woodworth from ministering, the Indiana Eldership praised her work in the ministry. Church records indicate that she was invited to come to Indiana and hold meetings there as quickly as possible.

Maria Woodworth maintained affiliation with the denomination's Indiana Eldership. As a result, the church in St. Louis had closer ties with the Church of God's Southern Indiana Eldership than with the Missouri Eldership. In fact, the pastor of the St. Louis church, H.H. Spiher, was elected several years as president of the Indiana Eldership.

Each fall, delegates from the church in St. Louis attended the Winebrenner Church of God's Indiana Conference. Because of his close Indiana affiliation, Pastor Henry H. Spiher transferred the church to the Southern Indiana Eldership on January 1, 1895.

This was done at the suggestion of Mrs. Woodworth. At the 15th Southern Indiana Eldership session, meeting at Anderson, Indiana, she recommended transferring the St. Louis members into the Southern Indiana Eldership. This resulted in controversy, however, among the members in St. Louis. In fact, it is said that some of the early members of the Woodworth Tabernacle later dropped out once they learned of the dependence on an Indiana organization.

Another controversy among the members of the Woodworth Tabernacle in St. Louis around this time centered around what was popularly termed the "second work doctrine." This concerned the holiness movement's concept of a second experience, one of sanctification, received after the salvation experience.

In fact, grievances were brought against Pastor Spiher at the 1895 eldership session by St. Louis members who believed in a second work of sanctification. Evidently Spiher did not share their views.

The rift was probably partly responsible for remarks Maria Woodworth made much later in her ministry in an undated booklet, *Questions and Answers on Divine Healing*.[344] There she cautions against insistence on particular doctrines about a separate sanctification experience or anything else that would tend to accomplish nothing but division among God's people.

The 1897 Southern Indiana Eldership again insisted that Maria Woodworth refrain from ministering outside of the eldership's geographical area. They told her that her license gave her no freedom to preach outside of the eldership's territory. While expressing high esteem for her, they told her to devote more of her time to ministry, as they put it, "in the bounds of our own eldership."[345]

At the same time, however, the elders strongly chastised their own denomination's Board of Missions for attacking Mrs. Woodworth. The board had denied funds to anyone not agreeing to cease all interaction with Maria Woodworth.

In response, however, the Missions Board refused to alter its stand. In fact, the board demanded that charges be brought against Mrs. Woodworth. The following year, 1898, the relationship between Maria Woodworth and the Southern Indiana Eldership could only be described as "strained," at best. The eldership met in its 1899 session at Shiloh Bethel in Daviess County, Indiana.

There, her license was said to have been placed "in the hands of the Standing Committee until she consents to work more in the bounds of this eldership or takes her transfer to the eldership where she expects to labor most in the future." During the same session, the elders adopted a stance "discountenancing physical healing and phenomena as not being the fruits of the Holy Spirit."[346]

Meanwhile, in the St. Louis church, there were 150 members in 1898. The 1899 *Encyclopedia of the History of St. Louis* by Hyde and Conard describes the church in the following terms:

> One of the peculiar doctrines of the church is that it adheres to the old-time apostolic demonstration of the power of the Holy Ghost and the miraculous healing of the body in answer to prayer.[347]

By this time, a second Winebrennerian Church of God had formed in St. Louis. This church sprang out of a work that had been established in 1896 by a certain F.T. Shore. Shore started meetings focused on what was then described as "primitive Christianity."[348] His followers refused to depend on any denominational hierarchy.

This group merged with a congregation started by Elder W.R. Covert once it was discovered that their beliefs and practices were nearly identical. This resulted in the formation of the Forest Park Church of God, with Shore as pastor. In 1899 they were meeting at 506 Tower Grove Avenue with a little over 40 members.

By 1896 another Winebrenner Church of God woman evangelist had appeared. This was Mrs. M. Sutliff, who was State Evangelist for Iowa. Both her methods and her preaching were said to resemble those of Maria Woodworth, although she never reached anywhere near the same level of fame.

A few years earlier Maria Woodworth had ministered in Iowa with another Church of God woman pioneer who was her long-time ministry partner, Emma Isenberg. Isenberg was an Indiana Church of God pastor and temperance advocate.

Also in 1896, Maria Woodworth was ministering in Syracuse, Kosciusko County, Indiana. Through her ministry, the tiny town of Syracuse seems to have become a mecca for those in need of healing. Many of the healings there were said to be nothing short of miraculous.

Maria Woodworth saw 400 saved and 200 healed in meetings in 1896 and 1897 in Fostoria, Ohio. She had conducted an earlier campaign in Fostoria which Church of God denominational historian C.H. Forney called "quite a revival."[349]

Denominational opposition continued, however, and in June of 1897 the Board of Missions of the Southern Indiana Eldership, of which she was a member, voted to expel Maria Woodworth. This was during the 52nd session of the Indiana Eldership in Whitley County, Indiana.

As proposed by the missions board, members would be required to, as their report put it, "withdraw all official relations from Sister Maria B. Woodworth."[350] The penalty for non-compliance would be a lack of financial appropriations from headquarters.

The Eldership's Standing Committee, however, came to her rescue. They vetoed the action, deciding instead to demand that Maria Woodworth, as Forney put it, "labor more within the bounds of the Eldership." In other words, apparently, she was to confine her ministry to Southern Indiana. The problem was, however, that by this time her ministry was nationally known. This meant that the denomination's demands could not possibly be met.

These squabbles with her denomination evidently were beginning to take their toll on Maria Woodworth. The increasingly severe attacks against her by her own denomination, despite the churches and converts added to the Church of God by her labors, seemed to be causing her emotional strain. In addition, the divorce and death of her husband—with the accompanying disposal of her lakefront Rochester, Indiana property—certainly must have contributed to a sense of frustration, discouragement, and stress.

C.H. Forney, in his history of the Church of God movement, assessed Maria Woodworth's ministry at this point. He declared that although she was still holding meetings, by 1898 the power that had been present seemed to be in decline:

> Mrs. Woodworth, licensed minister of the Southern Indiana Eldership, was still actively engaged in revival work, though less constantly, and apparently with waning power.[351]

The Woodworths' Rochester, Indiana friend Alfred Sibert said that he saw Maria Woodworth a couple years after the divorce. This was when she returned to Rochester to dispose of her Lake Manitou property. At the time, he said that she appeared "quite broken in health and spirit," adding that it was his impression that she had "dropped entirely out of the evangelistic field."[352]

In 1902, the discovery of a mineral water spring at what had been the Woodworths' home at Lake Manitou prompted the conversion of her hotel into what eventually became known as the Woodworth Mineral Springs Sanitarium. Some claimed medicinal effects from drinking the water. Later, it was analyzed and found to have healthful mineral content.

Local headlines in Rochester, Indiana in 1916 announced that a certain Dr. E.H. Southerland planned to erect a large sanitarium at the site. The location was referred to at the time by a local newspaper as "the celebrated Maria Woodworth place." Mrs. Woodworth, it can be assumed, would not have been happy with Southerland's plans for the site. She had used it as her ministry headquarters; now plans were being made to make the site into a center for "Mental Science:"

> Dr. E. H. Southerland, a prominent Mechano-Therapist formerly of Cleveland, Ohio, has taken an option on the celebrated Maria Woodworth Place on the east bank of Lake Manitou, embracing twelve acres of beautiful woodland, where he proposes to erect a thirty thousand dollar sanitarium for Mental Science having interested parties from Cleveland, Detroit and Chicago.[353]

The former Woodworth Hotel eventually became the Woodruff Hotel, and then, at least into 1922, was used as a private residence.

These developments at the property at Lake Manitou only came after it was no longer in the Woodworths' hands, however. After selling her Lake Manitou holdings, Maria Woodworth's ministry continued, but the problems she had undergone with her husband Philo, in addition to increasing attacks from her own denomination, appear to have grieved her heavily. Clearly, the trance evangelist needed a rest.

Maria Woodworth had been with the Winebrenner Church of God, General Conference, from at least close to the beginning of her ministry. She had spent years traveling all over the country, winning converts and building churches. Both those converts and churches were added to the Church of God.

She had become both a legend and a household name. Her revival meetings were the subject of countless newspaper articles, from small town papers to the *New York Times*. Because she achieved such wide press coverage, many of those articles have doubtless never yet been found by modern-day researchers. Probably many of them will never be found.

Whenever she was on pleasant terms with her denomination, the Winebrennerian Church of God acknowledged that they owed her a tremendous debt. She had been, by far, the most noteworthy evangelist among them. In spite of her contribution to the Church of God, General Conference, however, the denomination increasingly found fault with her and fought against her. Many of its ministers despised her ministry.

Perhaps they felt threatened by the healings and the visions of heaven present in her meetings. Perhaps they felt threatened by the presence of the love of God that was so intensely manifested in her revivals. She had attempted to fit the glory of God into a denominational structure in which it could never be fitted.

In writing about the Southern Indiana Eldership around the turn of the century, Forney noted that "At one time Mrs. M.B. Woodworth's influence dominated this Eldership, and her methods, views, and practices largely prevailed." He complained, however, that churches that sprang out of her ministry "disintegrated and died,"[354] implying that this was her fault. This ignores the fact that she and her first husband, Philo Woodworth, continually asked the denomination in vain for pastoral support after their evangelistic efforts in a given area were through.

BREAKDOWN

In October of 1896, Maria Woodworth was said to have bought a home in Gas City, Indiana. During the following year, 1897, she held meetings in several places in Indiana and her native Ohio. Then she seemed to have disappeared from the journalistic radar for a time.

She next surfaces at Butler, Indiana, a tiny hamlet near the Ohio state line in De Kalb County, Indiana in 1899. There, according to only a very brief mention in a Ft. Wayne newspaper, she had been lying for six weeks "at the point of death."[355]

The date was April 13, 1899. No further mention has been found pertaining to this apparent collapse.

In May of the following year, 1900, Maria Woodworth returned her papers to the Church of God's Standing Committee. At the same time she resigned from the Southern Indiana Eldership.

She somehow managed to recover from her near-death collapse. In fact, in the spring of 1900 she returned to St. Louis to hold meetings. Because of a streetcar strike, however, attendance was very poor. After a short time, she gave up the effort and canceled her meetings.

During that year, a census taker noted that Maria Woodworth was living with her granddaughter Mabel Ormsby in St. Louis. The two were sharing an apartment at 3133 Clifton Place, not far from Kingshighway and Arsenal. Also living with them were two boarders, one of whom—Hugh S. Deckard—is listed as a "minister and evangelist."

Then she held tent meetings in July of 1900 in Naron Township, Pratt County, Kansas. This was announced as a camp meeting at the Moore Schoolhouse. She again surfaces, this time at Poplar Plains, Kentucky in December of 1900. There the crisis that had her bedridden a few months earlier seemed over. Many in Poplar Plains fell into trances, lying for hours.

Later that same month, meetings were held by unidentified evangelists near Bloomington, Indiana, where, again, individuals lay in a trance state for hours. The press noted[356] that the same evangelists had ministered there seven years before. Perhaps this was Mrs. Woodworth and associates.

The ministry success in Poplar Plains, Kentucky took place just as 1900 ended. This was the year during which, in the face of denominational charges against her, Maria Woodworth gave up her license to preach. She returned her papers to the

Winebrennerian Church of God at a meeting of the eldership in Anderson, Indiana.

Back in 1891, the Kansas Eldership had, by a two-thirds vote, invited her to hold meetings in their state. When they again met in 1901, however, they made a point of formally noting that Mrs. Woodworth was no longer welcome in their midst. Church historian C.H. Forney quotes an unnamed source as indicating that this was because she "no longer affiliates with the churches of God."

The eldership went beyond this, however, to demand that its ministers "see that she does not labor on their fields or within the bounds of this eldership."[357] Clearly if Mrs. Woodworth was to return to Kansas it would not be with the help or sanction of the Winebrenner Churches of God.

Most probably believed that the 19th century came to a close at the end of 1899. Of course, it would be more mathematically accurate, however, to say that the 20th century began as 1900 ended. As clocks struck midnight on the evening of December 31, 1900, the century ended.

The coming of the new century marked a dividing line in the life and ministry of Maria Woodworth. The 19th century "trance evangelist" was about to become Maria Woodworth-Etter.

With a new husband would come new vistas for ministry. She would become known as "the hyphenated evangelist." In addition, not far into the new century, she would come into contact with a fledgling Christian movement that would increasingly be labeled "Pentecostal."

The beginnings of that movement are often traced to the moment the clock struck midnight on the evening of December 31, 1900, signaling the start of the new year, 1901. That was when a young woman at a tiny Bible school operated by Charles

F. Parham in Topeka, Kansas became the first at the school to speak in tongues.

Certainly others had spoken in tongues earlier, even in Mrs. Woodworth's meetings. This was likely the first time, however, that individuals sought for what the Bible calls the baptism of the Holy Spirit with the specific expectation of receiving the gift of tongues as evidence.

The resultant movement would wield tremendous influence on Mrs. Woodworth's ministry, yet to a large extent she had been walking in its basic tenets all along. Tongues were evidently manifested in her 19th century meetings, and certainly her meetings were always known for evidences of physical healing.

First, however, another major event would have to transpire in Maria Woodworth's life. That event came not at the moment the clock signaled the coming of January 1, 1901, but almost exactly a year later. On January 1, 1902, Maria Woodworth became Maria Woodworth-Etter.

A New Marriage and a New Start

1900 was a census year. Among those listed as living in Hot Springs, Arkansas, was a certain Samuel P. Etter, born in February 1843 in Pennsylvania. He is shown as living with his wife Martha and other relatives. Samuel's occupation is left blank.

By around 1901 Maria Woodworth had met Samuel Peter Etter of Hot Springs, Arkansas. Soon they would marry. This would be the second marriage for each of them. Mrs. Woodworth again surfaces in records on New Year's Day in 1902, this time not in a newspaper account, but in a marriage record.

Samuel P. Etter, the same man who was listed with his wife Martha in the census in Hot Springs, Arkansas in 1900, was the groom. The bride was Maria Woodworth, listed in the marriage record with her name misspelled as "B.M. Wodworth."

They married at the farm that Mrs. Woodworth then owned, which was located near Round Prairie in Wayne County, Illinois. Samuel Etter's residence is listed in the marriage record as Birmingham, Alabama, and he was said to be a contractor.

Samuel Etter was born in Pennsylvania in 1843, the son of William H. Etter and Sarah (Plastner) Etter. His first wife, Martha E. McKee, was born in Pennsylvania in 1841. Samuel and Martha married in Chambersburg, Pennsylvania on February 5, 1867.

Chambersburg was the same town in which Maria and Philo Woodworth had held revival meetings, suggesting that perhaps Etter was associated with the local Winebrenner Church of God. C.H. Forney, the Winebrenner Church of God historian, mentions several Etters involved with the movement in Pennsylvania.

References to an earlier Samuel Etter appear in Church of God periodicals in 1847 and 1852. One of those references connects an individual named Samuel Etter with a Winebrennerian meeting at Cherry Grove, Pennsylvania.

After marriage, Samuel and Martha Etter lived on a farm in Green Township, Franklin County, Pennsylvania. They appear there in the 1870 census, with their post office address listed as Scotland, Pennsylvania. Samuel became well established in Chambersburg area society.

By 1900, the two had moved to Hot Springs, Arkansas. There they lived at 112 Cove Street, in the north end of town. A little over a year and a half later, Samuel Etter married again—this time to Maria Woodworth.

They were married on New Year's Day of 1902 at what their marriage record called "her" home in Wayne County, Illinois.

This was near the village of Round Prairie in Berry Township. His age was given as 59, and his place of birth was listed in the marriage record not as Pennsylvania, but as "Pencelvaney."

Maria's age at the time was 58. Hugh S. Deckard, the boarder who was listed as a "minister and evangelist" and living in Maria Woodworth's St. Louis apartment in the 1900 census, was one of the witnesses. Samuel's occupation is given as "contractor."

In the 1910 federal census Samuel Etter appears in Berry Township, Wayne County, Illinois with his new wife, listed as Maria B. Etter. One column of the census report is used to indicate "Whether single, married, widowed, or divorced."

Both Samuel and Maria are designated as "M2," meaning that they had entered into their second marriages. Elsewhere in the same page, the designation "Wd" was used in order to indicate widowed status, but this designation is not used to describe Samuel. As a result, it appears that Samuel probably was not widowed, but that he and Martha (McKee) Etter were likely divorced.

Could this have been the reason for the relative obscurity of Maria's ministry for a few years after this point? One would like to think that Samuel did not leave Martha for Maria. Simply the fact that he was remarrying after a recent divorce, however, especially in those days, would have meant that the reputations of both Samuel and Maria could have been tinged with social stigma.

Maria then, at least in some people's estimation, totally abandoned ministry for a time. Whether or not a divorce was the reason, Maria seems to have pursued something of a low profile for the next several years, although she did not stay out of the ministry for long. Samuel Etter, who the Rochester, Indiana *Sentinel* described as "a religious crank,"[358] soon began to assist his new wife, Maria Woodworth, with her ministry.

At first, however, she appears to have sought an apparently much-needed rest from the slings and arrows of persecution and outright harrassment. After the battles with the Winebrennerians and after the divorce and harassment at the hands of Philo Woodworth, Maria seems to have simply wanted to get away, take a breather, and then make a new beginning.

After her marriage to Samuel Etter, Maria Woodworth-Etter became publicly known as "the hyphenated evangelist." Although she was listed in the 1910 census as "Evangelist," she seems largely to have begun pursuing a simple lifestyle as a farm wife. This was on her farm, which became known as the Etter farm, near Round Prairie, Wayne County, Illinois.

There Samuel and Maria lived with the family of Maria's daughter and son-in- law, John F. and Lizzie C. Ormsby. The 1910 census lists John Ormsby as a "Farm Laborer" on the "Home Farm."

Their property was located in Sections 10 and 11 in Berry Township. The farm's present-day location is around the area where County Road 1350 N makes some very marked sharp angles as it turns into County Road 1300 N, going east from Round Prairie.

LATER MINISTRY

Not long after establishing herself at Round Prairie, Illinois, however, Maria Woodworth-Etter became determined to revisit the churches she had formed earlier in her ministry. She desired to, as a newspaper put it, "install new life . . . into them" and to "place them on firmer foundations."[359]

In addition, the Church of God (Winebrenner) seems to have experienced a change of heart. Both Maria Woodworth-Etter and her long-time assistant Emma Isenberg were delegates to the Indiana Eldership's 1902 session at the Oak Grove Church of God in Whitley County, Indiana.

The year 1902 also saw court action involving Mrs. Woodworth in Marion County, Indiana. This case was appealed to the Indiana Appellate Court, where it was heard as Woodworth v. Veitch. A certain Mary J. Vinson had given Mrs. Woodworth a note for $100, payable at Mrs. Vinson's death. After she died, her estate's administrator attempted to block payment of the note. According to testimony, Mrs. Vinson wanted to give the money because she wanted to see the "pure gospel" preached.[360] The matter was decided in Mrs. Woodworth's favor.

Woodworth-Etter again held meetings, this time in Prospect Park in Davenport, Iowa, then at Sangamon, near Decatur, Illinois, in May of 1903. After her breakdown and remarriage, Maria Woodworth-Etter had clearly reemerged, but her anointing seemed to have waned. A newspaper headline, referring to her Sangamon meetings, termed her as "once a drawing card."[361]

She returned to St. Louis in order to minister in conjunction with the 1904 World's Fair. A persistent rumor, or, more accurately, a legend, insists that Mrs. Woodworth-Etter was on exhibit while in an extended trance state at the city's 1904 World's Fair. The legend insists that large crowds filed past her, while she remained in an extended trance state. No substantiation for this story has yet been found, however.

What is much more likely is that her ministry in St. Louis in 1904 was limited to meetings at Freimuth's Hall, at Clayton and Manchester Avenues. Those meetings took place in at least January of that year.

Unlike her 1890 meetings, although her 1904 St. Louis meetings were well-received, there were no huge crowds and there was no controversy. The local press contrasted the relatively uneventful 1904 meetings with those she had held in the same city in 1890:

> The meetings so far have been conducted quietly. Nothing approaching the scenes witnessed at the meetings here in 1890, when from 7,000 to 8,000 people nightly crowded the tent on a vacant lot at Jefferson and Cass avenues, has been enacted.[362]

The paper continued to further describe the 1890 meetings:

> Every night then there was a great outburst of religious zeal and excitement. Half the audience would be on their feet shouting and singing. Men and women went into trances and dropped in their tracks or lay on the platform as if dead. Sick persons were brought in on cots and stretchers and arose and walked after a laying on of hands. Cripples threw away their crutches and the blind announced that they had recovered their sight.

Even during the 1904 meetings, there were some noteworthy healings. Midwestern newspapers noted that the trance evangelist had returned. "Fifteen to twenty years ago," one paper noted, "trance evangelist Maria Woodworth was famous all over this part of the country as a woman preacher who hypnotized her converts and put them in dreamland or spirit spookdom for hours at a time."[363]

She was to still occasionally minister in St. Louis, even as late as 1916. In 1904, Maria Woodworth-Etter made plans to travel throughout the Midwest, ministering healing and the power of God. When she finally made plans to resume itinerant ministry throughout Indiana in that year, the Rochester, Indiana *Sentinel* noted that Mrs. Woodworth had all but totally disappeared after the death of Philo Woodworth. Since she had remarried, however, the paper reported that she and her new husband would "restage the trance business in a circuit of the state."[364]

As she re-entered ministry in full force in 1904, it seemed to many as though she had been raised from the dead. As she began to travel in ministry again, many of her converts saw her for the first time in years.

Her 1904 ministry re-entry was heralded by the press. One headline subtitle read "Famous Trance Evangelist Formerly of This City Comes Out of Seclusion: She Will Tour the Country Again But 'Pop' Woodworth is Gone and a New Husband is on Deck."[365] Another proclaimed "Trance Evangelist Woodworth Preaching and Healing Again."[366]

Once she entered back into the swing of things, it quickly became evident that persecution at the hands of the Winebrenner Church of God was not over. In 1905, Maria Woodworth-Etter tried to assert ownership of the tabernacle that had grown out of her work in St. Louis. This appears to have been because of her concern about the direction the work there was taking. Instead, the property was deeded to the Church of God eldership.

When this occurred, she tried to assert the right to spiritually direct the church during her lifetime. Because this was seen as tantamount to physical possession, this privilege was denied by the courts. When she tried to get back the property by legal means, this move appears to have weakened the church.

Maria Woodworth-Etter had stood against "hoodlums" and against doctors who wanted to have her committed to an insane asylum in order to establish that church in St. Louis. Her church, which was birthed out of one of the most noteworthy revivals of the 19th century in America, was taken out of her hands and given to the denomination that had told her they no longer had any use for her.

Woodworth-Etter, it would seem, was either loved or hated. The *Rochester Sentinel*, published in her former home town of Rochester, Indiana, said in 1904 that "Families were disrupted by her teachings and the effect of her visit did not die away for several years after she had gone."

Even the *Sentinel*, however, had to admit that she had achieved much in a positive sense:

> Out of trips through the state resulted the formation of the Holiness Christian, the Church of God[,] and Heavenly Recruit church associations, and all three are doing good in a way in many portions of the state today.[367]

The remark that they were only doing well "in a way" likely suggests that although these associations were flourishing, the writer thought but little of their practices.

Maria Woodworth-Etter moved on to Indianapolis. More healings resulted. Still, her ministry achieved nowhere near the notoriety it once had. Then, however, the press in Indiana noted in 1907 that Maria Woodworth, the woman who had ministered throughout much of that state about a decade earlier, had "broken out again."[368]

She announced meetings to be held near Windfall, Indiana. Reporters wondered whether her ministry would have the same power as displayed in earlier years. Then, she was known to preach for hours, but now she was about sixty. Further, if her life was characterized by the same anointing, why was she but little heard from in years?

As plans for meetings were announced, a Montpelier, Indiana newspaper observed that "a big time is expected."[369] A Ft. Wayne, Indiana newspaper noted,

> Maria B. Woodworth, the once famous trance evangelist, has emerged from several years' obscurity and is back in

Indiana. The usual crop of religious maniacs will follow her reappearance unless Maria has lost the strange power she used to exert over her "converts."[370]

In 1909, Maria Woodworth-Etter was back in Oakland, California, where her meetings were described by a local newspaper as "more or less sensational."[371] There, little else was noted about her presence in Oakland, except that, as had been the case nearly 20 years earlier, she was being forced to vacate the lot occupied by her revival tent.

The 1910 census showed her, listed as "evangelist," living with her second husband Samuel Etter, listed as farmer. They were still living on her farm near Round Prairie in Berry Township, Wayne County, Illinois. Living with them, still, was her daughter Lizzie, Lizzie's husband John F. Ormsby, along with their children.

In 1911 and 1912, Mrs. Woodworth-Etter was active in ministry in Indianapolis. One of her assistants in 1912 in that city was Mary E. Selby, mother of famed boxer Charles McCoy, known as "Kid" McCoy. McCoy took the name after determining that it was more marketable as a boxer and as a star of early silent movies than the name given him at birth. That name was Norman Selby.

The phrase "the real McCoy" is said to have originated when a man became involved in a fist fight with him, not realizing that he was attempting to fight the "real McCoy." Mary Selby wrote the Kid, pleading with him to give up prize fights and to give his life to God. She wanted him to accompany her on an evangelistic tour of the world.

"The Kid" refused to listen to her advice. Kid McCoy was sentenced to San Quentin after holding a dozen people at gunpoint, then committed suicide after he was paroled. "Sorry," his suicide note read in part, "I could not endure this world's madness."[372]

By around the time of the 1911–1912 Indianapolis meetings, Maria Woodworth-Etter was beginning to align herself with the new Pentecostal movement. This was after accepting an invitation to speak in Fred ("F.F.") Bosworth's church in Dallas, Texas.

Bosworth had been a part of John Alexander Dowie's Zion community and had participated in the 1906 Azusa Street Revival. He is best remembered today as the author of the book *Christ the Healer*. Maria Woodworth-Etter stayed in Dallas for six months, during which time many healings were reported.

Early Pentecostal figure Mack Pinson reported in 1912 that he attended meetings in Dallas, Texas featuring Mrs. Woodworth-Etter, who, he said, "has had the baptism in the Spirit over twenty years."[373]

Actually, such "Pentecostal" phenomena as speaking in other tongues is believed to have been manifested in some of her Illinois tent revivals as early as the 1880s. In fact, a resident of Scottsburg, Indiana, A.P. Dennis, specifically said that he found himself speaking in tongues during one of her meetings in 1888.

Dennis had been "laboring for Jesus" after becoming born again nine months earlier. Before attending any of Woodworth's meetings, he sometimes saw whole rooms full of people, in his words, "slain like men in battle under the mighty power of God."

Then he visited a Maria Woodworth revival. As he described it, "One night in October 1888, while many were slain, I became as a drunken man. I began to stutter, or stammer, and then suddenly began speaking in other tongues."[374]

He had a similar experience much later, during a camp meeting conducted by Garfield Thomas ("G.T.") Haywood in 1912 in Indianapolis. There he experienced the Holy Spirit in what he called "great glory" and again spoke in tongues. Dennis realized that he already had essentially the same experience in 1888 in Woodworth's meeting.

The year 1913 also saw Mrs. Woodworth-Etter ministering with noteworthy healings at several conventions. These included meetings in the Los Angeles area at the Apostolic Faith World-Wide Camp-Meeting, at the World-Wide Camp Meeting in Connecticut, and meetings in Castle Hall in Oakland, California. From Oakland she went on to San Jose.

She ran into a bit of hitch the same year in Connecticut, however. While ministering at the Apostolic World-Wide Camp Meeting at Long Hill, Connecticut, near South Framingham, Mrs. Woodworth was arrested. The charge was obtaining money under false pretenses.

The "false pretenses" were said to amount to practicing medicine without a license. This charge, which has since been directed at others who were termed healing evangelists, perhaps most prominently Jack Coe in the 1950s, was in response to the healings claimed from her meetings. Mrs. Woodworth-Etter was arrested along with two other ministers, Cyrus Fockler and Earl Clark.

"I've been doing the Lord's work for 35 years and I've never been arrested before," Woodworth-Etter testified in court. She continued,

> I'm not in the least disturbed about my arrest and I've plenty of faith in the Lord straightening out all this trouble. The devil gets in a few pieces of work every now and then. I suppose that he is working now, . . . for my annoyance. For 35 years I've been an enemy of the devil and he's always trying to get me. But the Lord is always stronger, and I'm not afraid.[375]

Samuel G. Otis, publisher of the Pentecostal magazine *Word & Work*, was also questioned by the prosecution. That was because Otis had leased the Montwait campground and had made arrangements for the camp meeting. *Word & Work* was published by Otis' organization, the Christian Workers' Union, at Montwait. Otis held a five-year lease on the Montwait campground from the local Chatauqua Association.

Offerings collected at the campground were to be divided equally between Woodworth-Etter's ministry organization and that of Otis. Otis said that his share would go toward such expenses as lighting and payroll.[376] Critics alleged that this money was collected under false pretenses, since Mrs. Woodworth-Etter was billed as a healer and, and in their view, such claims were false.

Testimony in Woodworth-Etter's behalf established, however, that she did not charge for healing. Testimony also showed that she acknowledged God as the healer and did not claim that any of the healings came from her. Further, it was testified that her first concern was with the salvation of the congregation rather than their physical health.

In fact, as one witness pointed out, Mrs. Etter would not pray for anyone for healing without first determining that they had been born again. The first question she asked before praying for healing was, "Is your soul right with God?"[377] Then she would tell the individual that healing comes from God, not from Mrs. Etter.

Witnesses testified that they had, indeed, received healing during the Montwait meetings. This, of course, countered the charge that Mrs. Etter had been collecting money for healing without individuals receiving healing.

During testimony in court, the judge seemed more interested in finding out about the general nature of "the power" present in

Sister Etter's meetings than about any specific allegations of illegal activity. The defense emphasized that she never took money for healing, and that she never claimed to have healed anyone herself. The power to heal, she insisted, was God's alone.

Mrs. Etter seems to have been questioned during the Montwait trial about all sort of things other than the matter at hand. This was an opportunity, evidently, to ask her pointed questions about all the aspects of her ministry that had puzzled and astounded others—including the trances.

Maria Woodworth-Etter explained that the "prostrations" were not the result of hypnotism. They were rather the result of the presence of the power of God. She testified that many times those who came to deride her meetings were among the first to fall, once the power hit. She also pointed out that a number of experts in hypnotism came to her meetings to try to discover her methods, only to realize that no hint of hypnotism was present.

When Mrs. Etter was asked if she had ever cured or claimed to have cured such diseases as cancer or deafness, she responded with "No, God forbid!" When asked if anyone had ever been healed by her, she answered, "No, nor saved."

On the other hand, when they asked if anyone had ever been helped through her ministry, she answered "Yes, thousands of them."[378]

Charges were soon dismissed. The clearly groundless trial against Mrs. Etter at Montwait was not the only attack against her ministry there. In acts reminiscent of her 1890 St. Louis meetings, boys threw rocks and eggs and even tried to start a fire.

Maria Woodworth-Etter also ministered in 1913 in Oakland, California. Regarding her meetings there, noted divine healing advocate Carrie Judd Montgomery wrote that "it seemed very easy to lead souls to Christ"[379] because of the powerful manifestation of the Spirit of God. Wave after wave of glory would come upon the congregation as they entered into praise and worship with great joy.

In somewhat vague terms Montgomery mentioned what she termed "a marvelous Heavenly Anthem" in one of the Oakland meetings. In that song, she said, "many voices joined." Whatever this "anthem" was, a musician was afterwards heard to say that she had never heard anything like it.

Carrie Judd Montgomery noted that a woman told her after the Oakland meetings that she did not expect to ever be, as the woman put it, "as near heaven again while on earth as I was in those meetings." The same woman also commented that Mrs. Etter would always point the congregation toward Jesus, and would never allow others to get their eyes on herself.[380]

Then, however, police were brought in during Woodworth-Etter meetings in Atlanta, Georgia in April of 1914, when a disturbance broke out. The disturbance began when Sister Etter asked a young man, who was standing on a chair in order to see manifestations of "the power," to sit down. He refused.

After retiring to the back, he stood on a bench against the wall. When again asked to sit down, such pandemonium broke out as to warrant coverage by the *Atlanta Constitution* and a visit from the local police. The local press called the resultant disturbance a "near riot."[381] Still, healings took place anyway.

Maria Woodworth-Etter arrived in Chicago later that year. In October 1914, a Chicago paper ran a large display ad with her photo. The ad read,

Mrs. M.B. Woodworth-EtterForemost
Living Woman Evangelist

The Woodworth-Etter Pentecostal Meetings at the big Gospel Tabernacle, 704–710 W. 63rd St.

Three services daily
10 a.m., 2 p.m., 7 p.m.

Salvation for the lost, healing for the sick, rest and joy for the heart-hungry, through Jesus, Savior, Healer, Baptizer in the Holy Spirit, and Coming King[382]

Before long, meetings of Chicago's Englewood Central Church, where Francis S. Bernauer was pastor, merged with those of Mrs. Woodworth-Etter at the Gospel Tabernacle. By this time, Bernauer had already worked with Essek ("E.W.") Kenyon, who has oftentimes (probably without justification) been called the father of the modern-day Faith Movement.

The Gospel Tabernacle was evidently the same facility that was also known as the Englewood Gospel Tabernacle. The following year, a local paper called the *Suburbanite Economist* referred to the Englewood Central Church as meeting at 704–710 West 63rd Street, the same address that was used in 1914 for the Gospel Tabernacle.[383] This facility should not be confused with the Chicago Gospel Tabernacle. The latter structure opened in conjunction with evangelist Paul Rader's meetings in 1922.

In 1915, Mrs. Woodworth-Etter was still holding meetings in Chicago. An ad promoting the meetings urged interested parties to contact "L.C. Hall, Pastor."[384] This was likely Lemuel ("L.C.") Hall, who had earlier been a supporter of John Alexander Dowie. Hall later left Dowie's Zion City, Illinois, and became one of the primary leaders of the early Pentecostal movement.

The following year, Maria's second husband died. Samuel Etter died August 14, 1914 in Indianapolis. By now Maria had experienced the deaths of both her husbands and all of her children but one—Lizzie Ormsby.

Maria Woodworth-Etter continued to minister, including appearances in St. Louis in 1915 and 1916. She continued to minister in a variety of locations around the country, but on May 19, 1918, she dedicated her own facility in Indianapolis. This was the Woodworth-Etter Tabernacle, which was established to draw interested seekers and believers from all over the country.

The Tabernacle, located at 2114 Miller Street, was next door to her Indianapolis home. Today, this location is at the corner of West Miller Street and South Belmont Avenue. The 1920 census shows Mrs. Woodworth-Etter living next to the Tabernacle, at age 75. There she is listed as "Evangelist."

In the same year, George Erickson, the man who predicted the destruction of Oakland, California by earthquake and tidal wave, was also listed in the census. Erickson, however, who was now 59, was living in the State Mental Hospital at Stockton, California. He had been there since Mrs. Woodworth's Oakland meetings in 1890.

Thirty years after his Oakland predictions, Erickson appeared in the 1920 census as an inmate in a "State Hospital Farm" in O'Neal Township, San Joaquin County, California. Although he was then 59, he was still not a U.S. citizen.

A Life Ends, and its Lasting Impact

The power of God had continued to be manifested in Maria Woodworth-Etter's meetings at the Woodworth Tabernacle in Indianapolis. Copies of the various versions of her autobiography which she published under several titles continued to circulate. In one of those editions, she addressed objections to the experience of falling under the power, an experience which had become the hallmark of her ministry:

> When we are praying for people to get saved or healed, some shout, some praise, some pray, but all are making the same sound. We put on the blood by faith, and get a

glimpse of His glory. Is it any wonder people lose their strength and fall prostrate under the new life which comes to them?

Is it strange we are people to be wondered at? You have seen all this here: singing, playing, making the same sound. Is it any wonder these people who come here, especially to get under the blood as never before, when they get a glimpse of Jesus, is it any wonder they fall prostrate?

You must prove God has changed, has taken His power away before you condemn us. His gifts and callings are "without repentance." He never changes; He is the same yesterday, today and forever.

No one has any right to condemn us, to say the people are hypnotized, crazy, have lost their minds, or I have put a spell on them. . . . You must throw the Bible away, or you must prove the gifts and callings have been taken from the church before you reject us.[385]

In an undated booklet (*Questions and Answers on Divine Healing*)[386] published while at her Indianapolis location, she described the presence of God in the Woodworth-Etter tabernacle:

He is now confirming His word with a great display of His presence, giving visible signs, and working miracles. The glory of God is being seen at times in various parts of the Tabernacle. It has rested over the pulpit as a purple cloud. A band of angels have also been seen a number of times. The Song of the Redeemed—the Song of the Dove—in the Spirit is wonderful. Angels, and also heavenly instruments, have been heard making melody in harmony with the Song.

She continued,

The presence of heaven generally rests on the congregation. Sometimes when the glory comes, and breaks like a cloud, saints in various parts of the house begin to dance before the Lord in the spirit. Among them are old men and women, young men and virgins, old men of eighty and children of two years. People are amazed at the manifestations of God's power.

Mrs. Woodworth-Etter's son-in-law John Frederick Ormsby operated a gas station at 1435 South Belmont, a little more than a block north of her Tabernacle, at least in 1922. The address of his gas station in 1924 was 1433 South Belmont. In that year, Maria Woodworth-Etter still owned the farm property she had lived on years earlier with her second husband, Samuel Etter.

By this time, however, Lizzie and John had divorced. Mrs. Woodworth-Etter's second husband, Samuel Etter, had died in 1914. Then Elizabeth ("Lizzie") Ormsby, his wife and Maria's daughter, was killed in a streetcar accident. Lizzie had been the only of Maria's six children to survive childhood, and now she was gone.

Mrs. Woodworth-Etter had often testified that one of the earliest and greatest sorrows of her life was when her father was killed when she was just nine years old. Now it was 1924, and she was nearly 80.

Philo was gone, Samuel was gone, and now Lizzie. After a lifetime of battles and disappointments, Maria Woodworth-Etter must have felt simply exhausted from a lifetime of service. Lizzie died August 10, 1924. Maria Woodworth-Etter died just a little over a month later, on Tuesday, September 16, 1924.

Many decades later, an early Assemblies of God employee recalled assisting with Maria Woodworth's meetings. In the

1910s Bertha Schneider had worked for the Assemblies of God's Gospel Publishing House when it was located on Easton Avenue (now Martin Luther King Drive) in St. Louis. Later, in the 1920s, she also assisted with meetings held by evangelist Aimee Semple McPherson.

In comparing the ministry of Maria Woodworth-Etter with later ministries, including that of McPherson, she emphatically declared that there was "no comparison."[387] The difference, she noted, was the level of prayer. Much power was manifested in the ministry of Mrs. Woodworth, later Woodworth-Etter, because her life was dominated by much prayer.

There was another factor that would explain the power evident in Woodworth's meetings, but even this was largely the result of prayer. Mrs. Woodworth explained it in her own words: "I was in a little church one day and prayed to be given the power of faith. Suddenly I felt that it had been given me . . . ."[388] Her subsequent ministry was based on that experience.

Yet one more factor was perhaps not as readily apparent, but no less real. Woodworth-Etter did just not minister from a mental concept of the Bible. She ministered from a place in which she truly lived while on the physical earth, that place being heaven. She saw the Lord; she heard his voice. She continually saw the angels of God.

She ministered in the power of her actual experience of the heavenly realms. In a day in which so many believe that only Bible college can equip one for ministry, we would do well to re-examine the ministry of Mrs. Woodworth. We would do well to note what it was that allowed her to minister with such obvious power.

A 1924 landowners' plat map for Wayne County, Illinois shows two adjacent plots of land in Berry Township as then still belonging to Mrs. Woodworth. One of these, consisting of 200 acres, is in Section 10 and is labeled as belonging to "M.B. Etter." The owner of a smaller 40-acre tract adjacent in Section 11 is labeled "M.B. Woodworth." Both of these designations pertain, of course, to Mrs. Woodworth-Etter.

That plat map was published in 1924. Maria Woodworth-Etter died that same year, on Tuesday, September 16, 1924. She was almost exactly 80. Her funeral was held in Indianapolis on the following Friday. Although at one time the name of Maria Woodworth could have appeared in literally any paper in the country, her passing was virtually ignored by national media.

Maria Woodworth-Etter's body was buried in Indianapolis in Memorial Park Cemetery. The cemetery is located on the east side of Indianapolis, at 9350 East Washington Street.

Once in a while, a few might visit her grave in Indianapolis. Probably nearly no one, however, ever visits the lot—still mostly vacant—where Mrs. Woodworth held her 1890 tent meetings in St. Louis.

At one time, those meetings rocked the community, and news of what went on there resounded around the country, with press coverage on both coasts. Her St. Louis were, arguably, her greatest meetings. Today, however, the spot is simply an empty, deserted, and utterly forgotten vacant lot. Most buildings for blocks around have been razed, leaving a vast, empty area. There are no tourists flocking to the site; there are no pilgrims who wish to see where it all took place.

The life of Maria Underwood Woodworth-Etter was both a powerful and a painful one. Her ministry was filled with controversy, but was also filled with glory. She left a trail of new churches and of profoundly affected lives wherever she went. Even those who despised her ministry found their attention riveted on the goings-on in Maria's tent, wherever it was set up.

She was hauled into court, she was mobbed, she was ridiculed, she was accused of all sorts of supposedly diabolical things. She and her congregations were pelted with eggs, rocks, and bricks. She was branded insane and labeled a hypnotist in papers all over the United States.

Was it worth it? That is something we cannot, at the moment, ask Maria Woodworth-Etter. That is because she is, at present, residing somewhere in the glory that she constantly saw before her, the glory that empowered her life and ministry.

SELECTED BIBLIOGRAPHY

Advertisement (for Eastern Hair Store), *Oakland Tribune*, Oakland, CA, Apr. 3, 1890, p. 8; Apr. 9, 1890, p. 5; Apr. 14, 1890, p. 8; Apr. 16, 1890, p. 8.

Advertisement (for Eastern Hair Store), *Oakland Tribune*, Oakland, CA, Apr. 24, 1890, p. 8; Apr. 25, 1890, p. 8.

"All-Night Trances: The People of North St. Louis Aroused by Occurrences at Sturgeon Market," *St. Louis Post-Dispatch*, Nov. 23, 1890, p. 3.

"Appears After Decade," *Evening Herald*, Montpelier, IN, Aug. 24, 1907, p. 4.

B., J.M., "Concluding Editorial Letter on the West," *Christian Advocate*, Apr. 30, 1891, pp. 288–289.

"Baptized from the Levee: Some of Mrs. Woodworth's Converts Submit to Immersion," *St. Louis Globe-Democrat*, Sept. 1, 1890, p. 10.

Barth, Harold B., *History of Columbiana County, Ohio*, Topeka and Indianapolis: Historical Publishing Co., 1926.

Berkstresser, W.I., "The Work of Mrs. Woodworth Criticised," *Chicago Tribune*, Oct. 7, 1887, p. 9.

"But it Will Be a Good Sendoff," *Chicago Tribune*, Oct. 3, 1887, p. 4 (citing the *Peoria Transcript*).

"By Wholesale: Fifty-Four of Mrs. Woodworth's Converts 'Dipped,'" *The Republic*, St. Louis, MO, Sept. 1, 1890, p. 1.

Campbell, John Bunyan, *Spirit Vitapathy*. Fairmount, OH: John Bunyan Campbell, 1891, pp. 348–349.

"Cancer Cured by Faith: Phenomenal Powers Possessed by a Woman Revivalist," *St. Louis Globe-Democrat*, Sept. 3, 1887, p. 12.

Carradine, Beverly, *Heart Talks*, Cincinnati: M. W. Knapp, 1899, p. 116.

"Casting Out Devils: Sister Woodworth Tells How the Job Can Be Done," *Ogden Standard Examiner*, Ogden, UT, Feb. 6, 1891, p. 3.

"Cataleptic Religion: An Evangelist's Wonderful Power," *Cincinnati Enquirer*, Jan. 25, 1885, p. unknown.

"Cat-Calls for Zionist Dowie: British Medical Students Give Faith Healer a Noisy Reception," *New York Times*, Oct. 16, 1900, p. 6.

"The Civil Courts: The Proceedings Against Mrs. Woodworth Virtually Dismissed," *St. Louis Globe-Democrat*, Sept. 6, 1890, p. 9.

"Claim to be Cured: Stories of the People Alleged to Have Been Benefited by the 'Power,'" *St. Louis Post-Dispatch*, Sept. 4, 1890, p. 4.

"Close of the Camp Meeting: Sister Woodworth Will Take a Rest and Then Go to St. Louis," *Decatur Republican*, Decatur, IL, Oct. 3, 1887, p. 3; Oct. 6, 1887, p. 1.

Cochrane, Clara, and Stella Watson. *Glad Tidings in Song*, Indianapolis: Woodworth-Etter Tabernacle, n.d.

Complaint for Divorce, Mari [sic; Maria] B. Woodworth vs. Philo H. Woodworth, Fulton County Circuit Court, Rochester, IN, Dec. 17, 1890.

Conard, Howard L., *Encyclopedia of the History of Missouri*, Vol. 1, New York: The Southern History Co., 1901, p. 612 (section headed "Church of the Apostolic Order").

Coroner's Inquest, City of St. Louis, Case No. 290, L. W. Burg, July 23, 1890.

Coroner's Verdict and Testimony on the Body of Philo H. Woodworth, Clerk of the Court of Common Pleas, Cuyahoga County, OH, filed Sept. 19, 1892. In the Cuyahoga County Archives in the Robert Russell Rhodes House, Cleveland, OH.

Crain, A.C., "Mrs. Woodworth: She is the Greatest Evangelist," *Los Angeles Times*, Oct. 1, 1893, p. 16.

Crain, A.C., et al., "Mrs. M. B. Woodworth: The Great Evangelist—Review of Her Work," *Los Angeles Times*, Nov. 12, 1893, p. 9.

"A Crop of Cranks: Col. Juan D. McCarthy's Stories of Oakland," *Oakland Tribune*, Oakland, CA, Apr. 22, 1890, p. 6.

"Dangerous Hysteria: Physicians Tell of the Serious Effects of Mrs. Woodworth's Meetings," *Oakland Tribune*, Oakland, CA, Jan. 10, 1890, p. 6.

"Devil in Them: Mrs. Woodworth Tells About Her 'Subjects,'" *Oakland Tribune*, Oakland, CA, Jan. 10, 1890, p. 1.

Diller, Theodore, "Correspondence," *Medical News*, Oct. 10, 1891, p. 443.

Diller, Theodore, "Hypnotism in a Religious Meeting," *Medical News*, Vol. 57, No. 13, Sept. 27, 1890, pp. 302–304.

Dilller, Theodore, "The Physician in the Apocrypha" (letter to editor), *Medical News*, Vol. 84, No. 4, Jan. 23, 1904, p. 179.

"The Doomsealers" (advertisement), *Oakland Tribune*, Oakland, CA, Apr. 9, 1890, p. 5.

Dowie, John Alexander, "Do You Know God's Way of Healing," *Leaves of Healing*, Sept. 14, 1894, p. 7.

Dowie, John Alexander, "God's Way of Healing," *Leaves of Healing*, Aug. 31, 1894, p. 7 (and verbatim in various subsequent issues).

Dowie, John Alexander, "Trance Evangelism," *Leaves of Healing*, Mar. 8, 1895, pp. 380–381. (The article is unattributed, but almost certainly by Dowie.)

"Driven Crazy by Religion: Victims of Mrs. Woodworth's Revivals in St. Louis," *New York Times*, Apr. 12, 1891, p. 1.

"Ein Öffentlicher Skandal: Das Treiben der 'Evangelistin' Woodworth—Das Frauenzimmer Scheint Wahnsinnig zu Sein" ("A Public Scandal: The Activities of the 'Evangelist' Woodworth—The Wench Seems to be Insane"), *Die Westliche Post*, St. Louis, MO, Sept. 2, 1890, p. 5.

"Electric Evangelist: An Entire Salvation Army in the Person of One Woman, Mrs. Maria Woodworth," *Chicago Tribune*, Oct. 4, 1885, p. 26.

"Elysium Seen by a Mortal: Wonderful Results of Mrs. Woodworth's Revival Powers," *Boston Globe*, Jan. 30, 1885, p. 1.

"Ended in Murder: The Disturbances at the Woodworth Camp-Meeting Result in Homicide," *St. Louis Post-Dispatch*, July 22, 1890, p. 2.

"Englewood Central Church," *Suburbanite Economist*, Chicago, Oct. 30, 1914, p. 2; Nov. 20, 1914, p. 2; Nov. 27, 1914, p. 2.

"Events of This Date: A Daily Resume of Events for Your Scrap Book," *Chicago Inter Ocean*, June 18, 1896, p. 6

"The Faith Cure: Marvelous Healing Powers of Mrs. Woodworth, the Celebrated Evangelist," *Atlanta Constitution*, Atlanta, GA, Sept. 18, 1887, p. 8.

"The Faith Cure Fever: Religious Excitement in Illinois," *Washington Post*, July 28, 1888, p. 2.

"Fleeing from the Doomed Cities," *Chicago Tribune*, Apr. 12, 1890, p. 1.

Flower Pentecostal Heritage Center. *Healing Evangelists 1881–1957* (DVD-ROM, which includes digital copies of some original Woodworth-Etter material).

Floyd, Halleck, "Mrs. Woodworth's Work," *The Christian Conservator*, Dayton, OH, July 15, 1886, p. 2.

Forkner, John L., and Byron H. Dyson, *Historical Sketches and Reminiscences of Madison County, Indiana*, Anderson, IN: John L. Forkner, 1897, pp. 293, 807–808.

Forney, C.H., *History of the Churches of God in the United States of North America*, Harrisburg, PA: Publishing House of the Churches of God, 1914.

"A Frenzied Revival: Strange Results of a Female Evangelist's Work in Indiana," *Boston Globe*, Jan. 25, 1885, p. 5.

"Der Geisteszustand der Frau Woodworth" ("The State of Mind of Mrs. Woodworth"), *Die Westliche Post*, St. Louis, MO, Sept. 3, 1890, p. 1.

"Go Into A Trance," *Ft. Wayne Sentinel*, Ft. Wayne, IN, Dec. 29, 1900, p. 20.

Godley, Albert, "The Field: Indiana," *Herald of Gospel Liberty*, Mar. 5, 1885, p. 149.

"Going's [sic] On in the Name of Religion" (under "Ministers and Churches"), *New York Evangelist*, Jan. 29, 1885, pp. 4–5.

"The Gospel Hypnotist: Mrs. Woodworth's Strange Power Over Her Audiences," *Washington Post*, Sept. 14, 1890, p. 14.

Hardesty, Nancy A. *Faith Cure: Divine Healing in the Holiness and Pentecostal Movements*, Peabody, MA: Hendrickson Publishers, 2003.

Harding, Lewis A., ed., *History of Decatur County Indiana*, Indianapolis: B. F. Bowen & Co., 1915, p. 269.

"Has Lost His Grip on the 'Power,'" *Chicago Tribune*, Aug. 12, 1890, p. 7.

Hayes, D.A., "A Study of a Pauline Apocalypse, I Thess. 4:13–18," *The Biblical World*, Mar. 1911, pp. 163–175.

Heisey, Paul Harold, *Psychological Studies in Lutheranism*, Burlington, IA: The German Literary Board, 1916, pp. 124–125.

"Her Husband Writes: Dr. Wellington Adams Receives a Letter from Mr. Woodworth." *St. Louis Post-Dispatch*, Sept. 11, 1890, p. 6.

Horton, John Theodore, Edward T. Williams, and Harry S. Douglass, *History of Northwestern New York*, New York: Lewis Historical Publishing Co., 1947, p. 121.

Hyde, William, and Howard L. Conard, *Encyclopedia of the History of St. Louis*, Vol. 1, New York: Southern History Co., 1899, p. 376 (section headed "Church of God").

"A Hypnotic Revivalist Disappears: Mrs. Maria B. Woodworth Shakes the Dust of St. Louis from Her Feet," *Chicago Tribune*, Apr. 24, 1891, p. 1.

"Hypnotism: Physicians Deem Mrs. Woodworth's Alleged Power Pernicious," *The Atlanta Constitution*, Atlanta, GA, Sept. 1, 1890, p. 1.

"Illinois—Seekers of Cure by Faith," under "News of the Northwest," *Chicago Tribune*, Oct, 1, 1887, p. 7.

"Is it Hypnotism? A Difference of Opinion Concerning Mrs. Maria B. Woodworth's Work," *St. Louis Post-Dispatch*, Aug. 24, 1890, p. 8.

"Kid McCoy, Glamorous Boxer, Suicide at 66," *Lewiston Daily Sun*, Lewiston, ME, Apr. 19, 1940, p. 8.

Kline-Walczak, Kenneth Richard, comp. *Testimonies of Signs and Wonders: Evangelistic Crusades of Maria Buelah Woodworth-Etter in Moline, Rock Island, Illinois and Davenport, Iowa in the Years 1902–1902–1907 or Redigging of the Wells of Holy Spirit Renewal: Our Forgotten Heritage in the Quad Cities*, rev. ed. Davenport, IA: Self-published, 2006.

"Lake Manitou Ground Under Option for Building a Large Sanitarium," *Rochester Republican*, Rochester, IN, Apr. 6, 1916, p. 1.

Lawrence, B.F., "The Works of God: Article V.—Details from Various Sources," *The Weekly Evangel*, St. Louis, MO, No. 140, May 20, 1916, p. 4 (section headed "A. P. Dennis, of Scottsburg, Ind.").

"A Legal Inquiry: Mrs. Maria B. Woodworth to Be Examined as to Her Sanity," *St. Louis Post-Dispatch*, Sept. 1, 1890, p. 1.

Liardon, Roberts, comp. *Maria Woodworth Etter: The Complete Collection of Her Life Teachings*. Tulsa, OK: Albury Publishing, 2000.

"Lost His Grip on the 'Power,'" *Decatur Republican*, Decatur, IL, Aug. 12, 1890, p. 2.

"Made Whole by Faith: Alleged Cures in York County, Pennsylvania, by a Trance Medium," *Chicago Tribune*, Feb. 27, 1888, p. 5.

"The Magic Belt Works Wonders" (Advertisement for Mrs. Ros. Sabine, fortune teller), *St. Louis Post-Dispatch*, Aug. 10, 1890, p. 19

"Manitou Musings," *Rochester Republican*, Rochester, IN, July 23, 1885, p. 4.

"Maria B. Woodworth: A Woman Who Has Caused Much Comment," *Oshkosh Northwestern*, Oshkosh, WI, Oct. 11, 1890, p. 3; also in *The Steubenville Weekly Herald*, Steubenville, OH, Oct. 17, 1890, p. 7.

Maria B. Woodworth vs. Philo H. Woodworth: Divorce, Fulton County Circuit Court, Rochester, IN, Feb. 26, 1891.

"Maria Stirs 'Em Up: Trance Evangelist Woodworth Preaching and Healing Again," *Rochester Sentinel*, Rochester, IN, Sept. 21, 1904, p. unknown.

"Maria's Miracles: The 'Power' Gets in its Work on Prominent Andersonians," *Rochester Weekly Republican*, Rochester, IN, Jan. 15, 1891, p. 6.

McDonald, W., Joshua Gill, Jno. R. Sweney, and W. J. Kirkpatrick, *Songs of Joy and Gladness* (Word Edition), Boston: McDonald, Gill & Co., 1886, song no. 80.

Minutes of the Annual Conference of the Methodist Episcopal Church for the Year 1870, New York: Carlton & Lanahan, [1870], pp. 260–261 (section headed "Genesee Conference, Held in Buffalo, N. Y., October 4–10, 1871").

"Miraculous Cures: Some of the Marvelous Effects of Mrs. Woodworth's Ministrations," *St. Louis Globe-Democrat*, Aug. 26, 1890, p. 12.

"MIraculous Healing: Remarkable Cures by Mrs. Woodworth, the Trance Evangelist," *Chicago Tribune*, Sept. 18, 1887, p. 10.

"Mobbed a Prophetess of Evil," *Washington Post*, June 19, 1890, p. 1.

Montgomery, Carrie, "Mrs. Etter's Meetings in Oakland," *Triumphs of Faith*, Mar. 1913, pp. 60–61.

"Maria Woodworth: Famous Trance Evangelist Formerly of this City Comes Out of Seclusion," *Rochester Sentinel*, Rochester, IN, Sept. 16, 1904, p. unknown.

Mrs. M.B. Woodworth-Etter: Foremost Living Woman Evangelist" (advertisement with photograph), *Englewood Times*, Chicago, IL, Oct. 23, 1914, p. 1.

"Mrs. Maria B. Woodworth," *St. Louis Globe-Democrat*, June 9, 1890, p. 3.

"Mrs. M'Intyre's Wonderful Cure: The Strange Things Happening at Mrs. Woodworth's Faith-Healing Camp," *Chicago Tribune*, July 28, 1888, p. 1.

"Mrs. Woodward [sic] Preaches an Orthodox Sermon to Christians," *St. Louis Globe-Democrat*, Apr. 21, 1890, p. 10.

"Mrs. Woodward [sic] Returns Thanks," *St. Louis Globe-Democrat*, June 29, 1890, p. 11.

"Mrs. Woodward's [sic] Sermon," *St. Louis Post-Dispatch*, Apr. 21, 1890, p. 4.

"Mrs. Woodworth," *St. Louis Globe-Democrat*, Apr. 28, 1890, p. 10.

"Mrs. Woodworth: A Journal Reporter's Talk with the Trance Evangelist," *Logansport Daily Journal*, Logansport, IN, 24 Jun 1886, p. 4.

"Mrs. Woodworth at Springfield: The Faith Cure Medium Continuing Her Professions of Power to Heal," *Chicago Tribune*, July 1, 1889, p. 2.

"Mrs. Woodworth at Xenia," *Ft. Wayne Sentinel*, Ft. Wayne, IN, Aug. 21, 1885, p. 1.

"Mrs. Woodworth-Etter in Chicago, Ill.," *Weekly Evangel*, St. Louis, MO, May 1, 1915, p,. 2; May 8, 1915, p. 2.

"Mrs. Woodworth Here," *St. Louis Globe-Democrat*, Apr. 6, 1893, p. 5.

"Mrs. Woodworth in Trance: The Evangelist Passes into the Ecstatic State in Her Meetings at Kokomo," *Indianapolis Journal*, May 31, 1885, p. 5.

"Mrs. Woodworth's Meetings," *St. Louis Globe-Democrat*, Apr. 24, 1890, p. 8.

"Mrs. Woodworth's Tent," *St. Louis Globe-Democrat*, June 10, 1890, p. 12.

"Mrs. Woodworth's Work: Fifty of Her St. Louis Converts Baptized in the Mississippi," *Chicago Tribune*, Sept. 1, 1890, p. 5.

"Near Riot at Old Tabernacle Breaks Up 'Healing' Meetings and Brings a Call for Police," *Atlanta Constitution*, Apr. 24, 1914, p. 9.

"O, Mamma! Mamma!" *Decatur Republican*, Decatur, IL, July 16, 1889, p. 3.

"Officially Postponed: Erickson Says God Made a Mistake in the Date of the Wavelet," *Oakland Tribune*, Oakland, CA, Apr. 15, 1890, p. 1.

"Once a Drawing Card: Mrs. Woodworth Begins a Meeting Today at Sangamon Station," *Decatur Herald*, Decatur, Illinois, May 23, 1903, p. 2; May 26, 1903, p. 2.

Pension Application No. 774977, Philo H. Woodworth, Civil War service, regular U.S. Army, Co. E, 3 U.S. Infantry, National Archives File No. SO 744–977.

"Philo Harris Woodworth (1839–1893)," reference page in Ancestry. com at records.ancestry.com/Philo_Harris_Woodworth_records.ashx-?pid=44294937, accessed Sept. 22, 2012.

Pinson, M.M.,"Trip to the Southwest, *Word and Witness*, Malvern, AR, Aug. 20, 1912.

"A Prophet of Woe," *Oakland Tribune*, Oakland, CA, Mar. 12, 1890, p. 1.

"Prophet Woodworth: The Seer in Particularly Hard Luck," *Los Angeles Times*, June 19, 1890, p. 1.

"Quackery and Emotional Religion," *The Republic*, St. Louis, MO, Sept. 3, 1890, p. 4.

"Quick Relief for the Woodworthites" (advertisement), *Oakland Tribune*, Oakland, CA, Apr. 9, 1890, p. 5.

Register of Enllistments, Enlistment Record of Philo H. Woodworth, Microfilm Publication M233, Roll Number 28, Naitonal Archives, Entry No. 306, Sept. 21, 1860.

"Religion Gone Wild: Wonderful Revival Meetings Held by a Trance Evangelist," *Atlanta Constitution*, July 12, 1886, p. 1.

"Religious Trances: Frequency of Physical Manifestations During Revivals," *St. Louis Globe-Democrat*, Sept. 7, 1890, p. 31.

"Repentance Run Mad: Mrs. Woodworth's Biggest Revival," *Indianapolis Times*, Sept. 22, 1885, p. 1.

"Rigid on the Altar Boards: Two Women in a Trance at the Faith Meeting in Springfield," *Chicago Tribune*, July 29, 1888, p. 9.

"Rigid Religion: Mrs. Woodworth, the Evangelist, at Hartford City, Revolutionizing the Town," *Ft. Wayne Sentinel*, Ft. Wayne, IN, Jan. 31, 1885, p. 1.

"The Rochester Sentinel 1879," web document from the Fulton County Public Library, Rochester, Indiana containing excerpts from the *Rochester Sentinel*, at http://www.fulco.lib.in.us/Tombaugh/Newspaper%20Excerpts/Html/Newspapers%201879.htm, accessed Sept. 21, 2012.

Rust, A., "Revival at Farmland," *The Christian Conservator*, Dayton, OH, Oct. 14, 1886, p. 1.

"Said to Be Religion: Strange Scenes at 'Revival Meetings' Held in Indiana," *New York Times*, Jan. 24, 1885, p. 1.

"Saunders Responsible: The Verdict in the Burg Inquest—Conflicting Testimony," *St. Louis Globe-Democrat*, July 24, 1890, p. 11.

"Say She is Insane: Drs. Wellington Adams and Theodore Diller Will Try to Stop the Woodworth Meetings," *St. Louis Post-Dispatch*, Aug. 31, 1890, p. 7.

"Says She Has Conversed with Christ: Ruth Hughes Knocks at the Pearly Gates, but Can't Get In," *Chicago Tribune*, Dec. 16, 1890, p. 9.

Schneider, Bertha, Oral history interview conducted by Bruce Gunn, Feb. 24, 1981 (audio tape). In the collection of the Flower Pentecostal Heritage Center, Springfield, MO.

"Secret Sorrow: The Inner Life of Mrs. Woodworth the Evangelist," *Decatur Republican*, Decatur, IL, July 17, 1889, p. 3.

"Seductive Mrs. Sabine: The Fortune Teller Secures $700 from Ignorant People," *St. Louis Post-Dispatch*, Sept. 21, 1890, p. 7.

"See Visions of Heaven: Strange Reports from Mrs. Woodworth's Meetings," *Chicago Tribune*, Dec. 21, 1890, p. 6.

Shaw, James, *History of the Great Temperance Reforms of the Nineteenth Century*, Cincinnati, OH: Walden & Stowe, 1875, p. 480.

"She Didn't Quake: Mrs. Woodworth's Followers Disappointed," *Ft. Wayne Sentinel*, Ft. Wayne, IN, Apr. 15, 1890, p. 1.

"She Will Be Tried: Drs. Adams and Diller File Application for an Inquiry as to Mrs. Woodworth's Sanity," *St. Louis Post-Dispatch*, Sept. 2, 1890, p. 4.

"Sheep Without a Shepherd: Mrs. Woodworth's Meetings Closed," *The Burlington Hawk-Eye*, Burlington, IA, Jan. 4, 1895, p. 4.

Sibert, Alfred B., "Lake Manitou Fish Tales." In Marguerite L. Miller, ed., *Home Folks*, Vol. 1, Marceline, MO: Walsworth, 1909, pp. 89–93.

Sibert, Alfred B. "The Truth of It: A Statement from the 'Manitou Musings' Man," *Rochester Republican*, Rochester, IN, Jan. 15, 1891, p. unknown.

"Sister Woodworth: She Has a Big Contract in St. Louis and Cannot Leave It," *Decatur Republican*, Decatur, IL, Aug. 16, 1890, p. 1.

Smith, Amanda, *An Autobiography: The Story of the Lord's Dealing with Mrs. Amanda Smith, the Colored Evangelist*, Chicago: Meyer & Brother, 1893, p. 187.

"Strange Cures by Faith: A Visit to the Woodworth Gospel Camp Meeting," *Decatur Republican*, Decatur, IL, Sept. 10, 1887, p. 3; Sept. 15, 1887, p. 3.

"Strange Scenes: The Remarkable Manifestations of the Woodworth Revival Tent," *St. Louis Post-Dispatch*, Aug. 21, 1890, p. 5.

"Taught Bob Ingersoll: The Infidel's Instructor Brought to Believe," *Chicago Tribune*, July 25, 1888, p. 1.

Teasley, D.O., *The Holy Spirit and Other Spirits*. Anderson, IN: Gospel Trumpet Co., 1904, pp. 332–333.

"Tells How She Got 'Power:' Mrs. Etter Calm on Witness Stand," *Boston Globe*, Aug. 30, 1913, pp. 1–2.

"They Use No Drugs: An Evangelist Who Attempted to Administer Medicine Repudiated," *St. Louis Post-Dispatch*, Sept. 7, 1890, p. 4.

"Think the City Will Be Destroyed: Mrs. Woodworth's Oakland Followers Fleeing from their Homes," *Chicago Tribune*, Apr. 7, 1890, p. 1.

"This Date in History: A Daily Resume of Events for Your Scrap Book," *Los Angeles Times*, June 18, 1896, p. 6.

"[Title unreadable]: It Charges Her Husband with Cruelty and Adultery." *Muncie Herald*, Muncie, IN, Dec. 27, 1890, p. 3.

"Took No Money for Healing: Mrs. Etter Gave God Credit for Cures," *Boston Globe*, Aug. 29, 1913, pp. 1, 4.

"The Trance Evangelist: Sister Woodworth Names Her Date for Fort Wayne," *Ft. Wayne Gazette*, Ft. Wayne, IN, May 23, 1885, p. 3.

"Twenty Years Ago in Oakland," *Oakland Tribune*, Oakland, CA, Dec. 4, 1909, p. 4.

"Unhappily Mated," *Pulaski County Democrat*, Winamac, IN, Dec. 31, 1898, p. 1.

Untitled advertisements (for Mrs. Woodworth's meetings), *Los Angeles Times*, Nov. 20, 1893, p. 8; Nov. 25, 1893, p. 10; Dec. 1, 1893, p. 6.

Untitled, *Albion Democrat*, Albion, IN, Apr. 20, 1899, p. 1.

Untitled, *Chicago Tribune*, July 26, 1888, p. 4.

Untitled, *Ft. Wayne Journal-Gazette*, Ft. Wayne, IN, Aug. 25, 1907, p. 4.

Untitled, *Ft. Wayne Sentinel*, Ft. Wayne, IN, Feb. 18, 1884, p. 1.

Untitled, *Ft. Wayne Sentinel*, Ft. Wayne, IN, Jan. 21, 1885, p. 3.

Untitled, *Medical and Surgical Reporter*, Sept. 13, 1890, p. 328.

Untitled, under "The City," *Ft. Wayne Sentinel*, Ft. Wayne, IN, Mar. 26, 1884, p. 3.

Untitled, under "The City," *Ft. Wayne Sentinel*, Ft. Wayne, IN, Apr. 11, 1884, p. unknown.

Untitled, under "The City," *Ft. Wayne Sentinel*, Ft. Wayne, IN, Sept. 4, 1885, p. 8.

Untitled, under "The City," *Ft. Wayne Sentinel*, Ft. Wayne, IN, Aug. 6, 1886, p. 8; same also under "Local Briefs," Aug. 11, 1886, p. 3.

Untitled, under "City Items," *Ft. Wayne Gazette*, Ft. Wayne, IN, Oct. 1, 1885, p. 6.

Untitled, under "City News," *Ft. Wayne Gazette*, Ft. Wayne, IN, Feb. 23, 1884, p. 6.

Untitled, under "City News," *Ft. Wayne Gazette*, Ft. Wayne, IN, Mar. 21, 1884, p. 6.

Untitled, under "City Personals," *Ft. Wayne Gazette*, Ft. Wayne, IN, Feb. 13, 1884, p. 6.

Untitled, under "Current Events," *New York Evangelist*, Oct. 1, 1885, p. 8.

Untitled, under "Friday's Daily," *Rochester Republican*, Rochester, IN, Feb. 6, 1891, p. 6.

Untitled, under "Friday's Daily," *Rochester Republican*, Rochester, IN, Apr. 2, 1891, p. 6.

Untitled, under "From Tuesday's Daily," *Rochester Republican*, Rochester, IN, Aug. 23, 1888, p. 5.

Untitled, under "General News." *Christian Union*, Sept. 4, 1890, p. 293.

Untitled, under "Indiana State News," *Martin County Tribune*, Loogootee, IN, Apr. 10, 1891, p. 1.

Untitled, under "Local Chat," *Ft. Wayne Sentinel*, Ft. Wayne, IN, Dec. 7, 1886, p. 2.

Untitled, under "Local Events," *Rochester Republican*, Rochester, IN, Feb. 12, 1887, p. 3.

Untitled, under "Local News," *Decatur Republican*, Decatur, IL, Sept. 22, 1887, p. 3.

Untitled, under "Local News," *Ft. Wayne Sentinel*, Ft. Wayne, IN, Sept. 9, 1884, p. 1.

Untitled, under "Local News," *Ft. Wayne Sentinel*, Ft. Wayne, IN, Nov. 23, 1886, p. 2.

Untitled, under "Local News," *Rochester Tribune*, Rochester, IN, Apr. 22, 1887, p. 5

Untitled, under "Notes," *St. Louis Post-Dispatch*, Apr. 29, 1890, p. 2.

Untitled, under "Personal Mention," *Ft. Wayne Gazette*, Ft. Wayne, IN, Sept. 11, 1884, p. 4.

Untitled, under "Religious Notes," *St. Louis Globe-Democrat*, Apr. 19, 1890, p. 10.

Untitled, under "Small Talk," *Rochester Republican*, Rochester, IN, July 2, 1885, p. 5.

Untitled, under "Small Talk," *Rochester Republican*, Rochester, IN, July 9, 1885, p. 5.

Untitled, under "Thursday's Daily," Rochester Republican, Feb. 6, 1891, p. 6.

Untitled, under "Women and their Doings," Indiana Progress, Indiana, PA, Feb. 24, 1881, p. 6.

"Vorgehen Gegen Frau Woodworth" ("Action Against Mrs. Woodworth"), Anzeiger des Westens, St. Louis, MO, Sept. 2, 1890, p. 8.

Wallace, Adam, A Modern Pentecost; Embracing a Record of the Sixteenth National Camp-Meeting for the Promotion of Holiness, Held at Landisville, Pa., July 23d to August 1st, 1873, Philadelphia: Methodist Home Journal Publishing House, 1873, p. 85.

"Wanted to See Wonders," St. Louis Post-Dispatch, Aug. 22, 1890, p. 4.

"Wanting to See a Miracle—From the Chicago Tribune," Current Literature, Apr. 1890, pp. 287–288.

"Wants to Cut the Knot: Mrs. Maria B. Woodworth Petitions the Court for a Decree of Divorce," Muncie Herald, Muncie, IN, Dec. 26, 1890, p. 3.

Warner, Wayne. Maria Woodworth-Etter: For Such a Time as This. Gainesville, FL: Bridge-Logos, 2004.

We Believe: The Doctrinal Statement of the Churches of God, General Conference (Draft as of October 1, 2009), Findlay, OH: Churches of God Publications, 2010.

"Went to the Lake-Front to Pray: 'The Rev.' Douglass Miller of Muncie, Ind. Unfolds a Prophecy," Chicago Tribune, Feb. 9, 1891, p. 3.

"Were Driven Crazy by Religion: Victims of Mrs. Woodworth's Revivals in St. Louis," Chicago Tribune, Apr. 14, 1891, p. 9.

"What Is It? Religion, Mesmerism or What?" Petersburg Daily Index-Appeal, Petersburg, VA, Jan. 26, 1885, p. 2.

"Why She Left Him: Mrs. Maria B. Woodworth Makes a Reply to Her Husband's Attack," St. Louis Post-Dispatch, Sept. 12, 1890, p. 4.

"Woman Claims to Be Divine Healer: Mrs. Woodworth Returns," St. Louis Globe-Democrat, Jan. 25, 1904, p. unknown.

"A Wonderful Cure" (Advertisement for Mrs. Ros. Sabine, fortune teller), St. Louis Post-Dispatch, Sept. 21, 1890, p. 22.

"Wonders of Faith Cure: Mrs. Woodworth's Great Success at Springfield," Chicago Tribune, July 26, 1888, p. 9.

Woodworth-Etter, Maria B., Marvels and Miracles God Wrought in the Ministry for Forty-Five Years, Indianapolis: Self-published, 1922.

Woodworth-Etter, Maria B., *Questions and Answers on Divine Healing*, rev. ed., Indianapolis: Self-published, n.d.

Woodworth-Etter, Maria B., *Signs and Wonders God Wrought in the Ministry for Forty Years*, Indianapolis: Self-published, n.d.

"Woodworth Hotel" (advertisement), *Rochester Tribune*, Rochester, IN, July 15, 1887, p. 4.

Woodworth, Maria B., *Revival Songs as Used by Mrs. M. B. Woodworth the Evangelist in Her Revival Meetings*, Dayton, OH: Self-published (printed by the United Brethren Publishing House, but "published by the author"), 1888. In the Essex Hymnal Collection, a part of the Essex Music Collection, Lovejoy Library, Southern Illinois University at Edwardsville.

Woodworth, Maria B., Rules of the Church of God, Arranged by Eldress Maria B. Woodworth in Springfield, Illinois, January, A.D. 1889 (found at the Circuit Court of the Seventh Judicial Circuit Court, Sangamon County, Illinois).

"The Woodworth Meetings: The Hired Bouncers Should Be Stripped of Police Power," Oakland Tribune, Oakland, CA, Jan. 13, 1890, p. 4.

Woodworth v. Veitch (Appellate Court of Indiana, Division No. 2, Oct. 15, 1902), 64 N.E. 932 (The Northeastern Reporter, Vol. 64, June 27-Nov. 21, 1902. St. Paul, MN: West Publishing Co., pp. 932–933); also in Charles F. Remy, Reports of Cases Argued and Determined in the Appellate Court of the State of Indiana, Vol. 29, Indianapolis: Wm. B. Burford, 1903, pp. 589–592; also in J.S. McMaster, McMaster's Commercial Decisions Affecting the Banker and Merchant, Vol. 6. Albany, NY: Weed-Parsons Printing Co., 1903, pp. 93–94.

"The Work of the Devil: That's What the Healer Says About Her Arrest," The Lowell Sun, Lowell, MA, Aug. 20, 1913, p. 14.

Zuma, Mon. T., "Branch Meetings: Auglaize Branch," Woman's Evangel, June 1883, p. 101.

ENDNOTES

1 Warner.

2 Hardesty, p. 122.

3 Warner, p. x.

4 Sibert, Lake Manitou.

5 Kline-Walczak.

6 Liardon.

7 Forney, p. 475.

8 Untitled, Albion Democrat, April 20, 1899.

9 Once a Drawing Card.

10 Woodworth, Revival Songs, pp. 5–6.

11 Forney p. 210.

12 J.M.B.; see also Forkner, pp. 807–808.

13 A previous biographer has referred to him as "Philo Harrison Wood-worth," but this is incorrect. His middle name was Harris. He appears as Harris Woodworth in the 1871 Columbia County birth record of his son Fredrick, and as Harris Woodworth in the 1880 census.

14 Electric Evangelist.

15 Ibid.

16 Philo Harris Woodworth, reference page in Ancestry.com; Ancestry public "tree" of Daniel Slevin.

17 Register of Enlistments; Pension Application.

18 Register of Enlistments.

19 Pension Application.

20 Ibid

21 Register of Enlistments.

22 Shaw, p. 480.

23 The Faith Cure.

24 Electric Evangelist.

25 Maria B. Woodworth: A Man Who Has Caused Much Comment.

26 Wonders of Faith Cure.

27 Ibid.

28 Miraculous Healing.

29 Sibert, Lake Manitou.

30 A Frenzied Revival; see also What Is It?

31 Going's On.

32 Electric Evangelist.

33 Forney, p. 209.

34 Ibid.

35 We Believe, pp. 5, 18.

36 Hyde and Conard, p. 376.

37 Maria's Miracles.

38 Sibert, Lake Manitou.

39 Horton, p. 121.

40 Minutes, p. 260.

41 Zuma.

42 See Visions.

43 Said to Be Religion.

44 Godley.

45 Untitled, under Women and Their Doings.

46 Untitled, Ft. Wayne Sentinel, Jan. 21, 1885.

47 Untitled, under Local News, Ft. Wayne Sentinel, Sept. 9, 1884.

48 Untitled, under Personal Mention, Ft. Wayne Gazette, Sept. 11, 1884.

49 Electric Evangelist.

50 Untitled, under City Personals, Ft. Wayne Gazette, Feb. 13, 1884.

51 Casting Out Devils.

52 Untitled, under City News, Ft. Wayne Gazette, Feb. 23, 1884.

53 Untitled, under The City, Ft. Wayne Sentinel, Ft. Wayne, Indiana, Aug. 6, 1886; same also under Local Briefs, Aug. 11, 1886, p. 3.

54 Untitled, Ft. Wayne Sentinel, Feb. 18, 1884.

55 Untitled, under City News, Ft. Wayne Gazette, Mar. 21, 1884.

56 Untitled, under The City, Ft. Wayne Sentinel, Mar. 26, 1884.

57 Untitled, under The City, Ft. Wayne Sentinel, Apr. 11, 1884.

58 Said to be Religion; A Frenzied Revival.

59 Cataleptic Religion.

60 Said to Be Religion; A Frenzied Revival.

61 Rigid Religion.

62 Mrs. Woodworth: A Journal Reporter's.

63 The Trance Evangelist.

64 Forney, p. 210.

65 Forney, p. 440.

66 Untitled, under Small Talk, Rochester Republican, July 2, 1885.

67 Untitled, under Small Talk, Rochester Republican, July 9, 1885.

68 Mrs. Woodworth: A Journal Reporter's.

69 Untitled, under Local News, Rochester Tribune, Apr. 22, 1887.

70 Untitled, under Local Events, Rochester Republican, Feb. 12, 1887.

71 Woodworth Hotel.

72 The Rochester Sentinel 1879, at June 21, 1879.

73 The Rochester Sentinel 1879, at July 5, 1879.

74 Close of the Camp Meeting.

75 Untitled, under From Tuesday's Daily.

76 Sibert, The Truth of It.

77 Ibid.

78 Sibert, Lake Manitou.

79 Ibid.

80 Floyd.

[81] Mrs. Woodworth's: A Journal Reporter's.

[82] Manitou Musings.

[83] Mrs. Woodworth at Xenia.

[84] Forkner, p. 808.

[85] Strange Cures by Faith.

[86] Close of the Camp Meeting.

[87] Mrs. Woodworth: A Journal Reporter's.

[88] Untitled, under The City, Ft. Wayne Sentinel, Sept. 4, 1885.

[89] Untitled, under City Items, Ft. Wayne Gazette, Oct. 1, 1885.

[90] Manitou Musings.

[91] Ibid.

[92] Ibid.

[93] Mrs. Woodworth: A Journal Reporter's.

[94] Mrs. M'Intyre's.

[95] Ibid.

[96] Taught Bob Ingersoll.

[97] Rust.

[98] Mrs. Woodworth: A Journal Reporter's.

[99] Said to be Religion.

[100] J.M.B.

[101] A Frenzied Revival.

[102] Said to be Religion.

[103] A Frenzied Revival.

[104] Elysium Seen.

[105] Repentance Run Mad.

[106] Ibid.

[107] Untitled, under Current Events, New York Evangelist, Oct. 1, 1885.

[108] Godley.

[109] Repentance Run Mad.

[110] Electric Evangelist.

[111] Religion Gone Wild.

[112] Ibid.

[113] Ibid,

[114] Ibid.

[115] Ibid.

[116] Forney, p. 210.

[117] Untitled, under Local News, Ft. Wayne Sentinel, Nov. 23, 1886.

[118] Untitled, under Local Chat, Ft. Wayne Sentinel, Dec. 7, 1886.

[119] Harding, p. 269.

[120] Ibid.

[121] Cancer Cured by Faith.

[122] Ibid.

[123] Ibid.

[124] Forney, p. 210.

[125] Miraculous Healing.

[126] Illinois—Seekers.

[127] The Gospel Hypnotist.

[128] Miraculous Healing.

[129] Ibid.

[130] Ibid.

[131] Ibid.

[132] Ibid.

[133] Woodworth, Revival Songs.

[134] Miraculous Healing.

[135] Ibid; Woodworth, Revival Songs, pp. 5–6.

[136] Woodworth, Rules of the Church.

[137] Wallace, p. 85.

[138] Smith, p. 187.

[139] Carradine, p. 116.

[140] W. McDonald, song no. 80.

[141] Woodworth, Revival Songs, pp. 8–10.

[142] Miraculous Healing.

[143] Ibid.

[144] Ibid.

[145] Strange Cures by Faith.

[146] Untitled, under Local News, Decatur Republican, Sept. 22, 1887.

[147] Forney, p. 621.

[148] Forney, pp. 526–527.

[149] Forney, p. 527.

[150] Berkstresser.

[151] Made Whole by Faith.

[152] Mrs. Woodworth at Springfield.

[153] The Faith-Cure Fever.

[154] Taught Bob Ingersoll.

[155] Untitled, Chicago Tribune, July 26, 1888.

[156] Secret Sorrow.

[157] Ibid.

[158] Ibid.

[159] O, Mamma!

[160] Secret Sorrow.

[161] Wonders of Faith Cure.

[162] Mrs. M'Intyre's.

[163] Rigid on the Altar Boards.

[164] The Faith-Cure Fever.

[165] Ibid.

[166] Ibid.

[167] Ibid.

[168] Ibid.

[169] Ibid.

[170] Has Lost His Grip; Lost His Grip.

[171] Sister Woodworth.

[172] Mrs. Woodworth at Springfield.

[173] Forney, p. 210.

[174] Ibid.

[175] Ibid.

[176] Ibid.

[177] Ibid.

[178] Forney, p. 621.

[179] Forney, pp. 356–357.

[180] Forney, p. 357.

[181] Wanting to See a Miracle.

[182] Ibid.

[183] Forney, p. 622.

[184] Ibid.

[185] Devil in Them.

[186] A Prophet of Woe.

[187] Officially Postponed.

[188] She Didn't Quake.

[189] But it Will.

[190] Went to the Lake-Front.

[191] Hayes.

[192] Dangerous Hysteria.

[193] The Woodworth Meetings.

[194] The Doomsealers.

[195] Quick Relief.

[196] Advertisement, Oakland Tribune, Apr. 3, 1890, etc.

[197] Advertisement, Oakland Tribune, Apr. 24, 1890, etc.

[198] Think the City.

[199] A Prophet of Woe.

[200] Fleeing from the Doomed Cities.

[201] Sibert, Lake Manitou.

[202] Ibid.

[203] Strange Scenes.

[204] Untitled, under "Religious Notes," St. Louis Globe-Democrat, Apr. 19, 1890, p. 10.

[205] Mrs. Woodward Preaches; Mrs. Woodward's Sermon.

[206] Mrs. Woodward Preaches.

[207] Mrs. Woodward's Sermon.

[208] Mrs. Woodworth's Meetings.

[209] A Crop of Cranks.

[210] Mrs. Woodworth's Meetings.

[211] Untitled, under Notes, St. Louis Post-Dispatch, Apr. 29, 1890, p. 2.

[212] Mrs. Maria B. Woodworth, St. Louis Globe-Democrat, June 9, 1890.

[213] Mrs. Woodworth's Tent.

[214] Mobbed a Prophetess.

[215] This Date; Events of This Date.

[216] Wanted to See Wonders.

[217] Prophet Woodworth.

[218] Wanted to See Wonders.

[219] Campbell, p. 348.

[220] Diller, Hypnotism in a Religious Meeting.

[221] Coroner's Inquest.

[222] Ibid.

[223] Ibid.

[224] Ibid.

[225] Ibid.

[226] Ended in Murder.

[227] Coroner's Inquest.

[228] Ibid.

[229] Mrs. Woodward [sic] Returns Thanks.

230 Vorgehen Gegen.

231 Mrs. Maria B. Woodworth.

232 Wonders of Faith Cure.

233 Woodworth, Revival Songs, pp. 22–23.

234 Mrs. Maria B. Woodworth.

235 Strange Scenes.

236 Diller, Correspondence.

237 Diller, Hypnotism at a Religious Meeting.

238 Untitled, Medical and Surgical Reporter.

239 Diller, Hypnotism at a Religious Meeting.

240 Pension Application.

241 Strange Scenes.

242 Ibid.

243 Ibid.

244 Wanted to See Wonders.

245 Mrs. Woodworth in Trance.

246 Strange Scenes.

247 Say She is Insane.

248 Ibid.

249 Miraculous Cures.

250 Why She Left Him.

251 Claim to be Cured.

252 Ibid.

253 Ibid.

254 Ibid.

255 Her Husband Writes.

256 Wanted to See Wonders.

257 Strange Scenes.

258 Ibid.

259 By Wholesale.

[260] Ibid.

[261] Baptized from the Levee.

[262] Ibid.

[263] By Wholesale.

[264] Ibid.

[265] Ibid.

[266] Ibid.

[267] Ibid.

[268] Ibid.

[269] Mrs. Woodworth's Work.

[270] The Gospel Hypnotist.

[271] Wanted to See Wonders.

[272] Ibid.

[273] They Use No Drugs.

[274] Claim to Be Cured.

[275] Teasley, pp. 332–333.

[276] The Magic Belt Works Wonders (Advertisement), *St. Louis Post-Dispatch*, Aug. 10, 1890, p. 19; A Wonderful Cure (Advertisement), *St. Louis Post-Dispatch*, Sept. 21, 1890, p. 22; 4 Convincing Proof.

[277] Seductive Mrs. Sabine.

[278] Claim to Be Cured.

[279] Ibid.

[280] Ibid.

[281] Her Husband Writes.

[282] Cat-Calls for Zionist Dowie.

[283] See Thomas R. Bullard, *Chained Lightning Doctor: A Biography of Arthur Wellington Adams*, Oak Park, IL, 1988.

[284] Diller, The Physician in the Apocrypha.

[285] Quackery and Emotional Religion.

[286] Wanted to See Wonders.

[287] Claim to Be Cured.

288 Said to Be Religion.

289 A Legal Inquiry.

290 She Will Be Tried.

291 Her Husband Writes.

292 Mrs. Woodworth.

293 Untitled, under General News, Christian Union.

294 Hypnotism: Physicians Deem.

295 The Civil Courts.

296 Ein Öffentlicher Skandal.

297 All-Night Trances.

298 Ibid.

299 Unhappily Mated.

300 [Title unreadable]: It Charges.

301 Wants to Cut the Knot.

302 [Title unreadable]: It Charges.

303 Wants to Cut the Knot.

304 Sibert, Lake Manitou.

305 Maria B. Woodworth vs. Philo H. Woodworth.

306 Complaint for Divorce.

307 Untitled, under Friday's Daily, Rochester Republican, Feb. 6, 1891.

308 Sibert, Lake Manitou.

309 Untitled, under Thursday's Daily, Rochester Republican, Feb. 6, 1891.

310 Forney, p. 229.

311 A Hypnotic Revivalist.

312 Driven Crazy by Religion; Were Driven Crazy.

313 Untitled, under Thursday's Daily, Rochester Republican, Feb. 6, 1891.

314 J.M.B.

315 Ibid.

316 Crain.

317 Ibid.

[318] Says She Has Conversed.

[319] Forney, p. 575.

[320] Forney, p. 695.

[321] Pension Application.

[322] Ibid.

[323] Untitled, under Indiana State News, Martin County Tribune.

[324] Untitled, under Friday's Daily, Rochester Republican, Apr. 2, 1891.

[325] Sibert, Lake Manitou.

[326] Coroner's Verdict.

[327] Ibid.

[328] Ibid.

[329] Ibid

[330] Pension Application.

[331] Ibid.

[332] Sibert, Lake Manitou.

[333] Untitled advertisements, Los Angeles Times, Nov. 20, 25, 1893; Dec. 1, 1893.

[334] Ibid.

[335] Dowie, God's Way of Healing.

[336] Dowie, Do You Know.

[337] Dowie, Trance Evangelism.

[338] Woman Claims.

[339] Forney, p. 475.

[340] Mrs. Woodworth Here.

[341] Crain.

[342] Crain, et al.

[343] Forney, p. 241.

[344] Woodworth-Etter, Questions and Answers.

[345] Forney, p. 625.

[346] Forney, p. 626.

[347] Hyde and Conard.

[348] Conard.

[349] Forney, p. 244.

[350] Forney, p. 237.

[351] Ibid.

[352] Sibert, Lake Manitou.

[353] Lake Manitou Ground.

[354] Forney, p. 257.

[355] Untitled, Albion Democrat, April 20, 1899.

[356] Go Into a Trance.

[357] Forney, p. 699.

[358] M'ria Woodworth.

[359] Ibid.

[360] Woodworth v. Veitch.

[361] Once a Drawing Card.

[362] Woman Claims.

[363] M'ria Woodworth.

[364] Ibid.

[365] Ibid

[366] Maria Stirs 'Em.

[367] M'ria Woodworth.

[368] Appears After Decade.

[369] Ibid.

[370] Untitled, Ft. Wayne Journal-Gazette, Aug. 25, 1907.

[371] Twenty Years Ago.

[372] Kid McCoy.

[373] Pinson.

[374] Lawrence.

[375] The Work of the Devil.

[376] Took No Money.

[377] Ibid.

[378] Tells How.

[379] Montgomery.

[380] Ibid.

[381] Near Riot.

[382] Mrs. M.B. Woodworth-Etter: Foremost.

[383] Englewood Central Church.

[384] Mrs. Woodworth-Etter in Chicago.

[385] Woodworth-Etter, Signs and Wonders, p. 519.

[386] Woodworth-Etter, Questions and Answers, p. 35.

[387] Schneider.

[388] Strange Scenes.

ABOUT THE AUTHOR

Steven Phipps, Ph.D. has taught as a faculty member of several colleges and universities, including the University of Missouri - St. Louis and Washington University in St. Louis. Academically, he is known as a media historian, with publications in the area of media history, as well as legal and regulatory aspects of the media.

He also has a passionate interest in the history of Christian revival movements, and has amassed many thousands of documents and materials pertaining to that subject. His research tends to follow a revisionist history approach, which entails using period source materials, such as first-hand accounts and newspaper reports, to construct a fresh, new view of historical events and movements. That approach often questions and challenges assumptions of previous historians.

Steven Phipps was born again as child while living in the part of Turkey which the book of Acts refers to as the Roman province of Bithynia. He later witnessed firsthand a number of the most significant Christian movements, ministries, and groups of the last several decades, including the Charismatic Renewal and Jesus Movement of the 1970s. He has personally met various Christian leaders who played vital roles in revival movements during those years.

His doctorate is in Radio-TV-Film from the University of Missouri - Columbia. He also holds a master's degree from Southern Illinois University at Edwardsville and a B.A. from the University of Missouri - St. Louis.

He has been trained at the doctoral level in historical research methodology, and has conducted historical research at various libraries and archives across the country. He has appeared on PBS as a media historian, and his publications in the area of media studies appear in various academic journals and books. He also actively pursues extensive research into Christian history, especially concerning revivalists and revival movements.

Even in the area of revival history, his research often emphasizes the role of the media in covering revivalists and revival movements. His current research emphasizes the Voice of Healing revival of the 1950s, the ministry of healing evangelist John Alexander Dowie, and the ground-breaking roles played by various little-known Pentecostal and Holiness groups during the 19th and early 20th centuries.

PRAYER OF SALVATION

God loves you—no matter who you are, no matter what your past. God loves you so much that He gave His one and only begotten Son for you. The Bible tells us that "...whoever believes in Him shall not perish but have eternal life" (John 3:16 NIV). Jesus laid down His life and rose again so that we could spend eternity with Him in heaven and experience His absolute best on earth. If you would like to receive Jesus into your life, say the following prayer out loud and mean it from your heart.

Heavenly Father, I come to You admitting that I am a sinner. Right now, I choose to turn away from sin, and I ask You to cleanse me of all unrighteousness. I believe that Your Son, Jesus, died on the cross to take away my sins. I also believe that He rose again from the dead so that I might be forgiven of my sins and made righteous through faith in Him. I call upon the name of Jesus Christ to be the Savior and Lord of my life. Jesus, I choose to follow You and ask that You fill me with the power of the Holy Spirit. I declare that right now I am a child of God. I am free from sin and full of the righteousness of God. I am saved in Jesus' name. Amen.

If you prayed this prayer to receive Jesus Christ as your Savior for the first time, please contact us on the Web at **www.harrisonhouse.com** to receive a free book.

Or you may write to us at

Harrison House • P.O. Box 35035 • Tulsa, Oklahoma 74153

The Harrison House Vision

Proclaiming the truth and the power

Of the Gospel of Jesus Christ

With excellence;

Challenging Christians to

Live victoriously,

Grow spiritually,

Know God intimately.

Fast. Easy.
Convenient.

For the latest Harrison House product information and author news, look no further than your computer. All the details on our powerful, life-changing products are just a click away. New releases, E-mail subscriptions, testimonies, monthly specials — find it all in one place. Visit harrisonhouse.com today!

harrisonhouse